II554913

Grief Diaries

SURVIVING LOSS OF A SPOUSE

A collection of intimate stories
about surviving the loss of a spouse

LYNDA CHELDELIN FELL
with
KRISTI SMITH
DIANNE WEST
MARY LEE ROBINSON
DIANE MCKENZIE-SAPP

FOREWORD BY CAROL SCIBELLI

AlyBlue
MEDIA

Grief Diaries
Surviving Loss of a Spouse – 1st ed.
A collection of intimate stories about surviving the loss of a spouse.
Lynda Cheldelin Fell/Kristi Smith/Dianne West
Mary Lee Robinson/Diane McKenzie Sapp
Grief Diaries www.GriefDiaries.com

Cover Design by AlyBlue Media, LLC
Interior Design by AlyBlue Media LLC
Published by AlyBlue Media, LLC

ISBN: 978-1-944328-01-6
Library of Congress Control Number: 2015916914
AlyBlue Media, LLC
Ferndale, WA 98248
www.AlyBlueMedia.com

PRINTED IN THE UNITED STATES OF AMERICA

GRIEF DIARIES

TESTIMONIALS

"CRITICALLY IMPORTANT . . . *I want to say to Lynda that what you are doing is so critically important.*"
–DR. BERNICE A. KING, Daughter of Dr. Martin Luther King

"DEEPLY INTIMATE . . . Grief Diaries *is a deeply intimate, authentic collection of narratives that speak to the powerful, often ambiguous, and wide spectrum of emotions that arise from loss. I so appreciate the vulnerability and truth embedded in these stories, which honor and bear witness to the many forms of bereavement that arise in the aftermath of death.*" -DR. ERICA GOLDBLATT HYATT, Chair of Psychology, Bryn Athyn College

"MOVING . . . *We learn from stories throughout life. In Grief Diaries, the stories are not only moving but often provide a rich background for any mourner to find a gem of insight that can be used in coping with loss. Reread each story with pen in hand and you will find many that are just right for you.*" -DR. LOUIS LAGRAND, Author of Healing Grief, Finding Peace

"A FORCE . . .*The writers of this project, the Grief Diaries anthology series, are a force to be reckoned with. I'm betting we will be agents of great change.*" -MARY LEE ROBINSON, Author and Founder of Set an Extra Plate initiative

"INCREDIBLE . . .*Thank you so much for doing this project, it's absolutely incredible!*"-JULIE MJELVE, Founder, Grieving Together

"STUNNING . . . Grief Diaries *treats the reader to a rare combination of candor and fragility through the eyes of the bereaved. Delving into the deepest recesses of the heartbroken, the reader easily identifies with the diverse collection of stories and richly colored threads of profound love that create a stunning read full of comfort and hope.*" -DR. GLORIA HORSLEY, President, Open to Hope Foundation

"POWERFUL . . .*I'm so glad that I have been a part of something so powerful.*" -MARY SUTHERLAND, participant in *Grieving for the Living*

"WONDERFUL . . .*Grief Diaries is a wonderful computation of stories written by the best of experts, the bereaved themselves. Thank you for building awareness about a topic so near and dear to my heart.*"
-DR. HEIDI HORSLEY, Adjunct Professor, School of Social Work, Columbia University, Author, Co-Founder of Open to Hope Organization

"OUTSTANDING . . .*Lynda and her team did an outstanding job of moving all contributors through the process in a gentle, yet efficient way. Most importantly, the project team set up questions for contributors that were fashioned to elicit thoughtful and insightful answers.*
-MARY LEE ROBINSON, Author, The Widow or Widower Next Door

"HOPE AND HEALING . . . *You are a pioneer in this field and you are breaking the trail for others to find hope and healing.*"
-KRISTI SMITH, Bestselling Author & International Speaker

"AMAZING . . . *This is so amazing that after all these years of dealing with all the issues I've had in my life, I'm finally feeling like I'm not alone in all this.*" -
DEBBIE PFIFFNER, Contributor to *Grief Diaries: Grieving for the Living*

"GLOBAL . . .*One of The Five Facets of Healing mantras is together we can heal a world of hurt. This anthology series is testimony to the power we have as global neighbors to do just that.*"
-ANNAH ELIZABETH, Founder of The Five Facets of Healing

"GRATEFUL . . .*This journey, while the intent has been to guide and encourage others through this path of darkness, has provided invaluable insights into my feelings, allowing validation of those feelings by the person who matters most - - me! I am grateful for this opportunity.*"
-NANCY HAMMINK REDMOND, participant in *Loss of a Spouse* & *Loss by Homicide*

"HEALING . . . *This was one of the hardest journeys I have led myself on and yet I would do it all over again. Healing is a hard process, of so many emotions but there is no time frame on how long it will take and through this project I have come closer to feeling healed.*"
-TERESA BROWN, participant in *Loss of a Parent* & *Grieving for the Living*

"REWARDING . . .*This experience has been very rewarding for me. Just being able to talk with others who have walked this road.*"
-MONICA MIRKES, contributor to *Surviving Loss of a Child*

SURVIVING LOSS OF A SPOUSE

DEDICATION

In memory of our beloved:
Ivor Cameron
Carl O. Gibson
Cara Gilsig
Jim Hickman
Kathy Hochhaus
David Edward Kenyon
Cameron Mjelve
Gregory Alan Owens Sr.
Kevin John Redmond
Ron Sapp
James Scibelli
Mike Smith
Vern West

CONTENTS

Foreword...................................... ix
Preface.. xi

1 The Beginning............................ 1
2 The Aftermath............................ 41
3 The Funeral................................ 55
4 The Transition............................ 71
5 The Question.............................. 85
6 The Dates.................................. 95
7 The Holidays.............................. 107
8 The Belongings.......................... 117
9 The Darkness............................. 131
10 The Friends............................... 137
11 The Relationships....................... 147
12 The Faith.................................. 157
13 Our Health............................... 169
14 The Quiet................................. 179
15 Our Fear.................................. 189
16 Our Comfort............................. 197
17 Our Silver Lining....................... 207
18 Our Hope................................. 217
19 Our Journey.............................. 227
20 Finding the Sunrise.................... 239

Meet the Writers......................... 247
Thank you................................. 263
About Lynda Cheldelin Fell........... 265
About the Series.......................... 267

BY CAROL SCIBELLI

FOREWORD

You are holding in your hands a portable bereavement group; no more sitting on hard metal folding chairs, no puffy-eyed strangers, and no one staring at your ratty pajamas. *Grief Diaries: Surviving Loss of a Spouse* features widows with perhaps little else in common besides answering identical questions about their widowhood. The varied responses underscore that there is no right way to grieve. Our marriages were diverse; why not its aftermath?

That said, whether our marriage was interrupted by death at the beginning, the middle or near the end, with children or without, financially stable or not, the core of each story is every widow's loss. Our lives were broken. When a widow meets another widow or widower, often the conversation begins with something similar to the jail sentence question: "How long has it been for you?" Once we establish the *when*, we can pinpoint the *where* on the grief scale. Then we're off and running, comparing long illness versus unexpected, accident, suicide, and all the possible nightmarish circumstances that made us eligible to join our unenviable club.

And, a club it is. Widows and widowers everywhere echo, "Nobody gets it!" About a year after my husband died, even my grown daughter called me and asked, "What's wrong, Mom?" I said, "Well, honey, your father is still dead."

Within these pages are our peeps. We get it. We lived it and we continue to live it long after our family and friends have gone back to their lives.

Lynda Cheldelin Fell gathered the writers for this collection. She did a magnificent job. It certainly wasn't fun to relive and detail the most painful experience of our lives, but Lynda's mission is to comfort the newbies. When I was a newbie in 2006, I sure would have preferred reading this book in my ratty pajamas than sitting on those hard metal chairs trying to focus on nine pained faces.

Wishing you happiness and laughter back in your life ASAP.

CAROL SCIBELLI
Author, *Poor Widow Me*
Award-winning playwright & comedian

BY LYNDA CHELDELIN FELL

PREFACE

Losing a loved one is a heartbreak unlike any other experience. It is an elusive language for which there are no words; one that is too profound to be taught in textbooks or college courses. Although a universal experience that transcends all differences, and thousands share the journey at this very moment, we often feel misunderstood and alone. Further, we wonder if our world will be robbed of beauty and joy forever, and whether we'll even survive the heartbreak. This is why I created Grief Diaries.

Grief Diaries first began as a weekly radio show in February 2014. A few well-meaning individuals gently asked why I would want to discuss loss every week in such a public fashion. I graciously replied that grief never leaves; it resides within every breath we take. Besides, I find comfort in discussing the crazy kaleidoscope of emotions with others like myself.

Like all good things, Grief Diaries grew and by summer 2014, I set out to create a national event to bring the bereaved together; all the bereaved, no exclusions. Naming it the National Grief & Hope Convention, I set my sights on April 2015. I selected the city of Indianapolis and a hotel I knew well, the magnificent JW Marriott. I signed the venue contract in June 2014, and began laying the framework of speakers, exhibitors, subcontractors, and more.

As the months passed and April drew closer, our excitement and momentum grew. It was all coming together almost effortlessly, like the universe itself had ordained such an event.

But then the unthinkable happened, an unexpected turn of events at the end of March 2015, that threatened to unravel an entire year of hard work. With just three weeks to go, the governor of Indiana signed a bill into law resulting in a national protest. The power of social media was harnessed, and the punishment was swift and harsh: a travel boycott against the Hoosier state, with Indianapolis squarely in the eye of the storm. Conventions and sporting events cancelled, state governors around the nation banned travel, and the beautiful city of Indianapolis came to a temporary standstill. Our convention offering comfort, company and hope was not spared from the fallout: attendees, exhibitors, and speakers began to cancel. Fighting my rising panic and with a year's worth of hard work at stake, I pondered our options. Should we proceed and hope for the best, or fold?

Aside from those who pulled out, the rest stood with me, and we agreed that even if only five people attended, those five souls needed us. My favorite quote from Mother Teresa played over and over in my head: "Never worry about numbers, help one person at a time." So we decided to move forward and hope for the best.

And a magical thing happened. The exhibitors, speakers, attendees and even the convention subcontractors united that weekend to form a beautiful little village full of comfort and hope. Our sorrow transcended all differences as we gathered to share our broken hearts and journeys through the depths of despair. We comforted one another, swapped stories, and shared contact information; friendships were born and hugs were abundant. Despite the odds, our little convention was so powerful that it gave birth to a village unlike any other.....a village full of company, comfort and hope.

Following the convention, I pondered what to do with this collective group of souls so full of compassion and kindness. Every story was heartfelt, every hug was healing. There must be a way to continue building upon what was born that weekend. But how?

To my mind, there is nothing more beautiful than one broken soul extending compassion to another in need. And it's true that when we swap stories, we feel less alone. Thus, there was my answer: A collection of voices sharing the same journey compiled into the same book. It is a gentle way to not only nurture our little village, but also grow and reach others in need of the same company and comfort we found that weekend in April.

And that, my friend, is how the Grief Diaries anthology series was born. Which brings me to this book, *Grief Diaries: Surviving Loss of a Spouse.* Contained within these pages are narrations from different writers about their journey through losing a spouse. In Chapter One, writers bravely share the moment when their familiar lives disappeared along with their dearly beloved's last breath. The writers were then presented with intimate questions pertaining to their loss, and their responses are compiled within the individual chapters. These narrations are unabridged, as every voice is unique. But no matter the age, the circumstances, or the number of days since the passing of their spouse, the stories contained within are a treasured reminder that none of us walk this journey alone. And that is what this book is all about.

Welcome to the Grief Diaries village, where grief transcends all differences and unites us on the journey. Welcome, my bereaved friend, to company, comfort and hope.

Warm regards,

Lynda Cheldelin Fell
Creator, Grief Diaries

CHAPTER ONE

THE BEGINNING

Tears have a wisdom all their own. They come when a
person has relaxed enough to let go to work through his
sorrow. They are the natural bleeding of an emotional
wound, carrying the poison out of the system. Here lies
the road to recovery. -F. ALEXANDER MAGOUN

Grief and sorrow is as unique to each individual as his or her
fingerprint. In order to fully appreciate the different perspectives,
it is helpful to understand one's journey. In this chapter, each writer
shares that moment when they lost their beloved to help you
understand when life as they knew it ended, and a new one began.

*

TANYA CAMERON
Tanya's 43-year-old husband Ivor
died of a heart attack in 2013

I met Ivor whilst I was working and traveling in the UK. Ivor
was from the UK and I am from Australia. We worked in the same
hotel where he was the chef and I was the head housekeeper. It was
a friendship right from the start that blossomed into love.

Ivor was such a beautiful and gentle person. We were kindred spirits. We spent a lot of time together and would go away on short trips for weekends to France and Scotland. Ivor had a sister in Scotland and spent a lot of his childhood in Inverness. He loved to show me all the places where he spent time as a child. Ivor migrated to Australia with his own visa as a chef, as chefs were high on the wanted list as a trade for Australia. Ivor had job offers like I had never seen them. A chef's life does not keep sociable hours. I was working early mornings and he would work late into the evenings. It put a slight strain on our relationship, but we worked through it. We married in 2008 having a small beautiful ceremony, surrounded by family and close friends. We decided to go on holiday the year after, so we could spend more time together back to the UK. Ivor wanted to see his family. A few weeks prior to us leaving for our trip at the end of 2009, I found out we were having a baby, well two babies, twins. We were so happy and life was coming together for us. We had two beautiful boys. Ivor was the proudest dad and I was the proudest mum.

The boys were just over two years old when I had a job offer to head into our country area to manage one of the retail shops for the business I work for. Ivor insisted that I take on the job, he loved the area and thought it was a great place to bring the boys up. Being in the country, they are very sport oriented and it's a lot different to being in a city environment. Ivor had just given up one of his chef jobs as he wanted to be there to see his little boys grow up. I was going to work fulltime and he wanted to be the stay-at-home dad. Ivor loved being home with the boys and they loved their daddy. I would come home after a full day of work, Ivor would have dinner on the table and was glad to see me, as he thought it was his turn to rest.

In January 2013, Ivor was asked by my company to work for them a few hours a week. We could manage it, and the little extra money would help us out. But during Ivor's routine medical exam, it was discovered that his blood pressure was unusually high. It was monitored over the next few months and he was given regular tablets to help keep it all under control. My parents loved where we lived so much that they decided to sell the family home after nearly forty years, to move closer to us. They bought a house twenty minutes away in a small but beautiful country town, mid north South Australia. Six weeks after my parents made the move, on the morning of April 27, 2013, our perfect world was turned upside down and inside out. Life was never going to be the same again. I found Ivor sleeping in his chair, though he wasn't sleeping, he had already left us.

How was I going to tell my three-year-old boys that their daddy wasn't coming back, when I didn't understand why myself? I sat the boys down and told them that daddy had gone to heaven, the angels had taken him there. He loved them so much but the angels needed him to help cook and prepare their food. One of my boys said, "But the angels never asked us if they could take Daddy."

Our lives have changed so much since; I have struggled financially and emotionally. At the time of Ivor's death, nothing much changed apart from the extra wage coming in. The boys still needed to go to daycare and the bills never stopped. I was trying to keep our heads above water financially. I am still managing the business, now working four days a week. We moved closer to my parents, I bought a home on the next street. My parents are my support network, they come around at breakfast to help with the boys, drop them off and then pick them up after school. They are so good to us, Dad cooks our meals, he now has dinner on the table when I walk in the door from work. The boys are now five and I am now starting to seek some help for the boys. I have been seeing a counselor on and off since, and noticed that the boys had been trying to deal with it the best they could. I have great family and friend support as well as sharing stories with friends that are in the same situation, losing their husbands and partners. I still miss Ivor every day.

*

JONATHAN DEAN
Jonathan's 36-year-old wife Cara
died of double pneumonia in 2010

I met my wife at McGill University in 1999. We hit it off very well and remained friends well after our studies. In 2000, she moved in with me to start a new life. She told me that in 1999 she was diagnosed with a progressive muscle disease. Right away, I became her primary caregiver and went beyond the call of duty to make sure she was well taken care of. During the nine years and eight months we were together, we had no children. She managed to have a few jobs but in the big picture, it was me who brought in the money because it was difficult for her. The disease kicked in stronger each year, and a walker and wheelchair were needed. The local rehabilitation center provided us with a wheelchair and my parents had the walker. Cara's mother gave us her cane. I stepped up even farther and did a lot more than met the eye.

In February 2010, Cara asked me to bring her to the hospital. Right away I knew something was up. I managed to get her in the car and get her to the local hospital as fast as I could. She was called into triage and not even five minutes in, a Code Blue was called which meant that Cara had been in respiratory distress and went into cardiac arrest. She was rushed into the emergency ICU. I was told to wait in one of the rooms. It was three hours later when I asked a nurse what was happening, and she brought me to the emergency ICU where they were working on my wife. After I left the ICU, the nurse asked me if there was someone to call.

Cara's eighty-four-year-old father was in Los Angeles. I was on the computer each night updating the extended family on my wife's condition. Her father came home Sunday evening, and on Monday at 6:10 a.m. my wife passed away. The hospital called and my wife's brother and her father came. I was so lost, I did not know what to do. I talked to the ICU social worker and when I brought her in to see Cara, right away she told me she knew my wife as they had worked together a few years back. As of this writing, it has been five years and seven months since my wife passed, and I still have difficulty at times. It is a long journey we are on. I LOVE YOU, CARA!!!!!

*

BONNIE FORSHEY
Bonnie's 43-year-old husband Carl
died in a car accident in 2005

I was married the first time in 1971. I married my pastor's son, Bill, who had just returned from two tours in Vietnam. We went on to have two beautiful children, a boy and a girl. I don't think that he was ready for marriage, because he vanished without a trace. I was left with two toddlers, ages two and three, no job and no car. I had to file for divorce, and start all over again.

I found a position at the hospital working as a unit secretary. I also enrolled in the local community college and started training to become an R.N. Our lives were starting to come together again. We became very active in church and the ladies were constantly stopping by with food and taking the children shopping for clothing. The Lord works in mysterious ways. They brought us groceries every week, helped me with my bills, and wouldn't take no for an answer. Years later, I met someone in the community. His name was Carl, and he was a true Southern gentleman. We dated for a while, and he was perfect. We were married and bought a new home and the children flourished. I went to work in a bigger hospital and he became a foreman for Asplundh Tree Company. Our lives were so perfect, I couldn't have asked for anything more. I decided to go back to school to get my Bachelor's in Nursing so I could obtain a better position and increase my salary. During the last month of class, there was a knock on the door and I was called to the Dean's office. When I got there, I was told that there had been an accident. My husband had fallen 115 feet while trimming the trees along a power line and had been airlifted to the hospital. As I drove to the hospital, scenes of my life were going through my mind. I was hysterical and I was trying to prepare myself for what I was about to see. When I arrived, I was taken to a quiet room and briefed about Carl's condition. He had a fractured spine, various fractured limbs, punctured lungs, and they didn't know if he was going to pull through or not. I went to the chapel to pray and gave it all to God. Two weeks later, I brought Carl home.

He was left as a functioning quadriplegic. He would always be in a wheelchair, unable to walk, and only having limited use of his hands and arms. I was so thankful that he was alive. I adored him. My husband fell into a deep depression, and that once active, happy and vibrant man changed in front of my eyes. He had someone convert his vehicle so he could use hand pedals to drive. One day Carl went for a drive to clear his head when a drunk driver drove across his lane. I was told that Carl swerved to avoid hitting him, but ended up hitting a concrete barrier. His car caught on fire and he could not get out because his wheelchair was in the back seat. I miss Carl so very much. Not a day goes by that I don't think of him. What a blessing he was to me.

A year after, there was a knock on my door. I thought I was seeing a ghost: it was my first husband Bill stopping by to see his children and asking for forgiveness. He said that he had been sick and had gone through a liver transplant and that he had remarried, and had two more children. It was hard to bite the bullet, but I did so for the sake of my children. I wish that Bill had never located us. He promised my children everything and gave them nothing. His new wife didn't want Bill to visit the children or support them. She changed their phone number to an unlisted number and Bill simply forgot about them again. It was bad enough to cause my sixteen-year-old son Billy to end his life. Oh, how I wish that I had never answered the door!

Seven years later, my ex-husband was at a bonfire. Someone threw an accelerant on the fire to make it burn faster. It blew out the other side and totally engulfed Bill in flames, and he fell into the fire. He was transferred to the burn unit and placed on life support. My poor daughter had seen her brother die, and was now having to see her father in this horrible condition. Bill was suffering so much and there was no chance of survival. My daughter made the choice to take him off life support and to let him go. It was so hard to see Bill like that because he was my first love and the father of my children. I am happy that he is at peace now. He must have really struggled with the demons in his head. They say God never gives us more than we can handle, but sometimes I wonder.

*

MERIDETH HICKMAN
Merideth's 64-year-old husband Jim
died of pancreatic cancer

The beginning, well that does bring a smile to my thoughts. I had been alone for several years after a divorce. The kids and I were okay and had settled into a routine of work and school and getting by. I took a job at a store to help make ends meet and met a really good friend there who was also doing the juggle between a divorce and kids. And he introduced me to Jim. It was a blind date and we had both agreed after much prodding and coaxing to go out once if our friend would agree to just stop asking us! Jim and I had a casual date for pizza and he called me by the wrong name all through dinner. I didn't correct him, thinking this would be a short-lived thing because I wasn't looking for a relationship at the time. For the next date Jim continued to call me "Mildred" and I didn't stop him. But after a few dates I finally said, "I guess I should tell you that Mildred is not my name, I'm Merideth." He looked shocked and asked why I hadn't corrected him. I said that I really hadn't expected to see him again after that first date but that I was really liking him, so I thought he should know because it looked as though we were going to continue to see each other! We laughed together and continued to see each other more and more.

Jim had been alone for nineteen years after his divorce and had never had children, so he came into this relationship with challenges to say the least! As we all know, kids are noisy, messy and expensive, none of which Jim had experienced before. But we became so connected and we were a family from the start. I completed Jim and he completed me in many wonderful and amazing ways. Sure there were many challenges, but we always beat the odds and made it through.

One Friday the thirteenth, my world changed in ways that I couldn't even know at the time. I never believed in the Friday the thirteenth lore, although I had a healthy respect to watch and observe just in case! Jim had been feeling bad for about six months without being able to voice any real symptoms except for what he called indigestion. He had trouble eating much and had some pain with that feeling. He had trouble lying flat and slept in his recliner more and more. Jim had retired in the last six months and was told that he wasn't handling it well emotionally and was given pills for anxiety. I knew that wasn't it because I knew Jim. I insisted that we see a new doctor. We went in to see the new doctor who poked and prodded and said he felt there was some sort of issue but needed a CT scan to see what was really going on in there. We went for the CT scan the next day. It was hard because Jim had to drink a quart of contrast for this scan and, as I said, eating was not easily done at this point. But we made it through and it stayed down and his scan was completed. The results came on Friday the thirteenth.

The doctor called to say that he wanted to see us both and in person but would give no other information. I knew in my mind that meant it was bad but told myself and Jim that it would be okay, that we could do surgery and chemo and whatever we had to do and that we would be okay. I think I knew it would be cancer even before the diagnosis. After we arrived I noticed we were the last appointment of the day and the office was empty and quiet. We were seated in the exam room and the doctor came in with the scans in hand. Very calmly and without much feeling he told us that the scans confirmed what he had suspected. Jim had advanced pancreatic cancer with metastatic cancer of the liver. Stunned, we asked what the next step was and I asked how soon we could get into surgery. He looked at us without expression and said that was not an option, that the only option was aggressive chemotherapy that might extend Jim's life by months. Jim stared at him and asked how long that meant he had. The doctor responded with a shake of his head and said maybe six months. If Jim opted for chemo, he might get a year at best. His cancer was already well advanced, there was no hope. The doctor then looked at me, took my hand and said, "You will need to be strong for him, he needs you." I gave him a small smile, shook my head in agreement and asked if there was a restroom I could use. He showed me and I excused myself and calmly walked to the bathroom. I closed the door and locked it and stared into the mirror. I threw some cold water onto my face, and went to the floor. I sat on the cold tile and sobbed into the wad of paper towels I had gathered in my hands to wipe my face. I was trying to be silent so no one would hear me, especially not Jim. This man whom I loved, who had come into my life and made me laugh, made me complete like I had never experienced before, made a life and a home with me, raised my kids and shared the good and the bad for the last twenty years was dying. And I couldn't stop it, couldn't make this better, and couldn't even slow it down. I had just learned that Jim would leave me, he would have no choice, and he would have to battle this disease before he left.

I felt numb and breathless. How would I tell the kids? Why us? All I could think was how much I did NOT want to do this thing before me. Be strong for him...he needs you now... REALLY??? That's your best advice to me??? As I cried and tried to gain my composure I just kept thinking to myself, "And who will be strong for ME?? Who will take care of ME? What will happen to ME?"

I still feel that this seems so selfish, after all Jim just found out he was going to die, so how could I be thinking of me? But I felt totally out of my element and capabilities, and had no idea how to help Jim die well and with dignity. Was I even up to this challenge or would I break before the end? And this was not the last time I would ask this last question.

*

STEPHEN HOCHHAUS
Stephen's 51-year-old wife Kathy
died of soft tissue sarcoma in 2011

Katherine Alice Thomas was born in Calgary, Alberta, Canada on March 24, 1959. She was adopted at two months of age by David and Shirley Thomas and raised on a farm in Langdon, Alberta. Kathy went to school there and received her real estate license before finishing her Bachelor's degree in accounting in Phoenix, Arizona. Under a business investment visa, she bought a home in Scottsdale, Arizona, and opened a clothing store. Kathy later started an accounting business where she began doing work for my company when we fell in love and married in 1998 on the anniversary of the day we met.

Kathy was an avid quilter and started a wearable art business called Lilacs and Ladybugs. She became a U.S. citizen in 2009. We traveled often to Canada to spend time with her aging parents and eventually built a second home near them to assist with their care. On the trip up to close on our new home, Kathy felt a lump in her leg which turned out to be the cancer that would end her life four months later.

After receiving chemo and radiation for six weeks, Kathy and I flew up to visit her parents who were not in good enough health to come down to Arizona for Kathy's surgery. While in Canada, Kathy had a cough that turned out to be cancer that had metastasized to her lungs. From the hospital in Calgary, Kathy was air transported to Phoenix. We had hoped that the Mayo Hospital where Kathy had received treatment might somehow be able to save her life. She had no chance and died five days later as I slept next to her.

Kathy never asked, "Why me?" She never felt sorry for herself and even when I had to tell her that she had but days to live, she simply said, "It is what it is." She was the bravest woman I have ever known.

I was and still remain deeply in love with her and only with grief counseling and group support was I able to continue living. I think of myself as half the man I used to be. Only with time was I able to become strong enough to continue living and accept the fact that I am no longer half of a couple who truly were in love but instead just a man truly in love. I now travel alone, eat out often by myself, and still celebrate anniversaries and Kathy's birthday with more joy than sorrow. I honor Kathy by doing things we would have done. I have also grown comfortable living alone and often can sleep through the night. But do I miss her? You bet I do, but I have discovered that I cry a little less. I smile a little more. I have found myself alive again.

Before Kathy died, she told me she would try to reach me from the other side if she possibly could and yes, she found a way. I am driven by a simple concept, "Death cannot stop true love. All it can do is delay it for a while," from *The Princess Bride*.

*

MARLISE MAGNA
Marlise's 36-year-old partner Blaine
died by suicide in 2010

I met Blaine about three years before his death, as a friend of a friend on Facebook. We clicked immediately and always engaged in happy banter and debates. He was involved at the time and so was I, so it was always aboveboard and just a good conversation. After almost two years of being friends, circumstances changed and we decided to meet up. Our first encounter was literally all of two minutes but we KNEW we were meant to be. After that we spent a lot of time together, although it wasn't easy. We didn't live near each other and his ex-girlfriend who was the mother of his son, caused a lot of problems. She withheld his son as a form of punishment and I firmly believe this was the most pertinent factor in his decision to take his own life. I so wish I could meet up with his little T-man, as Blaine called him, and tell him how awesome the father he never knew was.

We were set to get married on 11/11/2011, it was a number that Blaine simply loved and insisted on. He then wanted to move to Bali and live an idyllic island life. Towards the end he would say many times, "Baby girl, I'm gonna kill myself. It's gonna be epic," and "See you on the other side."

Blaine was a Microsoft Certified systems engineer and loved always expanding his fields of knowledge. Music was another passion we shared. He was a huge lover of Pearl Jam and would often quote their lyrics. We had released a few tracks of trance-type music on iTunes. Blaine also had an amazing penchant for writing. He loved scuba diving and often wrote stories about dives and finding black pearls (which I was apparently, to him). He loved coffee and his favorite food was chicken lasagna (he was a body training expert!).

I knew in the week leading up to Blaine's death that he wasn't one hundred percent himself, but I never dreamed things would escalate at such a rapid rate. On the day Blaine took his life, he left me a few Facebook messages saying, "I love you baby girl." He was very quiet but I ascribed it to his erratic sleeping patterns and assumed he'd fallen asleep in the morning hours. About 2 p.m. I received a text message on my cellphone saying to please call regarding Blaine, but it came from his number. Fear set in. I called and a close family friend answered and told me what had happened. At first I said that if Blaine wanted to end things with me, to just say so and not to make sick jokes. Eventually I realized it was no joke and I frantically started calling morgues to find Blaine. After I got the details, I drank myself into a fitful sleep.

First thing the next morning, I made the long and arduously heart-wrenching trip to the state morgue where all suicides go to be autopsied. I met Blaine's mom there for the first and only time. It was surreal, his family thought Blaine had made me up in his mind. I wasn't allowed to see his body alone but the head of the morgue took pity and said if I waited until closing time, he'd allow me a few minutes alone. Imagine seeing the man you love, your best friend and lover, lying cold and lifeless, still blood splattered from the autopsy. I died a million times over and then some. After that it was surviving day to day until the funeral. His family told people that Blaine had suffered a heart attack. My life stopped after that. I became totally depressive and tried taking my own life. I ended up under psychiatric supervision for three weeks. For months after I partied hard, I guess to try and numb the pain. I became a total insomniac and suffered great anxiety and depression.

Blaine was an only child and I cannot imagine his mom's agony. She has been left utterly alone. My life has never been the same and will probably never be.

Yes, I thank Blaine for sharing his last time on earth with me. I thank him for enriching my life and broadening my horizons and encouraging me to be the authentic me and loving me without condition. I thank him for being there for the good and the bad. I thank him for changing my life path. I thank God for lending him to us for a little bit. We always said "two hearts beating as one," and "two against the world baby, two against the world." To quote "Just Breathe," one of his favorite Pearl Jam songs: "Nothing you would take. Everything you gave. I hope until I die... Meet you on the other side." From Blaine to me:

Love at first sight is a fantasy.
The make believe or the imaginary.
To some it's a gift that becomes real.
When the imaginary dream becomes real,
the ecstatic joy and freedom is a rare gem,
that few get to share.
I'm glad that I know,
that I have found that gem.
In you.
You are my fantasy and God willing my reality.
I Love you, mind, body and soul.
Under the sun, the moon, the stars.

DJ Zer0.1 and Mia Magna, forever. See you on the other side.

*

DIANE MCKENZIE-SAPP
Diane's 65-year-old husband Ron
died from renal failure in 2006

I was the beauty queen, the "Miss Congeniality" type, and didn't see marriage in my future. I had seen *The Stepford Wives* and decided I wouldn't stifle my individuality. What if I found a partner who would make me a better person, if he was my other half, melding together like oil and vinegar making a great dressing? What were the odds of that? I decided to become a stewardess.

Ron was the kid from the poor side of the tracks, shining shoes and selling vegetables as a child. He loved the Baltimore Colts, hanging out with family, guy friends, rock and roll, his car and playing baseball. A natural athlete, Ron was the best shortstop that ever played. He worked to finish high school. No one in his family had ever finished high school. I went to Catholic school, played varsity field hockey, basketball and softball.

Ron saw the good in people; he was optimistic, and always had a smile on his face. I was an opportunist and liked dogs more than people. Ron did everything because it was the right thing to do. I had always calculated the risk versus benefit of my actions. He was oil and I was vinegar. By our second date, I knew Ron would be the father of my children.

He drove a soda truck when we met and later a tractor trailer. I sold my crafts, worked in retailing, and began to teach porcelain doll making. The trucking industry failed with deregulation so Ron went to work at GM assembling, Martin Marietta, and the State of Maryland, each job paying less but with family insurance. The labor market, the economy and equal opportunity act were not kind to us. Each failed company would bring me back into the workforce. I would work in retailing as a store manager or department manager in large retail stores.

While gardening, my diamond fell out of my engagement ring. Ron worked an extra job to replace it. It meant so much to him that I wear my rings. It was important to him that my finger declared my love for him. It was more important to him than to me. Now I honor the man with a widow's ring to declare that our love knows no boundary.

In my forties, our son Mike went to an expensive college. With two people in college, his tuition was reduced so I went back to school to become a nurse. I was a nurse at the Fort Howard VA until Rhonda, our oldest, was hit by a drunk driver and suffered a traumatic brain injury. I nursed in hospice while Kadie, our youngest, could choose any college east of the Mississippi, and not use her full scholarship in California. Like the wolf mother, I wanted my pups close. I was a federal nurse inspector for Medicare and the State of Maryland.

on was diagnosed with colon cancer in May 2007. Baltimore Orioles baseball stars Boog Powell and Eric Davis were diagnosed with colon cancer about the same time, had the same surgeon, and both did well. I made an appointment with that surgeon but Ron chose the surgeon our primary physician recommended. If I had made that appointment, Ron might be alive today.

Never have surgery in the summer. During the summer months the new doctors arrive in hospitals and the surgeons turn over their operating rooms to kids who have never done surgery before. The student who removed the cancer used the same cancer-infected instrument to remove the bowel and pierced Ron's right kidney. We were not told; the hospital, the doctors and our primary physician did not report the incident and conspired to hide the record. The young man who did this "mistake" told me himself with tears in his eyes, or I would have never known. Colon cancer is very treatable and has a protocol. A kidney laced with colon cancer cells has no treatment. Ron's health spiraled down from that day on. August 1997, Ron had "successful surgery," yet he began to die that day.

The doctors "did all they could;" hospitalizations, countless surgeries, seeping wounds, wrong medications, unapproved chemo concoctions, radiation burns, chemo illness, impotency, ventilators, foot-drop, internal blockages, infected stents, misdiagnosis, misread scans, wound vacuums, delirium, ventilators, rare-infections, dialysis, adhesions and constant mind numbing pain. Some medical errors include:

- An ER doctor ordered Lipitor 2000 mg which ruined Ron's liver. The usual dose is 20 mg.
- Rehab and hydrotherapy were ordered. Ron was infected with MRSA from the clinic's water bath.
- The pierced kidney developed colon cancer, leaving Ron with one kidney.
- Ron's stent failed leading to removal of his remaining kidney which then required dialysis.
- The doctor reading the scan said Ron's entire gut was necrotic. He would die without surgery. They only found a stent with a rare microbe and adhesions that they misdiagnosed as necrosis.

Ron suffered and never complained. He never had a bad word to say about his doctors. He said they were doing the best they could. He joked that without doctor appointments he would never get out of the house.

I was diagnosed with breast cancer in 2005. I had surgery and radiation. I opted not to get chemo as I needed to work for medical insurance and be Ron's caregiver. In 2014, I was diagnosed with angiosarcoma, a deadly cancer that shows up several years after radiation treatment.

In 2006, scans indicated that Ron's cancer had spread to his bones. His liver was three times the normal size. Ron chose to stop dialysis and opted for a renal failure death over colon cancer. He died in hospice.

The night he died, he laughed with his kids, family and friends. The Beatles song "Let It Be" looped as I got into his bed. He rested when touching me. We were together when his guide came for him. He went, I stayed.

I would be "okay." As a hospice nurse, I should be. I didn't know I would die that day as well. There was the constant grayness, the tears, and my broken heart. The pain of grief is real like the phantom pain of amputees. My heart bled tears. He did not break my heart by dying; rather my heart and soul were torn in half and would never be the same. Everything that was good was gone. I felt incomplete, broken and had no reason to welcome tomorrow. Tornadoes, earthquakes and volcanoes leave the destruction I felt in my soul. My words "I'm fine" belied the woman inside. She was lost without her other half, melting away, broken and fading into nothingness with each passing day.

I had lost my partner, my future and myself. The third finger on my left hand was "me," my history and a symbol of our love. My wedding rings were artifacts of a time that no longer existed, an exquisite memorial to what had been. To remove them was unthinkable, but they mocked the widow. Once upon a time those rings told my story; now they taunted. There is no Happily Ever After.

*

JULIE MJELVE
Julie's 42-year-old husband Cameron
died by suicide in 2011

I met James Cameron Mjelve in 2005 while we were both living in Edmonton. At the time he worked for a laborer's union. We married in 2007 and had three beautiful children together, one boy and two girls. In 2009, Cameron decided to go back to university and finish his Education degree. In 2010, during his second year, I began to notice that he was struggling more with the course load. During Christmas break Cameron seemed different, a little off from his usual self. Perhaps a little depressed, but nothing to be overly concerned about. In January 2011, our youngest daughter was born with a disability and the stresses of life became overwhelming for Cameron. He began to struggle even more with his university courses.

On July 21, 2011, my husband committed suicide. We were both forty-two at the time and our children were three years old, two years old, and five months old. There is much that has changed in my life from losing a spouse. Perhaps the first is that I've had to learn how to use the word "widow" when speaking about myself. That alone has been a tough adjustment. I've become single again and I've had to learn how to be comfortable in a room full of couples. I've had to become comfortable in a room full of widows. I've had to become comfortable crying in front of both those groups of people. It has been a difficult experience, losing a spouse. I've had to face major decisions for myself as well as the children alone. At times this has been very stressful, especially when I've had to make decisions which impact my children's health or our financial stability. It has been so difficult not having anyone to bounce ideas off of. Friends will always tell you they are there to help you and listen to you, but it's still not the same. I miss my friend who shared everything with me.

But, I have learned from my experience, and developed a stronger decision-making process. And, as a result, I have been able to become more confident in the decisions that I make. Another way my life is different as a result of losing a spouse is that I simply cannot do the things I want to do. I cannot run to the store at 10 p.m. at night, there is no one to watch the children. I cannot sleep in on a Saturday if it's been a tough week of being up in the night with a variety of sick children. Even something so simple as taking a vacation has become a major undertaking. Not only is there no one to help me with the children, but there's no one for me to share the experience with. Even if we as a family are on vacation and the children are enjoying themselves, who did I get to tell about my experience? In that same regard, life is lonely. I don't have anyone to share even the small moments with. There is no spouse who laughs with you or remembers with you. There is also no one who touches you. Yes, the kids hug and climb all over me, but it's different than the simple loving touch of a husband.

Life has been different and even difficult, for sure. But I also see it as an opportunity to grow. Although my life will never be what I had dreamed it would be, I am discovering that there is a new life that I can make. It unfortunately doesn't include my husband, but it does include my children and we take Cameron's memory with us wherever we go. And we are learning that we can still live a life that is full of meaning and adventure, even if it wasn't the life we originally chose. And I do feel like I have a choice. We live in a society that is very focused on couples. This is not the life that I chose, to be single at forty-two years old, but I also feel like I'm presented with a choice on how to react. I can sit and wallow in self-pity and despair over broken dreams, or I can get up and start life over again.

I will always, always remember my husband. I will always grieve his loss. I will still cry over his loss. But I will choose to keep on living and to help my children find their life as well.

*

LILIAN MORTON
Lilian's 58-year-old husband Michael
died in a plane crash in 2012

The first day I met Michael, I was working at a medical software company. When I got to the office one Monday, there were two gentlemen there. It was Michael and his partner. They had been hired by one of our investors to turn the company around. As Michael explained, the company was in bad shape and had a really rough road ahead but they had a plan and he explained to us what was going on and what they were going to do. For the first time since I took the job, I felt like someone was being straight with me. I trusted Michael immediately.

The U.S. Securities and Exchange Commission was investigating the company. A crazy time, previous management's shenanigans made the local and national news including the front page of the Wall Street Journal. Michael often talked of writing a book about our experiences there. He received about a hundred messages a day from people who had invested their life savings, be it two hundred dollars or two hundred thousand dollars into this company, and were given "fake" stock certificates. Michael returned every one of their calls and met with anyone who came to the office. He handled all of the investors with such compassion and understanding, regardless of the size of their investment.

We were from different parts of the country and the odds of us ever meeting were slim to none. It was a fluke that I took that job and, as he later explained, he refused the job at our company multiple times until his partner begged him to just come down for the week and meet everyone. He agreed and he never left except to visit his kids. We got married and moved to Florida where he and his partner started a business. Michael loved his family deeply. He had three children and I had three children. It was chaotic but wonderful every time we got all of our brood together.

We both loved to read. I would buy the books, Michael would read them and leave me notes in the margins about his thoughts, or just to say he loved me or something silly. I still find these today, three years later. He would regularly write me letters or cards and sometimes give them to me, other times leave them for me to find later. Michael always kept journals. I bought him a beautiful red leather journal. He immediately began writing in it. The next night I found it lying on my pillow. I opened it and he had written in it to me. I wrote him back and left it on his pillow. This continued off and on for the remainder of our days together. That journal is one of the things that I cherish most.

After a few years in Florida, Michael's best friend and business partner was diagnosed with cancer and died about a year later. His wife didn't honor his burial wishes and it caused a great amount of turmoil in his family. It also caused us to discuss our own wishes in this regard at great length. Michael did a turn on the company that we decided to purchase. Michael was also a long-time pilot and decided to start flying again. He was looking on the internet and posting at the airport for a small plane to purchase. He was so excited about flying again. Once he got current, he was anxious to take me flying with him. He wanted to show me what he saw. I had only flown with Michael once before, when we first met.

We scheduled a time one weekend to go up in the plane. We got up, had coffee and headed out toward the airport, hoping that the haze would burn off by the time we got to the airport. When it was apparent that wasn't going to happen, we had to reschedule for another time. The last weekend we had together, we woke up and we were both sick with the stomach virus. We had to cancel flying plans again. This was the third time in one month. I jokingly told Michael that I guess I'm not supposed to be flying in that plane with him, and we had a good laugh about it.

Wednesday, we were feeling a little better and felt that we needed to get back to work. It had become our weekly ritual to stop at a restaurant down the street from our house and have a drink and share an appetizer and talk about everything that was going on with us. Michael called it the State of the State. We usually did this Friday or Saturday but occasionally when we had weekend plans, we would do it Thursday. This was one of those Thursdays. We talked about the kids and how much Michael was looking forward to seeing them on Easter break and we made big plans to go to the lake again. We talked about how the company, although not doing great, was certainly moving in the right direction. We talked about how lucky we were to have each other and how blessed we felt. Michael told me he was going flying the next day and asked me to go with him. Friday morning came and we had a few issues come up at work that I had to deal with. Michael came into my office to get me to go flying, I apologized and told him that I wasn't going to be able to get away.

When I returned that day from a quick lunch, I had a message from someone at the airport. I called back and was told that Michael's plane had gone down and there was a fatality and he was the only one on board. That was the day my world stopped spinning. I just started screaming. I couldn't believe it was real. I lost my best friend, my husband, my partner. The police wouldn't allow me to go to the crash site. I just sat in Michael's office for several hours until one of our friends took me home.

The funeral home didn't want me to view Michael's body because they didn't want my last memory of him to be the condition he was in now. I insisted. I told them that the last memory I would have of Michael would be when he was alive and kissing me goodbye as he left for the airport. For me, I needed to know it was really him. They reluctantly agreed and my sister went with me. I'm so glad I did. It was hard but it was necessary.

I sat down with the funeral home to discuss the arrangements. I didn't have to give it much thought because Michael and I had discussed it when his friend died. I knew exactly what Michael wanted. He was cremated and we had a memorial service. The following week, I flew Michael to his hometown where we had another memorial service for all of his extended family and friends. His kids and I scattered some of his ashes on his parents' graves.

*

LISA OWENS
Lisa's 50 year-old husband Greg
died of pancreatic cancer in 2014

Greg was the love of my life, my first love, and I was his last. We actually went to school together, but never talked or had classes together. We met via CupidJuntion.com, an online dating site. We started talking online, and discovered that we had mutual friends. Our first date was in March 2002, and we either talked or saw each other every day until we married in 2004.

Greg had one son who had a child at a young age, so Greg adopted the child to keep him out of the system. Matthew was two when we started dating and four when we married. I was able to experience motherhood, something I had always wanted. Life was good! Greg was a computer programmer and together with my job, we were able to do whatever we wanted. We were so blessed. During our second year of marriage, we bought a brand new house and life continued on like a dream.

Matthew had some behavior issues and some problems with being biracial. He couldn't understand being black in our white world. His pediatrician suggested therapy and this is when our dream turned quickly. Matthew was diagnosed with early onset childhood bipolar and, on his twelfth birthday, he was hospitalized. We ended up losing the house, our car, and our dream life to get the help Matthew needed. Greg had to leave his career to be Matthew's caretaker, because I was his target and unable to fight off his attacks.

On Matthew's twentieth hospitalization in less than two years, Greg went to the emergency room and was diagnosed with an ulcer due to stress. He was then hospitalized for two weeks with pancreatitis. It took the doctors three months to locate cancer in the head of Greg's pancreas; they gave him six months to live.

Greg immediately went to work on getting everything in order. He gave guardianship of Matthew to his son, who was now old enough to care for him. Greg moved us to the basement apartment in my parents' home so I would be taken care. We were blessed that my job allowed me to spend as much time with Greg as possible. Greg fought every day to live! He loved the ocean, and we were able to go to Florida for a vacation. Friends gave us a Christmas trip to Callaway Gardens just outside of Columbus, Georgia, so Greg could see the Christmas lights. Greg was on hospice the last seven months of his life; I spent most of those days with him. He rarely slept, so most mornings we went to Wal-Mart so Greg could walk and get some exercise.

Slowly, Greg began to put the finishing touches on the life he fought so hard for. He bought cards for his family and friends, and gave each a handwritten letter telling them just how much they meant to him. He went to the funeral home and cemetery with me to finalize each detail. One morning while in Wal-Mart, Greg bought a black-striped polo shirt from the clearance rack and said that was the shirt he wanted to be buried in. He was an amazing man, and we treasured our time every day.

One Tuesday morning, Greg walked into the hospital. He died five days later, on Saturday, October 11, 2014. Surrounded by his mother, sister, and me holding his hand, Greg passed peacefully. We watched him take his last breath; we prayed he would take another breath, but he did not. He was at peace and, for the first time in two years, was pain free!

The days ahead were a blur, but the service was beautiful and his presence was felt. Greg touched so many lives, and I continue every day to see the joy he brought to so many, especially me! I was so blessed to have had him love me! This last year has been hard, but knowing Greg is now free of pain has allowed me to survive. I haven't moved on yet; our place is still just as Greg left it. His razor and shampoo still grace the shower, and it brings me daily comfort to see them as I try to make it through one more day without him. I go to Greg's grave every week and talk to him. I sing to him, and have an unpublished Facebook page where I'm journaling my journey without him. I know Greg knows what is going on, and is my guardian angel.

My best friend lost her husband five months ago. They were married just three months when he died in a motorcycle accident. Helping her deal with her loss has helped me to see how blessed I was to have Greg, and share all the special moments we had. We had time to say our goodbyes, we had time to say the things that my best friend didn't get to say to her husband. I am a better person by knowing, loving and being loved by Greg Owens. He gave me a life, and made me smile!! I am the blessed wife of an angel.

*

MARY POTTER KENYON
Mary's 60-year-old husband David
died of heart failure in 2012

My husband David used to shake his head when I'd tell him he was beautiful, but he was. By early 2012, I thought we'd discovered the secret to a perfect marriage. In the five years after his cancer, I could count on one hand the number of times we'd even exchanged strong words. We'd become true partners in every sense of the word. It hadn't always been like that. While we may have started out that way, eight children and financial struggles contributed to our relationship becoming stagnant. I believe the turning point in our marriage came during David's cancer treatment. One day when he sat exhausted in a chair, I knelt down in front of him, removed his socks and shoes, and began rubbing his aching feet. In twenty-seven years of marriage, I'd never touched that man's feet. For the first time in a long time, maybe ever, I was putting him first. For the next five and a half years, we reaped the rewards of what marriage could be. We were enjoying each other and grateful for our life together. We had eight healthy children and I was having some success getting things published and teaching classes and workshops. David reveled in all my activities, telling me it was my time "to fly." I'd remind him he was the wind beneath my wings, encouraging me and caring for our children while I attended conferences, conducted workshops and worked on a book that had been his idea. Life was good.

Our grandson Jacob, who'd been diagnosed with cancer in 2010 at the age of five, was also doing well, with his cancer in remission. Then in March 2012, Jacob's cancer returned, and I don't think David could bear to imagine what his little body would have to endure. David had a heart attack and ended up in the hospital for a stent surgery. Three days after he came home, his heart stopped sometime during the night, and I thought mine would break in two. Our youngest was just eight years old.

How would I live without my beloved at my side? I began journaling the day after David's death, filling three pages with all that I was grateful for: those bonus years with David after his cancer, my children, my siblings, good friends. I also wrote about the pain and anguish I was experiencing in bereavement. I was determined to continue doing those things David had encouraged me to do: the writing, workshops, and conferences. I finished the book that had been his idea, and seven months after his death, signed a contract for it. I will never forget seeing a display of that book filling the window of a Barnes & Noble bookstore. It was a surreal moment, an experience that should have been exhilarating, but instead was bittersweet and painful. David should have been there.

I've signed three more book contracts in the ensuing years, and have continued doing workshops and public speaking. I love helping others who are grieving, so I do a lot of public speaking at churches and for grief support groups. I also wrote a book chronicling my grief journey in losing a mother, husband and grandson in the space of three years. I want other grievers to have something to hang on to in the darkness of grief.

My world is so much bigger now. I began a Bible study at my church, have developed strong friendships with other women, and got a job as a library director. A day doesn't go by that I don't miss David. I absolutely hate being a single parent, but I appreciate each and every day I have here on earth, just like David did. I think about what David said to me when I'd asked if he dreaded those birthdays that ended in zero the year he was going to turn sixty. "Not at all! Think of the alternative," he'd commented. He didn't live to see sixty-one years. These last few years have been a faith journey for me just as much as a grief journey. I believe I will see my parents, David and Jacob again someday. In the meantime, I resolve to be a better person than I was before. I'll mine my pain, instead of wasting it, reaching out to others to help them on their own path.

*

NANCY REDMOND
Nancy's 40-year-old husband Kevin
died of a heart attack in 2012

I met my husband Kevin in March 2002, in a spiritual chat room when we were introduced by my sister (she and I were both moderators in this chat room). Kevin and I had never met nor even seen a picture of each other when we chose to begin our lives together, and he moved across country from Wyoming to Minnesota! I had three children from a prior marriage and Kevin had a daughter from his first marriage. After seven years, we finally took the ultimate leap of faith together and were married just prior to the Keith Urban concert in St. Paul. As luck would have it, Keith's people found us in the audience and Keith came over and sang "Making Memories of Us" to us on our wedding day with fifteen thousand of our "closest personal friends" in attendance!

For three years, we lived the most perfect marriage anyone could imagine – when we were not at work, we were together, truly making memories of us, and went out of our way to experience life to its fullest. Kevin truly taught me to live in the moment each and every day. Kevin was the most amazing drummer I had ever seen. He not only marched with the Casper Troopers Drum & Bugle Corps as a young adult, he also marched with a senior drum corps here Twin Cities, Minnesota, as well as playing in the Keith Urban Drumline in 2008 in St. Paul. I always told Kevin that the three loves of his life were in this order: Drumming, his dog Chloe, and me. And I was okay with that! I adored his "drummer's heart" and miss that constant drumming as we went about our everyday existence.

After Kevin's retirement from drum corps, he began driving the equipment truck for Minnesota Brass which led to his career as a truck driver. We had our lives so "together" in the three years of our marriage that his sudden death tore the rug out from under my feet and there isn't a day that I wouldn't give my own life to have him back here.

On May 10, 2012, Kevin woke at his usual time of 5:30 a.m. to leave by 6:30 a.m. for his job as a truck driver for an ice company. I remember that day so vividly. He always rubbed my leg to ever-so-gently wake me up to say goodbye. That day in particular, he took off his uniform baseball-style hat and laid his cheek so gently on mine. I swear I can still feel the warmth of his cheek when I miss him the most. He kissed me goodbye and I remember thinking, "Oh, I could just pull you back into this warm bed and keep you next to me all day!" He hugged me like it was the last time he'd ever do so. It was. It was such a beautiful springtime morning, and I started my day feeling so happy and peacefully.

I received a call before I left for work that morning inviting us for a night out in support of a friend going through a rough time. I phoned Kev and asked if he'd be done in time to join the group for dinner, and he sounded so "different." I remember telling Kevin that he didn't sound okay and asked him if he needed me to come get him or call help for him. He assured me that he was fine, and that he was looking forward to a night out after work. It was just a gut feeling but I called him right back to check on him – a wife's intuition, I guess – and he didn't answer. An absolute feeling of panic ensued for me in that instant, and at that exact moment, a little gray bird with a red breast landed ON THE SCREEN of my bedroom window – not the frame of the window but his little claws were wrapped around the screen of the window. The exact same thing happened the morning my stepmom was murdered in Hawaii. Recognizing that sign, in that instant, my heart knew Kevin had gone Home to God.

I attempted to phone him several times during the day and always got his cellphone voicemail. I even drove home at lunchtime to see if maybe he had an early end to his day and had perhaps gone home to catch up on some sleep. I prayed and called him constantly for ten hours straight. I called everyone who could possibly have had contact with Kevin that day, and the fear built. I finally filed a missing person report at 7:00 p.m. that evening. Soon after, my daughter and a dear friend came to sit with me and wait. My friend's son was Kevin's co-worker and he contacted the plant manager at the ice company, who drove to the ice plant to see if Kevin's car was still at work. When word came in that Kevin's truck had been located by GPS, my son drove the thirty-five miles to the Target store where Kevin's truck had been parked and unfortunately had to identify Kevin's remains. My sweet son was the one who had to deliver the most horrible news he'd ever have to share.

By 11:00 p.m. that evening, fourteen hours after I had last spoken with Kevin, it was confirmed that Kevin had died of a massive heart attack around 9:30 that morning – shortly after I last spoke with him. Our last words to each other were, "I love you." In my times of greatest periods of grief, I cling to that fact.

*

MARY LEE ROBINSON
Mary Lee's 63-year-old husband Pat
died from a sudden stroke in 2013

My husband Pat was widowed when I met him in 2003. His wife had died after a brief struggle with pancreatic cancer. When we met, he was the saddest man I ever saw. Gaunt, way too lean, drawn and without much color. His two teenage sons were completely out of control, submerged deeply into the world of drugs. While Pat and I dated, they seemed to turn around and were headed in positive directions.

In 2005, we married in South Carolina where we both wanted to retire. By then, Pat had also regained his normal healthy weight, his color and the sparkle in his eye. He was a handsome man, a cross between Sam Elliott, Tom Selleck and Doc Holliday, at six-foot two-inches and 200 pounds with silver hair. With six elderly relatives to care for, and needing some distance from the kids to encourage independence, we moved to West Virginia. Our plan was for Pat to continue working for a few more years while I traveled to care for our family. The pace was brutal as relatives fell

29

or became ill, and the kids returned to their downward spiral. The day came when we were able to realize our hopes and move to coastal South Carolina and build a home of our own design on a lovely lake. The seven months that we spent building the house and then the eleven months that we lived in it together were the happiest and most peaceful we'd known. Life was grand for the Robinsons.

Pat had suffered an aneurysm in his carotid artery a year and a half before we met, and then had a mini stroke in West Virginia. Medically, we thought it was resolved and Pat appeared to be the picture of health. One afternoon, he happily waved and walked out the door to go play pool with his buddies. Pat was an excellent player, and it was his favorite thing in the world. He never came home again. He had a stroke in the pool hall and was rushed to the ER. When I arrived at the hospital, his neurosurgeon gave me the very bad news that Pat would not survive. The best that could be hoped for was that he would be permanently in a vegetative state, and that wasn't likely to last long.

With no family or friends around, I had the very tough decision to remove my husband from life support. Since we'd talked about it many, many times while caring for our elders, and had prepared the legal documents, I knew with certainty what I must do. It was devastating. Five days later Pat was gone.

He could not speak in the beginning, but he knew I was there and squeezed my hand. As the hours rolled by, he slipped farther and farther away from me. The first indication that he had been deteriorating neurologically for about six months before he died, was when I went to the bank two weeks later to begin settling his affairs. Pat died in the middle of February 2013. On the prior Halloween of 2012, he changed all the beneficiary designations out of my name into the names of his drug-addled sons without telling me. It explained why his files were a mess and many missing. Pat was a certified public accountant, he kept meticulous records normally. All of our income producing accounts were gone, and so was half my income. I was shattered initially, thinking he didn't love me. It helped when I talked with Pat's dearest friend who told me that he too was shocked, as Pat had told him again, most vehemently, that the kids would never see a dime. They'd just put it in their veins. It took some time, but we began to put some of the pieces together as we looked backwards. There were signs, but they were very subtle. It was very likely that for months Pat had been having mini strokes on the side of his brain that affected memory and judgment.

The task fell to me to see that the kids got their money, as I was still executor. I did, and they did. It was a promise to keep to Pat. My next task was to pick myself up off the ground, by myself as I have no children and very little family. It was then that I began to receive strong indications, I call them signs, from God and my family who had already passed, that I had work to do. My mission, my purpose, was and is to serve other widows and widowers. Of the eight family members that had died and to whom I was closest, five were widowed, two of them twice, and a living cousin lost a spouse and a child. I've often talked with two especially dear friends. When I told them that I felt I was being "called" they said, "Yes, you are, and you can tell God that you are not deaf!" The signs were loud, clear and multiple.

There have been many obstacles to what I have done, and yet every time I meet one, the way seems to be cleared to continue. I miss my husband enormously, and yet I feel his presence daily. I have a purpose and a mission that is my driving force. It's also a way to begin to replace lost income. I lost half the income, but not half the bills. Because of this calling, I've also met some incredible people and made very special new friends. It's not the life either Pat or I envisioned, but it's a good life. Daily I strive to be "The Widow My Husband Would Be Proud of.......Still."

*

CAROL SCIBELLI
Carol's 56-year-old husband Jimmy
died from lymphoma in 2006

At our ninth grade graduation in 1965, Jimmy pointed me out to Fanny, his Italian mother, and said, "You see that girl with the blonde flip trying to hide the gum in her cheek? That's the girl I'm going to marry." Her response: "Good that she's Jewish. Jewish women want things. She'll make sure you're successful." I would like to believe that my future mother-in-law was in awe of her son's early devotion to me, but it's clear that Feisty Fanny aspired to lock him in as the son who would take care of her in her old age.

We were married at age twenty-two in 1972, and for the next thirty-three years Jimmy did take care of Fanny, and me, and our children. If he could have, he would have given birth to our daughter and son. He wasn't bossy or pushy: He was a nurturer, and even as a young man he seemed to understand how the world worked. I certainly didn't. We had arranged to meet somewhere, and the moment I saw him I breathed easier.

Wherever we were, Jimmy was the smartest, loudest, funniest and most likable man in the room. Jimmy was a big man with big dreams. He owned horses and a gold mine and oil wells and a casino and guess what? We weren't crazy rich. We had our ups and downs, and we did all right. It was all about sharing the adventure with friends and family. Holidays meant making memories. For several Thanksgivings we took his two brothers, their families, our kids, and my cousins to upstate New York for a weekend of karaoke, sledding, and football on the lawn. And, Jimmy didn't just cook traditional fish on Christmas Eve. He made a volcano out of shrimp and little boats from calamari. That was just one year's theme.

Everyday life was good, too. We laughed often. Our marriage wasn't perfect, of course. As the kids became teenagers, I wanted to tighten our grip on them, keep them close. Jimmy was more permissive. We'd fight about this. His opinions were rigid, and he could be moody. He could build a wall and stay on the other side of it for days. Naturally, this is my version of our marriage. Since my husband isn't here to contradict me, I was the perfect wife!

The first week of March 2006, six weeks before he died, Jimmy began to have severe stomach pains and he was unable to lie down without tremendous discomfort. It never occurred to me that it was serious. He was only fifty-six and although overweight, just months before he danced as smoothly as Fred Astaire and as always, he spun me around like a Raggedy Ann doll. But the doctors suspected pancreatic cancer, and the prognosis was not good. The next several weeks was a cyclone of tests and the doctors held back a definite diagnosis until the results "told the story." Jimmy was convinced from the start that he was doomed. He would say things like "After I'm gone...," and "Sayonara!" I was in denial. I told my friends that I couldn't understand why he was being so negative. They would try to tell me with their eyes. and I would purposely look away.

Every so often reality did creep in. Once, I fell apart in Jimmy's arms and sobbed, "I don't know how to do anything!" I immediately felt small and selfish. He was comforting me. I was astounded at how stoic and altruistic he was. When it was clear to Jimmy that he was dying he announced to me, "This is going to be a life changer for you. It will be an adventure!" I couldn't believe that he was thinking of me. Many years later, I joked that if I was the one dying I'd be the same way – I'd also be thinking of me!

We never did get a definite diagnosis. The educated guess was Burkitt lymphoma, a rare and aggressive cancer that took Jimmy on April 13, 2006, six days after he entered Sloan-Kettering Hospital. Now, almost ten years later I can still hear, "I'm sorry Mrs. Scibelli, your husband has passed." Our kids, Jacki and Doug, friends and family stood around in the hospital hall, stunned, not knowing what to do, or where to go. We lingered by the elevator. It opened, and out stepped a friend holding a bouquet of flowers. I remember feeling sorry for him. He had walked into a minefield. Much later I wondered what he did with those flowers, and if he ever brought flowers to a hospital again.

I was numb for longer than I can say. Widows talk about the first year fog. Well, I was immersed.

Writing about my marriage and the initial sting of widowhood is more upsetting than I expected it would be. I've become an independent, happy woman yet here I am a decade later feeling overwhelmed and teary as I recount "my other life." I want to get it right. I want to accurately replay our time together for the readers, for myself, for Jimmy, and for all who knew us as a couple. I hope I did. I often think about what Jimmy said, "This will be a life changer for you. It'll be an adventure." I say to him in death what I rarely said to him in life, "You were right, honey."

*

KRISTI SMITH
Kristi's 48-year-old husband Michael
died from cardiac arrest in 2011

Michael James Smith was the best hugger. Ask anyone and they will tell you that no one gave better hugs than Mike. He would wrap his arms around you and give you a giant squeeze. Men and women alike: after all, everyone needs a hug. Mike's personality was bold and his heart was big. He loved people and he had a way of making just about everyone feel special. He noticed and included everyone. It was his mission to involve people into life; real life, true life. It was like he was some sort of life coach and when he gave you a jersey and invited you onto his team, you felt honored. To Mike, each person had a place of importance and mattered, regardless of their background or status. His magnetic presence drew you to him. His bright eyes and smile filled the room.

Mike was a catalyst for change. He had a lot of energy and he wasn't going to waste any of it. He was a pilot, a pastor and a powerhouse. Flying first for Piedmont Airlines, which then became US Air, Mike was born to fly. He loved to fly. He used to say he loved it because it was the only job where he could see the sun shine every day. Climbing above the clouds seemed to clear his heart and head and he always came back with clarity. When airline schedules took him away from family too much, he left the airlines and flew commercial for local companies. It was more important for Mike to see his girls grow up than to climb some ladder.

Mike was hardwired to be the center of activity so he channeled that energy and used it everywhere he went. He used it most powerfully in his role as an involvement pastor. His passion and enthusiasm to serve God, as you can imagine, dramatically changed the climate at church. For the most part, people loved him for it but a few did not like it, because the church started to grow and grow fast. Mike did not care what people thought. He took his orders from God. Getting more people to know the love of Jesus and the grace of God was his mission and he took it very seriously. But let me tell you, no one had more fun at his job, or in life for that matter.

Mike was truly the best dad I have ever known. He loved our girls, and Abigail and Faith adored their dad. Mike was a dad who was "in there" with his kids. He was not a standoff or come across harsh dad. The girls had a soft spot in his heart and he was crazy about them. He read to them, played games with them, and taught them everything that he knew. The best thing he taught our girls was how they should expect a man to treat them by watching how he treated me as his wife. He called me his bride until the day that he died. Most important, Mike showed the girls what a father's love should look like, and pointed to God as their father. Grace was not just something spoken at the dinner table. Grace was his way of life.

At the age of forty-eight, Mike died suddenly and without any warning. It happened one evening in October, while riding back from a meeting with a friend. They were almost to our house when Mike said he felt tired and leaned his head over to rest. He never woke up. Arriving in our driveway less than a minute later, Mike's buddy was not able to wake Mike up and that's when we got the dreaded knock on the door. His friend was in a panic because he could not wake Mike up and he was afraid something was seriously wrong. Chaos ensued as the girls and I ran out to the car to see what was happening. I could tell Mike did not look right so I sent the girls, ages fifteen and seventeen, to get the doctor who lived three doors down from us and someone to call 911. His friend and I got Mike out of the car just in time for the doctor to start CPR, but Mike just lay there. Pale. Too pale. Ten minutes later when the paramedics arrived, we all stepped back to give them room. For ten more minutes they did CPR and used the shock paddles on Mike's heart several times, but no revival. It was then that I realized he was probably gone.

The neighbors heard the sirens and came out to see what was going on. No one expected that Mike would die. But standing there something came over me. That whole slow motion thing they show in the movies started and I knew I had to get the girls away from all this drama. Two neighbor ladies huddled with the girls and me at the other end of the driveway and we began to pray. As I prayed out loud it was then that I knew for sure that Mike was not coming back. In the darkest moment of my life I looked up into heaven and God gave me peace. Supernatural peace. The paramedics came and told me they were going ahead of us to take Mike to the hospital and for us to meet them there. The girls and I grabbed our shoes and drove silently with Mike's friend toward the hospital. About half way there I called my sister and let her know Mike was being transported to the hospital and that I didn't think he was going to make it. She assured me that he would be fine but I knew in my heart he was already gone. Our lives were drastically changed that day.

Almost an hour later when the doctor came and told us that Mike had died, it was like the wind got knocked out of us. The girls and I were heartbroken; literally shredded emotionally. The whole town, our church, our families and friends were as shocked as we were. Mike was the most alive man we ever knew and now he was dead. That was four years ago. Sometimes it feels like a lifetime ago and sometimes it feels like last night. Everything has changed since then. Everything.

Today Abigail is happily married and lives in Germany. She is a gifted photographer and her husband Jared is studying in seminary. Together they hope to help revitalize the church there. Despite her loss, joy lives on. Faith is graduating from the Aveda Institute in cosmetology and already has a job lined up in one of the best salons in Charlotte. She is engaged and will be getting married next fall. Her fiancé is a personal trainer and he has a heart for ministry, too. Despite her loss, faith lives on. And I am an empty nester who has moved down South and I am figuring out that the baby birds are not the only ones who can fly. My heart has wings and I am excited to see where they can take me. Despite my loss, love lives on.

*

DIANNE WEST
Dianne's 69-year-old husband Vern
died from multiple myeloma in 2010

Vern West was born in Castalia, Ohio, in 1941. A natural athlete, he excelled at basketball and tennis and headed off to Defiance College to get his teaching degree. He arrived at Sand Creek High School (Michigan) in 1964 as a first year teacher and basketball coach. I arrived there as an eighth grade student. No one – especially us – would have ever guessed that five years later we would fall in love and marry. But one magical moment in the summer of 1969 changed my life forever. A chance meeting. A spark. A love that was meant to be. A love that defined me. A love I will carry with me forever.

From 1969 to 1981, Vern moved around to different schools in Lenawee County due to coaching opportunities. We were blessed with a son in 1976. But in 1982, when the Michigan economy tanked, Vern was pink-slipped and we moved to Las Vegas where hundreds of teachers were being hired. He loved Las Vegas and was positive it was the right place for us to be. I wasn't so sure that first year, but I grew to love southern Nevada. Vern stopped coaching after the first year and began his career at Thomas & Mack Center, UNLV's sports arena, as the usher supervisor in addition to teaching. He retired from both teaching and UNLV after twenty years to open the Orleans Arena as guest services manager. Vern was an amazing teacher, a fabulous coach and an inspiring mentor to many.

Vern had always had back issues that flared from time to time, so we weren't initially alarmed when the pain began in 2006. His work at the Orleans Arena had him on his feet a lot, running up and down stairs and throughout the arena. However, when he got to the point where he could hardly walk I convinced him to see a doctor. A CT scan was done but didn't show anything, so Vern was sent to a physical therapist. And he got worse. We finally begged his primary physician to get insurance approval for an MRI. We weren't home too long after the procedure when the doctor called and said, "My God, man, you have a tumor on your spine." I don't think I'll ever forget those words.

The doctor had already set up an appointment for us to meet with a surgeon early the next morning. We were numb. We just held each other tight that night. A small room. Vern in a wheelchair, me on a stool, the doctor showing us the MRI scans. The tumor. The hot spots. Spinal compression fractures. And so many lytic lesions. Multiple myeloma. Cancer. Metastasized. Not a good prognosis. Surgery needed immediately, told to check into the hospital when we left the doctor's office. Surgery tomorrow?? I got Vern back into the car and drove down the street to a residential area. Found a shaded spot and stopped the car so we could talk. But there were no words. We just held each other. I finally asked

Vern if he wanted to get a second opinion and he said no. He trusted the doctor. So we drove to the hospital. And so it began, four plus years. Surgeries. Mistakes. Rehab. Physical therapy. C-diff infections, GI bleeds, pleural effusions, pneumonia, pulmonary embolism, chemo, radiation, many blood transfusions. Colostomy. Kidney failure, dialysis. Abdominal aortic pseudoaneurysm caused by a screw in the titanium cage they put in to support Vern's spine after removing the tumor. He went through so much. And then there was nothing more they could do to him. For him.

Vern's final days were spent at Nathan Adelson Hospice. No more pricks and prods or waking him up for rounds. He was peaceful. As I had done whenever he was hospitalized, I stayed with him twenty-four hours a day. And those final four days were a gift. He spoke very little the first two days and then was silent, but I have no doubt at all that he was able to hear my words. When the death rattle arrived, I gently slid into his bed, held him close and spoke to him until he slipped away hours later.

Those who lose their loves suddenly often express jealousy over those of us who knew death was coming. Oh, how differently I think they would feel if they had to experience watching their love waste away and go through such horrible things. But we only know what we know. There is no room for comparisons. Yes, I was able to say goodbye to my Vern. Yes, I was able to tell him I love him. And I am so very grateful for that. But was I prepared? Did I start to grieve early? No and no. I spent every waking moment doing everything in my power to keep him positive, to care for him, to ease his pain, to learn how to take care of a colostomy bag and a PICC line and to hang IVs at home and give Vern shots in his belly, to research possible treatments, to be his advocate with the many doctors and nurses and CNAs and techs, to get him to the dialysis center three mornings each week, to administer meds and keep track of all of this.

I married at eighteen and went from living with my parents to living with my husband. I was fifty-nine years old and had never lived alone in my entire life. I grieved the loss of my love and I even grieved the loss of being his caregiver.

I returned to work immediately. I needed the normality of the workweek. So I cried on the way into work. Fixed my makeup in the parking lot and walked through the gate as I had done before I was widowed. I "acted" normal all week long and I crashed on the weekends. I worked four ten-hour shifts, so when I arrived home at 7 p.m. on Thursday I put on my pajamas, closed the blinds, and did not step outside, answer the phone or answer the door all weekend long. Didn't eat well, didn't sleep well. But during those forty-plus hours on the job, no one had a clue of how close to the edge I was living. And no one seemed to care.

It's now been five years since I last held Vern in my arms. It actually doesn't feel like it's been that long. And some days it feels like it's been forever. Time has eased the pain but has not changed how much I miss him and the tears can still come. I've recently retired. I'm spending a lot of time volunteering. I've done some traveling. I'm living my life. And I'm doing my best to live it well to honor Vern, because I am who I am today because he loved me.

*

CHAPTER TWO

THE AFTERMATH

Somehow, even in the worst of times, the tiniest fragments of good survive. It was the grip in which one held those fragments that counted. -MELINA MARCHETTA

Following loss, the first questions we often ask ourselves are: How am I going to survive this? How can I function when I have no feeling or when my emotions are so strong they threaten to paralyze me? There we stand in the aftermath, feeling vulnerable and often ravaged with fear. How do we survive?

*

TANYA CAMERON
Tanya's 43-year-old husband Ivor
died of a heart attack in 2013

I was trying to come to terms with the fact that my husband was not ever coming back. How was I going to cope with bringing up my little boys on my own? It was survival time, sink or swim. I had two little ones who depended on me. They had just lost their dad; they can't lose their mum as well. I chose to swim at all costs. It was my little boys that kept me going. I felt like I was in a daze for weeks, trying to realize that Ivor was gone. I was trying to keep the boys in their routine, going to daycare four days a week, trying to keep myself together. Financially I struggled. A lot of this time afterward is blurry and I just kept trying to stay focused, that was my way of getting through, along with a lot of help from a counselor.

*

JONATHAN DEAN
Jonathan's 36-year-old wife Cara
died of double pneumonia in 2010

I immediately joined an eight-week support group. I also saw a bereavement counselor and in January 2011, I saw a psychologist. I had to manage as best I could because of my job. I am a driver for the elderly, and also a volunteer medical driver for a nonprofit organization called Abovas. I am one of fifty drivers who take medical clients to their appointments. It was like a huge explosion. At times, I was lost. I had no friendship support. All in all, I managed ALONE.

*

BONNIE FORSHEY
Bonnie's 43-year-old husband Carl
died in a car accident in 2005

I was at work when I received the news. I, of course, fell apart and left early. My husband had died in a car crash. He swerved to avoid hitting someone, and now he was gone. I was angry because this could have been avoided. Another drunk driver takes a life and walks away. I had to go on antidepressants for about a year. I also went to see a therapist to help me deal with things.

*

STEPHEN HOCHHAUS
Stephen's 51-year-old wife Kathy
died of soft tissue sarcoma in 2011

I was in shock and numb through the first two months so I stumbled along until finally collapsing in the third month and found grief counseling.

*

MARLISE MAGNA
Marlise's 36-year-old partner Blaine
died by suicide in 2010

Honestly, I couldn't face the initial aftermath. I resorted to handfuls of pills, copious amounts of alcohol, and eventually a suicide attempt which landed me in intensive care in hospital. After I was classified with what would be called a nervous breakdown, I went for a three-week long psychotherapy clinic which helped a lot.

*

DIANE MCKENZIE-SAPP
Diane's 65-year-old husband Ron
died from renal failure in 2006

Do the tears ever stop? After my husband died, some things were constant such as never-ending grayness, the tears and my broken heart. Grief had filled my heart with pain, and my broken heart bled a river of tears. I just wanted the tears to stop. They controlled me; they were a constant reminder of how weak I was. Once before when I had wanted to stop crying, I remembered myself as that four-year-old girl who decided she would not cry ever again. That decision lasted for over twenty years and I would not, could not, cry even if I wanted to. Was this what I wished for? I thought about stopping the tears, and I knew I could if I made up my mind to do so. Was I willing to not cry again? Would I mourn for those unshed tears? Were the tears a weakness and where were these despised tears coming from? I imagined the source of this river of tears to be the blood of my broken heart, and it measured the depth of my sorrow. If those tears were not respected for what they represented, would I disrespect and dishonor Ron's memory? Suddenly my perception of those tears changed as I realized that the tears were not a weakness, rather my heart was sending a token of respect and honor. I thanked my heart for its valiant effort and knew that the tears would only stop once I had found a way to preserve their integrity. I spoke to my tears and promised them a place of honor, to be a place that remained close by, so if they stopped I would always have a tear or two on hand. I would never need to be dry-eyed if I kept the tears I had now. "Waste not want not," rang true.

How do you save a tear? Not with the boxes of disposable tissues, not with rolls of toilet paper, and not on the sleeves of my clothes. So how do you save a tear? With a hanky! Hand•ker•chief: noun - a square of cotton or other finely woven material, typically carried in one's pocket and intended for blowing or wiping one's nose. Synonyms: hanky. I had my recently deceased mother's collection of 1940s hankies. These were the perfect color, and unused. But I wanted something older, something with lace and the feeling of a relic, a worthy resting place for my tears. With the lyrics of Celine Dion's "My Heart Will Go On," flowing through my head I outbid antique dealers and brides searching for something old to carry down the aisle. I bid for antique Irish linen, and French tatted silk, and gently embroidered cotton handkerchiefs. I had a mountain of lovely works of art from an age where tears were caught and slipped into a long mutton sleeve. I imagined that any of these would befit a widow. Turns out I only needed one.

I sat and called the tears. I said, "Dearest Tears, you can come anytime you want or need to. I will save each one of you on these beautiful pillows made just for you. I do not despise you as I once did, I am sorry. I did not see you for what you are. You are my past and my future; you are my memories and my pain. I will accept and love you for what you have brought forth from my heart. I will never deny you again." The tears began slowly at first, and then the river as usual. I caught them all in the first Irish linen handkerchief, refolded it carefully and placed it in my cedar chest. I have kept my promise to revere, honor and respect my widow's tears and continued that promise with my signature design ring, the Broken Heart design which is made of two teardrops aligned next to each other. It signifies that our heart has been forever broken and that our tears make the heart and soul of this ring. The "Tears" design has been patented and is worn by the brokenhearted all over the world. This is the Story of Tears and how they did wane away. Yes, I tear up once in a while when I hear an old Celine Dion song or see the smile of a grandchild, but those tears are not the same as I cried for my love. Those Broken Heart Tears are resting in a place of honor in a ring of remembrance.

I have fifty antique handkerchiefs if anyone needs one.

*

JULIE MJELVE
Julie's 42-year-old husband Cameron
died by suicide in 2011

The initial aftermath was very difficult. One of the choices I made was not to tell the children right away. I took a day to find out what was the best way to tell them. It sounds strange to talk about in a section about surviving the aftermath, but it was an important piece that made the rest of the aftermath a little more bearable. Because I had taken that time to think things through, I didn't say anything I had to go back on, but instead said things I could build upon.

A lot of my survival has centered around my children, because they were so small when my husband passed away. At the time they were three years old, two years old, and five months old. So a lot of my survival of the initial aftermath was simply that: survival. There wasn't much more that I could do other than take care of the children. Surviving meant we made it out of the house to a playground, even if it took us all day to get there. Surviving meant we made it to school or to church, not that we were on time or prepared, just that we made it. Surviving meant I got supper made. I survived by not even trying to get my kids to sit at a table. We all sat in front of the TV with kid-sized lawn chairs and little trays for their plates. Not my ideal way to share supper with a family, but I had to survive.

Surviving the fact that my husband committed suicide has not been easy either. I felt I had to talk about all the events that led up to his death, over and over and over again. I needed to analyze every decision that I had made, that led up to the events he found too stressful to cope with anymore. I went for counseling, and went often in the initial phases. I really needed someone to talk with who wouldn't get tired of hearing me question everything again and again. I also coped by making what I called a Truth Journal. For every action on my part that I questioned if I had done the right thing, I countered it with the truth about the situation and the choices that my husband made. Although people talk about the aftermath being the first few weeks and months, for me I found that the aftermath lasted years. It's only now, four and a half years later, that I feel like the aftermath is over and that I am coming out of the initial crisis of it. I think part of the coping has come in simply recognizing that it does take a lot longer than society traditionally gives us.

*

LILIAN MORTON
Lilian's 58-year-old husband Michael
died in a plane crash in 2012

My sisters and my parents came in and stayed with me. My family helped me with my daughter who was in high school at the time. They made me eat and sleep. I went to bed but I didn't sleep much. My sister slept with me. I slept in the shirt Michael wore the day before he died because it still smelled like him. I continued to do this until his smell was no longer on the clothes. I couldn't stop crying. I couldn't think. I still talked to him all the time as if he was there. Every time my phone rang or someone knocked on the door, I expected it to be him. Every morning I would wake up and think I was going to find out that it was just a bad dream but it wasn't. I would dream about Michael still being alive and we would be driving or talking, just doing ordinary things and I would tell him about the nightmare I had that he had died in a plane crash. But that was just a dream and the nightmare was real.

I woke up the first morning after Michael died and in the dish next to my bed where I kept my jewelry there was a handful of pocket change. I figured that someone found it somewhere and just put it there. When I went to the bathroom to brush my teeth, there was a dime in the sink. I took a coffee can and went through my entire house that day and put all the pocket change in the can, put the lid on it and put it in the closet. The next day it happened again. I pulled out our journal and wrote to Michael. I told him that I know he always told me that if there was any way he could contact me after he left this world that he would. I said, "If this change is your way of contacting me then I'm great with it and do it again." I checked the entire bedroom and bathroom once again before I went to bed and there was nothing. I woke up the next morning and there was the dime in the sink again, change in my bedside dish, and coins on the windowsill in the bathroom. It was the first time since it happened that while awake, I smiled.

A week to the day after Michael died, I had to get on a plane with his ashes and take him home to let his extended family say their goodbyes. I sat there in the airport with him sitting next to me and suddenly realized that I had to get on the plane. I was frozen and having an anxiety attack. I was afraid that I wasn't going to be able to get on the plane. I called my sister and she talked me through it. She said, "You know how he loved a deal and you know that he is thinking right now that he is getting to fly for free." I laughed because I knew that was probably exactly what Michael was thinking. I managed to get us on the plane and I looked out over hills Michael flew over just one week earlier and it was so beautiful. And I know that was the last thing Michael saw before he went down. It somehow made me feel close to him.

*

LISA OWENS
Lisa's 50 year-old husband Greg
died of pancreatic cancer in 2014

I was numb! Greg died at the hospital, and I was there with his mother and sister. I made the phone calls that I needed to make while waiting for the funeral home, and then I drove home alone. I cried and cried; that's all I did. I hugged his clothes and our cat, and touched everything Greg had touched! I miss him so much.

It has been almost eleven months, and I haven't moved anything. Greg's shoes still sit by his chair; his bathroom stuff is still where he left it, and the shampoo bottle he dropped the morning we left for the hospital is still laying where it landed. I've cleaned around it, but it just needs to be there. It's comforting to see Greg's stuff. I changed out my pillowcases for his favorite T-shirts, so I hug and sleep on them at night. I go by the cemetery three or more times a week just to check on him. I know he is not there, but it is a place to talk and sing to him. Greg was a strong man whom I absolutely adored. He fought pancreatic cancer for two long years, hurting constantly every day. His death was a relief for him; he was no longer suffering, no longer hurting and in pain.

Every day has been a struggle, starting with just getting through minute by minute and then hour by hour. I feel guilty when I am happy, but I have had some happy moments. I never knew there was really such a thing as a broken heart, but it is very real. My heart will never heal, because a piece died when my husband earned his wings. My faith in God has been tested but still remains strong; I have to keep it because I'm waiting to be reunited with my love.

*

MARY POTTER KENYON
Mary's 60-year-old husband David
died of heart failure in 2012

My husband's death was such a shock to all of us: he was a five-year cancer survivor who then survived a heart attack and stent surgery, only to die sometime in the night three days after he came home from the hospital. I was immediately surrounded by my children (four of the eight had left home) and my sisters. I remember being just numb with shock and grief that first day, wondering how I could possibly survive the kind of pain I was feeling. I was certain I would die with it. My children stayed near me at all times and, in fact, four of my five girls slept in the living room with me the first night or two. I ended up sleeping in the same room with the youngest two for a few nights before I finally braved the bedroom I had shared with my husband. My three youngest girls and I slept with one of David's shirts for a long time.

The morning after David's death, I sat down at the kitchen table with an empty journal and immediately filled three pages with things I was thankful for; having those bonus years with David after his cancer, my children, my siblings, the recent talks David and I had shared...there were many things I could be thankful for, even while I was reeling with grief.

I instinctively knew I needed two things: the kind of praying I'd heard from the women and men I'd met at Christian writer's conferences that past year, and God's word. I didn't know how to get either. It wasn't the rote prayers of my childhood religion I craved, but the outpouring of heartfelt personal prayer. As for the Bible, I'd never even held a study Bible, nor was I sure how to search for answers in one. My anguished cries must have reached heaven; within days a young woman sent me notebook pages full of Bible verses, my daughter Emily gave me a study Bible, and her youth leader stood with me and held my hands, praying out loud. It wasn't long after my husband died that my writing mentor, author Shelly Beach, asked me to write devotions for a grief Bible. To write them, I HAD to learn to search the Bible for answers. I also started reading everything I could get my hands on about grief. I am a writer and researcher by trade so it seemed natural to begin studying grief. Books written by authors like Madeleine L'Engle, C.S. Lewis, and Joan Didion, who had gone down this road of grief before me, helped tremendously. Obviously, they had survived the loss of a spouse. I studied the science of bereavement; if we will experience loss in our lives (and all of us will) then our bodies and minds must be designed to handle it. Journaling, praying, reading the Bible and the words of others who had faced loss sustained me. I also blogged about widowhood, and soon had a following of other widows. Pieces of that blog and my journal ended up in my own book, *Refined By Fire: A Journey of Grief and Grace*, which was published two years after my husband's death.

*

NANCY REDMOND
Nancy's 40-year-old husband Kevin
died of a heart attack in 2012

I remember being absolutely numb. Kevin was missing for fourteen long hours before being found in his work truck. I had called the police department to report him missing after I got home and had received no contact from him all day, so my biggest memory of that night was the chaplain from the police department telling me how sorry she was for my loss. I wanted to scream at her, "You're sorry? Why? Because you had to get up at 11:30 p.m. at night to come to my house to deliver this news? Or because you had to walk half a block to my house for all the cars parked in front?" All I could think was that I wanted her to leave.

I remember snuggling up in two of Kevin's sweatshirts and wanting so badly to NOT fall asleep because if I woke up, it was real and as long as I stayed awake, it wasn't. Irrational? Of course, but then who IS rational at these times? I remember the big bear hug from my son, Christopher, who burst through my front door and wrapped me in the biggest hug I have ever received. I remember my daughter's sweet voice as she talked to her brother, my oldest son, Ryan, who had to identify Kevin. I remember the enveloping LOVE that was so present in my home. I also remember the little red-breasted bird who landed on my screen at the approximate time of Kevin's death. In my heart of hearts, I knew intuitively at that moment that Kevin had gone home. I remember the pain in everyone's eyes as they looked at me and struggled to make sense of what had happened and even more so struggled to find the right words or actions to comfort such a loss. I remember having to make the phone call to Kevin's mom to tell her the news.

*

MARY LEE ROBINSON
Mary Lee's 63-year-old husband Pat
died from a sudden stroke in 2013

My husband died quite suddenly; he walked out the door healthy and happy one afternoon and never came back. He had a massive brain hemorrhage while playing pool. The neurosurgeon found me almost immediately after I arrived at the emergency room. The news wasn't good. He told me that Pat was unlikely to survive this devastating stroke, and if he did, he would never really recover. He was very much going to be a vegetable. The surgeon asked "Does your husband have an advanced directive? If he does, if it were my family member, I would implement it."

I am fortunate to be the child of a nurse practitioner and a combat veteran. By this time, I had also had a ringside seat at the passing of several other family members. The concept of death, sudden or otherwise, was not a foreign notion to me. In fact, Pat and I had buried some close family members together already, and were mentally preparing ourselves for more losses that were imminent in our aging family.

We talked many times, in practical gloves-off terms, about our respective wishes. This certainty about what I knew my husband wanted was a great deal of comfort when I had to make this monumental decision all by myself. There was no one to consult. Beyond the two of us, some elderly relatives, and my husband's very drug-involved estranged sons, I had no close family in any sense. We had just relocated to our new retirement destination and friendships here were not deep or numerous.

So, in a moment of strength I don't know where I found, I signed the pivotal papers.

Pat was admitted to the ER the day before Valentine's Day. We had plans to celebrate, but they were not going to work. Instead, that day I dressed carefully, including Pat's favorite perfume, and took two pens to the hospital with me. Once there, we squeezed hands and I released his and asked him to open his palm for me. There, I drew a red heart and wrote inside "my heart" and closed his fingers around it. I told him that this was his present for Valentine's; he held my heart in his hand and always would. He made a fist and the nurses told me that he resisted opening it for them. Hard. The heart stayed there permanently at my request.

Dying takes a long time. I knew that from previous experience. Despite the "no life extending measures" orders in place, the medical staff continued to administer saline and a feeding tube. Having walked the final walk with other loved ones, I knew that the morphine dosages were so high that the patient does not suffer any discomfort by removing those last two ministrations. Confirming that knowledge with the doctors, I requested that they, too, be pulled. Pat could not speak initially, but after the third day he was no longer responsive in any way to the nurses or to me. He was just uncomfortable from the tubes in his throat. It was time to let go. With a very, very heavy heart, I did. He died two days later. I said "Goodbye, I love you." Once he was pronounced dead, and a funeral director was chosen, I drove myself home.

*

CAROL SCIBELLI
Carol's 56-year-old husband Jimmy
died from lymphoma in 2006

"Stunned," says it best. When the doctor told us Jimmy passed, we all hugged and cried. Once we left the hospital I needed to be alone. I can still feel myself clutching my husband's pillow, insulating myself as I sat in the back seat of someone's car as we headed for home. I rested my face on the cold window not really looking out or focusing. My arm was squashed against the metal door handle. My daughter and son must have been next to me in the car but the images are spotty and foggy and I couldn't say for sure. Once home, I went right to bed. My sister-in-law Carmela and my friend Jade came in to sit with me, but sometimes when they peeked in I pretended to be asleep. I stayed on my side of the bed, purposely not allowing myself to look at the empty space next to me. I could hear voices and dishes clanking from the kitchen downstairs. I didn't want to face anyone and it was a relief to have no responsibilities, nothing expected of me. I wished I could just disappear.

Immediately, I had a running conversation in my head with Jimmy. When I was sure that no could hear me I talked to him out loud. I would sit on our closet floor and have lengthy conversations with his Dockers. I filled him in on how each person was reacting to losing him. He always liked to gossip, and I needed to fantasize that he was experiencing this ridiculous situation with me. It was completely unreal and unnatural that I was facing something so traumatic without Jimmy by my side. "How could this happen? How could this happen?" was my mantra from the start. I repeated it many, many times each day for at least a year.

*

DIANNE WEST
Dianne's 69-year-old husband Vern
died from multiple myeloma in 2010

My loss followed a long, hard cancer battle and when Vern entered hospice, I knew we would only have a few more days together due to his kidney failure. Well I "knew" that, but I didn't allow myself to actually feel it. It was surreal. I was numb as I drove home from the hospice facility four days later, and that feeling continued as I planned Vern's service and returned to work. I remember feeling I had stepped outside my body and could watch myself behaving "normally," doing all of the "right" things – but it wasn't really me. I felt robotic, in a fog, just going through the motions. Doing what I thought was expected of me. Maybe it was the shock that at fifty-nine years old I was alone for the very first time in my entire life. I continued to do the things I needed to do at work and in public, but I was a real mess at home.

I've used the term cocoon when describing my weekend behavior during those early months. I closed myself off from everyone and everything. I didn't sleep nor eat well, didn't answer the phone or the doorbell, didn't open the mail. I slept in Vern's hospital bed or his recliner rather than return to the bed we had shared prior to his diagnosis. The thought of being in that king size bed alone was just too much to handle. I suspect I needed to do these things in the privacy of our home in order to "act" the part I was playing in public. It was probably not the healthiest way to do it, but it worked for me.

I didn't see a counselor or therapist, but I did participate in an online bereavement group through the Cancer Support Community that gave me a safe space to share my feelings with others those first few months. I think having that safe space made a real difference.

*

CHAPTER THREE

THE FUNERAL

Can anyone understand how it is to have lived in the White House and then, suddenly, to be living alone as the President's widow? -JACKIE KENNEDY

For many the funeral represents the end while for others it marks the beginning of something eternal. Regardless of whether we mourn the absence of our spouse's physical body or celebrate the spirit that continues on, planning the funeral or memorial service presents emotionally-laden challenges shared by many.

*

TANYA CAMERON
Tanya's 43-year-old husband Ivor
died of a heart attack in 2013

Ivor's two sisters flew out from England and Scotland. Thankfully they were there to help me prepare for his funeral. He was buried. I never knew what he wanted, it was something we never talked about, and we were too young to expect anything to happen. So we thought! I knew Ivor would have wanted a small service, not over the top, and nothing religious (as we aren't religious) for his funeral. His sisters wanted a church service with the aisles decked out with flowers. I had to put a stop to that. They were fine when I stepped in and said that wasn't what Ivor would have wanted. The last thing I needed was too many people interfering, but then again I needed someone with a slightly clearer thinking brain than what I was having at the time.

I arranged for a viewing of my husband, I needed this to make sure it was real for me and the funeral home advised us to do this the day before the funeral. The funeral was going to be a hard enough day as it was without trying to have a viewing on the same day. I am glad I saw my husband, as sad as it was. I could not touch him; I just wanted to sit next to him. His sisters didn't take to seeing him very well. Sometimes it is best to remember your loved ones the way you remembered them.

The funeral director, his wife and staff were all so wonderful and they made us feel a part of their family. Nothing was a hassle for them. The funeral director came up to me after we had just buried my husband and told me to ring him anytime, he didn't care if it was 3 a.m., but if I needed any help with my boys I was to call him. That was just such a lovely thing that anyone could have said to me. I never made that call.

*

JONATHAN DEAN
Jonathan's 36-year-old wife Cara
died of double pneumonia in 2010

My father-in-law and his brother paid for everything. I was there for the initial meeting with the funeral director and helped pick out the casket, but they paid for everything. My wife was not cremated. Some of the extended family were at the funeral. I did not want certain people at the funeral but that fell through and I saw them and nearly lost it. Anger set in, but I was comforted by my wife's aunt.

*

BONNIE FORSHEY
Bonnie's 43-year-old husband Carl
died in a car accident in 2005

My in-laws took care of everything. I simply could not handle it. I had just buried my son, and now my husband was also gone. I felt like I was losing my mind. I had to take a leave of absence from work so I could try to make sense out of everything.

*

STEPHEN HOCHHAUS
Stephen's 51-year-old wife Kathy
died of soft tissue sarcoma in 2011

My wife wanted no funeral, so I had to deal with the cremation, as she requested, by myself the next day. Kathy's parents wanted a service for her in Canada, so I had to transport her through Customs and deal with being upset and alone among a lot of people most of whom didn't have a lot to say to me.

*

MARLISE MAGNA
Marlise's 36-year-old partner Blaine
died by suicide in 2010

A close family friend planned the funeral. Blaine was an only child and his mother simply couldn't cope. We only met at the morgue and the entire family was in a state of shock. What stunned me at the funeral was that not only was the family not honest about the cause of death, but also that I was the only one falling to pieces as the hearse drove off; the rest were already sipping on coffee and eating snacks. Made me question the value of our lives to others.

*

DIANE MCKENZIE-SAPP
Diane's 65-year-old husband Ron died
from renal failure in 2006

Ron's time was limited from the day of his "successful operation." I was working and he was on medical disability. For his funeral I pre-ordered laminated remembrance cards online and then the day he died, I added that date and had them overnighted. They were given to family and special friends. Weeks prior to his death, we chose the pastor and friends to speak. He was reinstated into the Masons and a Masonic Honor Guard gave their moving tribute ceremony.

All the family picture albums were stored on my computer. For weeks, after coming home from the hospital or hospice I made several different CDs and selected music from Elvis Presley's gospel albums, the Beatles and the Wings of a Dove album. They looped on laptops around the funeral parlor. Friends and family gathered in front of these photographic memorials smiling and remarking to each other "I remember that." I made copies of the photograph CDs and music for all who requested them so they could relive those memories when they chose. Ron was remembered with love by all who knew him.

He always wore his wedding ring even at work where it was not wise to do so. When his wedding ring was lost during a hospital nursing home stay, he was devastated. I found him a gold plated band on eBay and although it was not his real wedding band, he found comfort in wearing it and would not take it off. I requested the ring remain on his finger. I could not have him buried without his precious ring. It is the one thing of his that I did not keep. I "acted" my way through those days and was relieved when the show closed. It is at this time that we are most sensitive to words and feel with wounded hearts. What you can say to the wounded is "I am so sorry."

What Not to Say To a Widow:

1. I know just how you feel
2. It was for the best
3. It just takes time
4. You are young, you will find…
5. What are you going to do with ….
6. What about your rings (you aren't married any more)
7. It was God's will
8. Anything that starts with "at least"
9. Anything that starts with "You need to"
10. (Fill in your own here) _____

Ron had always been my voice of reason and common sense. I wondered if that willful, self-destructive calculating devil that hid from Ron was now walking free. Where was my conscience now? I miss him. I promise to remember him and his memory. I will make my broken heart visible for all to see.

*

JULIE MJELVE
Julie's 42-year-old husband Cameron
died by suicide in 2011

I planned most of the funeral, along with my husband's parents. They came with me to meet with the funeral director and we made a lot of the choices together. They were very good at deferring to me for most things, but speaking up when they had a strong preference about something. Although things went smoothly and there were no disagreements, it was a difficult experience in a different way. At the time I felt it was my responsibility to plan and organize the funeral, as well as to say the eulogy, since it was my husband who died. However, looking back, in some ways I wish someone would have just done it all for me, and all I would have had to do was show up and be the grieving widow, and just allow myself to be sad, rather than having to participate.

*

LILIAN MORTON
Lilian's 58-year-old husband Michael
died in a plane crash in 2012

I made all of the arrangements according to the lengthy discussions Michael and I had following his best friend's death. Michael wanted to be cremated and wanted his ashes scattered. He said he wanted some of them scattered on his parents' grave and the others we could scatter wherever we wanted. He said, "I don't want an urn sitting on someone's mantel making them sad, or a headstone sitting in a cemetery for them to visit. Scatter them or I will haunt you." Michael said he didn't want a service but if we wanted to just get together and talk about the good times we had with him, that was okay with him. I had him cremated and we had a small memorial service where we lived but no formal service. I stood up and shared some of my memories of him with the group and invited others to do the same. We had quite a few people stand up and talk about their memories of Michael. Some of the things that were said I had never heard before. It was very nice.

Afterwards, we went to the local restaurant where Michael and I had our weekly outing and we all had appetizers and toasted him. He was a Mason so we booked his hometown Shriner's temple to hold his memorial service. His son and I met with the manager and chose the food to serve. I stood up in front of his friends and family and shared some of my memories of Michael; others joined me in sharing memories as well. The Masons did their scroll ceremony and we opened up the doors, had drinks and appetizers, looked through photo albums, laughed, and told stories about the wonderful times we had with Michael. I gave several of Michael's family members some of his ashes. I told them of his wishes to please scatter the ashes. I took the rest back to Texas with me. I drove into the country and scattered some of Michael's ashes in the area where we were going to take the kids for Easter. I scattered his ashes in many places that were meaningful to us, at our house in Texas and in New Orleans where we went many times together.

*

LISA OWENS
Lisa's 50 year-old husband Greg
died of pancreatic cancer in 2014

Greg had planned his funeral; I just followed through with it. We worked with disabled adults, and Greg wanted them to have a big part of the service. They were honorary pallbearers and their choir sang three songs. It was perfect! I didn't want a spray of flowers on top of the casket, so I had one of our "Team Greg" T-shirts made, and everyone who had supported Greg during his journey put their name on it. We all wore blue jeans and our "Team Greg" T-shirt because Greg didn't want anyone to go out and buy something to wear. We planned it after work, so anyone who wanted to come, could come. It was an awesome service; he would have been so proud of. The chapel was full and was such a blessing of support that included Greg's friends, family and special friends. Greg told his family that I knew his wishes, and they let me carry them out. They were pleased, and there were no disagreements.

*

MARY POTTER KENYON
Mary's 60-year-old husband David
died of heart failure in 2012

My husband and I hadn't broached the subject of funerals and gravestones so I had to make those kinds of decisions by myself. I knew David had loved the beautiful wooden coffin my mother had from a nearby monastery, so that was an easy decision. My two oldest children, son Dan and daughter Elizabeth, went with me to the funeral home and our heads were reeling with the choices, but we agreed on something simple and tasteful. The funeral dinner was held on a Friday during Lent at our Catholic church, and I find this humorous now though it was somewhat scandalous at the time. I'd chosen roast beef as the entree. Roast beef for Catholics on a Friday during Lent? Some there didn't eat, including the priest who'd performed the funeral. You would think the person from the church who was helping me plan would have reminded me it was Friday and Lent, but they didn't, and honestly, in my state of mind I really didn't know what day it was!

I put off choosing a gravestone much too long. Each time I passed the cemetery, I felt like crying. Did no one care about this man who lay beneath the ground? It was four months before I could bear to put the order in, and another four before the gravestone was installed. I chose the single photo my husband had loved to be put in the middle; one we'd had taken in a Chuck E. Cheese photo booth. As a private joke, I'd submitted it to the newspaper for our thirtieth anniversary announcement and David got a kick out of the comments from coworkers who'd loved it. Only we knew it had cost twenty-five cents. I also had a butterfly etched into the stone because David had been the "wind beneath my wings" in recent years, supporting and encouraging my writing.

*

NANCY REDMOND
Nancy's 40-year-old husband Kevin
died of a heart attack in 2012

I was surrounded by family as I went to plan Kevin's funeral. We made it a celebration of all the things Kevin loved in life and found so much comfort knowing that he would have loved it. Our funeral director was a Minnesota Brass alumni and he made everything so gentle for me. We brought Kevin's dog Chloe to the service. My niece had bathed Chloe and bought her the prettiest "evening dress" to make her Kevin proud. We had the Minnesota Brass Drumline play the Santa Clara Vanguard warm-up exercise at the funeral. My family and friends commented again and again on the LOVE and beauty of the simple yet very heartfelt service to honor Kevin's life.

*

MARY LEE ROBINSON
Mary Lee's 63-year-old husband Pat
died from a sudden stroke in 2013

The job of planning my husband's funeral was mine. My husband had two sons from whom he was estranged for several years. Both were heavily drug involved to the point of living in that seamy underworld of dealing hard drugs. After consulting with the chaplain at the hospital who also happened to be a former police detective, it was decided it would be better not to have them travel to our town. They were notified immediately after Pat died and told that no arrangements had been made, but it was going to be a very small private memorial.

New to town, I had no idea which funeral director I wanted to use. I just picked one from the phonebook. Pat wanted to donate his body, as do I, to the state anatomical board for study. We'd discussed the positive aspects of being able to do some good in our afterlife, as well as the fact that most such organizations will return the cremains to the family for a mere six hundred dollars. My husband was an accountant and tighter than two coats of paint. The idea appealed to him. Unfortunately, we hadn't been in our new home state long enough to get those papers signed. Nix one final wish. An acquaintance called with pricing for cremations that she researched for me. Unfortunately, I didn't get the information before Pat was on his way to the most expensive place in town. I wish I had received that call. It would have saved me about two thousand five hundred dollars. On to the next of my husband's wishes.

Pat wanted to have a small memorial service and, in the Irish tradition, a wake to follow. Read: party. He loved them. I got this; this is a piece of cake, it's what I do. I wrote the obituary and submitted it to the funeral director and the papers in the two cities where we used to live. I was very, very careful not to name the little town where we lived. My stepsons never knew our physical address and I needed to keep it that way. I explained that to the funeral director. The local paper printed Pat's obituary, but attached their promotional byline which revealed the town name. If you don't know, a thirty-second Google search will bring up a complete obituary very easily. I learned of another relative's passing that way, before my aunt was able to phone me. My stepsons would be able to locate me in nothing flat. The funeral director looked a little alarmed when I went flying into his office, demanding that he pull that internet link down, which he did, promptly.

I set about making the arrangements with the church we were planning to join. Difficulty number one surfaced here. While the pastor was most kind, the only date available to have this service in the immediate future was on my birthday. I found a bagpiper, but he too was only available on my birthday. Since it's on St. Patrick's Day, I thought, well, that would still be fitting. We held a St. Patrick's Day party more years than not. Pat would like that.

Since the memorial service couldn't be published in the paper, and since we knew few people in town anyway, I had invitations to the service printed up. Painstakingly, I hand addressed each one and mailed them. I arranged to rent the room at our neighborhood's clubhouse. I went to our favorite restaurant and set up the catering arrangements. Maryland blue crab cakes. Nothing else would do; Pat loved them.

As a gift from my mom, I went shopping for an appropriate outfit and was pleased with my selection. I bought a pretty navy blue duster, matching skirt, white blouse and heels. Thinking I had made it past the hardest part, I made a trip to the bank two weeks later, with my Power of Attorney in hand. I needed to get the funds to pay for all this. I had another shock waiting for me.

It was becoming evident in the aftermath of Pat's death, that in the six months leading up to his death he was having mini strokes. Another indication surfaced when I learned that he had changed the beneficiary designations on all of the income producing assets, a half a million dollars in all, from me into the names of his heroin-addicted sons. He did this on Halloween, before he died in mid-February. I had no idea. We were enjoying the happiest time of our marriage with the greatest amount of harmony, I made it to the car, but just barely, as my knees began to buckle. That meant that the arrangements for the memorial all had to be canceled. No friends or family were coming. I was on my own, completely.

*

CAROL SCIBELLI
Carol's 56-year-old husband Jimmy
died from lymphoma in 2006

Plans for the funeral didn't exactly magically happen, still much was done without my participation. That was fine with me. I was grateful for the support and the level heads swarming around me. Easter Sunday came in between Jimmy's death and the day he was buried. While the world was celebrating Holy Thursday, Good Friday and Easter Sunday, my family and I were suspended in time. Those five days between April 13 and April 18 were surreal. I was aware of others in my house but like a three-year-old, I'd wake up from my nap and wander downstairs where food and drinks were waiting for me.

The casket and the mausoleum where Jimmy was laid to rest was planned by Jimmy's two brothers and two of his best friends, but I found a man to officiate a non-religious service in a church. I was determined to honor my husband's disapproval of organized religion and also have his service in a spiritual setting. He was a spiritual man. We had a one-day wake. My son used the video from his dad's forty-fifth birthday party and looped it to play continually on a TV at the funeral home. My son and daughter chose the photos for the easels placed near the casket. At home, they sat at my feet like six-year-olds playing on the living room carpet organizing the photos. I felt ancient, invisible and oddly detached. All I thought was, someday they'll be doing the same for me.

As I zipped up my black skirt the morning of the funeral, the material hung loosely and spun around my waist. I was thrilled to realize that I must've lost some weight. An instant later I turned to Jimmy's photo on the night table and apologized to him. I was horrified to catch myself feeling happy about being thinner on the day I was burying my husband. How could that have even entered my thoughts? Much later, I appreciated how human and funny this was so I included this scenario in my memoir, *Poor Widow Me*. I called it, *I Lost My Husband and Three Pounds*. As early as the funeral I became aware that I could still find humor during dark times. I sat in the front row between my children. At the time, my daughter Jacki was twenty-nine and my son Doug was twenty-five. Everyone knows that the first row is reserved for the immediate family and my daughter whispered to me, "I feel like everyone is staring at us." She was right. I'm sure they were, so I put my arms around both of them and bent down into a huddle and said, "I know what you mean, honey. This is probably the only time in life that people don't want the best seats in the house." We sat up laughing. Our bodies were shaking and I hope the people in the back assumed we were crying. Aside from me saying something funny and realizing, "Wow. I can still think funny," it was a major moment for our family. It jumped out at me that I was "it" for my children now. I was the Last Parent Standing and my job would be to set the tone. That encouraged me to keep trying to dig for and find the old me. And, the old me was someone who was wired to be funny.

*

KRISTI SMITH
Kristi's 48-year-old husband Michael
died from cardiac arrest in 2011

My husband was always the life of the party, so he wanted his funeral to be a celebration of life. Mike wanted a party that would make his life eclipse his death, but when he died I was not in the party mood and this seemed like an impossible task. Death hung in the air. I knew if we had the memorial too early it would not be a celebration of his life but instead a dirge of his untimely death. Mike was only forty-eight years old and in perfect health when he suddenly died. My husband had touched so many lives as a pastor and through his magnetic personality and I needed time to figure out how to celebrate this wonderful man. The best decision I made was that we scheduled his memorial service for three weeks later. This would allow friends and family to come from out of town and give us the breathing space we needed to plan something special.

Since the memorial would be so delayed we had to figure out a way to honor the people who needed more immediate closure. We decided to invite our families to the funeral home for a private viewing of Mike. This provided us opportunity to say our goodbyes as a family and still honor Mike's request for a party. The party would have to be later.

There was another group that desperately needed a way to show their respect and that was the Young Life kids. For over three years there had been twenty to thirty high school teens meeting at our house weekly for home-cooked meals, Young Life bible studies, and lots of fun. We hosted bonfires after the home football games and up to eighty teens would show up. These kids needed to say their goodbyes to Mr. Smith, so they quickly planned a candlelight service and held it two evenings after Mike passed. At twilight, the girls and I stepped out onto our upper deck to see the lower lawn twinkling with hundreds of lights. Each candle illuminated the face of one of the lives my husband had touched. For over an hour we sang, cried, and prayed. Impromptu speeches spoke of the influence Mike had on their lives. And then with hugs and tears, they all said goodbye to Mr. Smith. It was breathtakingly beautiful and unforgettable.

For the next three weeks we planned the celebration of Mike's life while we adjusted to his death. The neighbors had asked if they could host a run at the local park in honor of Mike so on the chilly autumn morning of Mike's memorial, the girls and I joined hundreds of runners at the park. There was live music, which Mike would have loved because he always said that music is what makes the party. Everyone was wearing yellow bandannas with the words "Run Like Mike" across their foreheads. The course was laid out with signs with scriptures on them for runners to read as they ran. The chill in the air melted with the warmth of their hearts. This officially set the tone for us to celebrate Mike's life that day. We all had time to go home and shower before meeting at the church.

The memorial service was called, "The Legacy of Love, Joy and Faith." Everyone received a yellow wristband with those words inscribed on it as they came in the doors. The service was beautiful. To open, I had called on my favorite buddies in the praise band to play a couple of meaningful songs. Next, we treasured seeing pictures of Mike scrolling across the screen with his bright eyes. His smile still illuminated the room even though he'd been gone for almost a month. An older gentleman, who was like a father to Mike, prayed. Mike's best friend spoke. His sisters cried through memories. And then the girls and I took the stage. The three "Smith girls", as we were affectionately referred to, stood together and one by one we honored the most important man in our lives with words of timeless love and respect. The grand finale happened when this lovely young woman sat down to her keyboard and belted out, "People Get Ready." It was the finishing touch. The most important element to Mike would have been to give an opportunity for everyone there to get ready for life after death and that song brought it all home.

Then we invited everyone to lunch and the first round of drinks was on Mike. Of course, there was music, lots of hugs (because Mike was renowned for his famous Mike Smith hugs), and a "fly by" to salute his life as a pilot. I know Mike felt honored and it was a celebration of life. A life well lived.

*

DIANNE WEST
Dianne's 69-year-old husband Vern
died from multiple myeloma in 2010

My husband did not want a funeral. Well, actually, he didn't want me to have to endure a funeral. Nearly all of our friends had disappeared during the long cancer battle and he feared no one would come to his service and that would hurt me. But when I shared this with our son, he was shocked and felt strongly that a service had to be held. Vern wasn't talking much by the time he entered hospice, but I shared our son's concerns with him and he said he wanted me to do whatever I felt would be best for me. So a service was planned. A dear widowed neighbor worked for the local mortuary and made an appointment for me to meet with someone she knew well; another friend went with me that day. It was good to have her there with me, as I was not really thinking clearly at all and she asked the right questions. Because the mortuary was gearing up for Tony Curtis' funeral, we were asked to use the King David Chapel located in a separate building. We're not Jewish, but they assured me I could have Christian songs played and a cross by the casket. It turned out to be a very lovely choice as we had the whole building to ourselves with a large chapel.

A friend brought in refreshments for those arriving early for the viewing which preceded the service, and the food was able to be placed in one of the viewing rooms. I did not spend any time with those gathered in that room, instead I greeted people at the entrance to the building. I remember thinking afterward that it was quite odd for me to have done that and I don't know what led me to stand in that location. I was genuinely happy to see so many people who came to the service. It warmed my broken heart. But there were also a few who attended who had hurt me deeply with their behavior during Vern's illness. I was able to allow all to hug me, to offer condolences, and I said nothing but kind words. I felt only gratefulness that they took the time to be there to honor Vern.

Long before he became ill, Vern had shared that he wanted to be cremated; however, the cremation was done after the service because our son wanted an open casket for the service. Hundreds showed up including students Vern had taught and coached, teachers he had taught with at different schools, coworkers from his arena employment, my coworkers, and nearly all of those who had disappeared during the cancer years. Vern's parents, my parents and his only brother were deceased; my siblings live in Michigan and did not come out for the service. It was standing room only. At that point I was grateful I had agreed to have a service. My Vern deserved to be remembered and honored that day. Of course, those people all disappeared again within days and weeks, but that's another story.

Five days after the service I received the call from the mortuary that Vern's ashes were ready to be picked up. A friend offered to go with me, but I wanted to do this alone since I wasn't sure how I was going to react. David, the gentleman who had handled the arrangements, came out to take me back to his office. I had to show my ID, sign some papers and verify it was the correct urn. Again, I felt removed from myself. I knew what I was doing and what I had to do, but was strangely unemotional. David placed the urn – a beautiful wooden box – inside a carrying bag with the death certificates and carried it out to my car. David gave me a hug and we were alone, my Vern and I. I actually smiled a little at that moment when I realized Vern was sitting in the passenger seat of my car. That had been our goal … to get him strong enough to ride in my car and not have to use the wheelchair van. I drove home in tears and lifted the carrying bag with the urn from the car. I recall being surprised at how very heavy it was. I carried my Vern back into our home, where he remains today five years later.

*

CHAPTER FOUR

THE TRANSITION

The bereaved need more than just the space to grieve the loss. They also need the space to grieve the transition. -LYNDA CHELDELIN FELL

As we begin the transition of facing life without our spouse, some find comfort by immediately returning to a familiar routine, while others find solitude a safe haven. Sometimes our circumstances don't allow choices to ponder, and we simply follow where the path leads. But the one commonality we're all faced with is the starting point that marks the transition from our old life to the new. Where do we begin?

*

TANYA CAMERON
Tanya's 43-year-old husband Ivor
died of a heart attack in 2013

It was really important for me to try and keep some normality in the boys' lives. They were attending daycare at the time, which was helpful to me to try and come to terms with everything that had just happened. It was easier to do all the paperwork, phone calls etc. that needed my attention while my boys were being cared for and safe. I had six weeks off work, and I knew the more time I stayed away the harder it would be to go back. I can say it wasn't easy returning. I could just sense the sadness and pity that everyone had for me. It took me many months to get back to work as normal as I could. I had only been in this country town for eight months so I didn't know a lot of people, most of my customers did not know my circumstances. I would just break down and cry at the counter for no reason. I still wonder what a lot of them must have been thinking. Anything would set me off, someone just saying, "Hello," or "How are you?" I just felt like I was dying inside myself.

My work has supported me all the way through and even until now and beyond. My team has been a great support. I still have my moments when I just cry at the drop of a hat and sometimes you don't know why you do it, but I have learned to go with it.

*

JONATHAN DEAN
Jonathan's 36-year-old wife Cara
died of double pneumonia in 2010

It took three months for me to get back to work. I was able to do grocery shopping but nothing else. After three months, I slowly started driving again and it became easier after a while. I was treated kindly by my clients but had no support at all. I was completely ALONE at the end of each trip, back in my apartment.

*

BONNIE FORSHEY
Bonnie's 43-year-old husband Carl
died in a car accident in 2005

I didn't return to work for at least a year. I had been through so very much. I was lost and spent time with my daughter. She was all that I had left. Most of my friends avoided me. I think it was too difficult for them to see me so sad. They didn't know what to say.

*

STEPHEN HOCHHAUS
Stephen's 51-year-old wife Kathy
died of soft tissue sarcoma in 2011

Being alone and running my own business, I had to be there every day from day one. I broke down often with escapes to the restroom.

*

MARLISE MAGNA
Marlise's 36-year-old partner Blaine
died by suicide in 2010

I never really returned to work fully after the ordeal. My entire life spun out of control and I lived not even day to day but hour to hour. Embarrassing to say now but for a few weeks I became a total hermit, lived off alcohol and medication, sitting in front of the TV in a state of suspended disbelief. I couldn't even bring myself to bath, brush my hair or change my clothes. I was a hot mess. To this day I only do freelance work and about two years after his passing, I became born again and am currently in ministry. That has given me some peace but I am still very anxious and scared to commit to this day. I am very fortunate that my family, my mom especially, have all been very supportive, both financially and emotionally. I am also surrounded by an awesome support structure of friends.

*

DIANE MCKENZIE-SAPP
Diane's 65-year-old husband Ron
died from renal failure in 2006

I had taken all my vacation time and used family leave to be with Ron, and that ran out within a few days after he died. I was not able to function in my position and told them that I could return, however I could not control unexpected tearful relapses. I had breast cancer the previous year and they let me take that as personal leave for the rest of November, December and January. I had worked about four years for Medicare and the state as a Nurse Inspector of Health Facilities and did the yearly inspections of nursing homes in our state. It was a demanding, precise and very exacting professional position. I could not become tearful or appear emotional during these visits, or my evaluation of the official visit would appear invalidated and unprofessional and the team that I worked with could not depend on me to support their work as well.

I had a new boss who was a challenge to work alongside. I needed to work five years to become vested in the state retirement system as I wanted the health insurance and medication plan that this would cover. Each personal leave had incurred additional time for me to make up to count toward the five years. I worked an additional year and one month past my hire date to make up the necessary five working years. I loved the field work and when I returned I was cleared to do the inspection visits. However, the last year I was sent to the complaint division at the end of a dreary hall where paperwork and occasional phone calls were handled. The complaint department was where they punished people by turning a thinking rational person into a paper pusher. And as a nurse, I found the isolation maddening. I don't know what I did or said, perhaps it was the nursing home doctor I called a murderer. He had allowed a patient to die without medical intervention. I felt as if I was an outcast as I did my time. I felt invisible. I felt useless. I listened to people telling me I needed to get out and date, and to other inane advice from people who had no clue. I finally learned to just mutter a noncommittal hum and ignored whatever bit of wisdom was being force-fed. I left there with a sense of closing a door and not looking back.

After retirement I had too much time and little to do. I dreamed of rings and I dreamed of becoming the Zorro of nursing homes. I dreamed of midnight raids into nursing homes with my official badge that I hadn't turned in. I would threaten the lazy midnight crew with citations, unless they changed their ways with a flurry of medication runs, clean beds and answered call bells. I would not write them up only if they corrected their problems before the sun rose. I would leave before dawn without a single clue. With no paperwork, there would be no record of the Zorro raid and the nursing homes wouldn't complain about the timing of the visit since there was no write up. It was a great dream though I could end up in jail for impersonating a federal agent. In the past, whenever I had a "really great idea," it was always run by Ron. Ron was my idea leveler. He would tell me if an idea was really good or a bit nutty, as I could never tell the difference.

Now he's gone so if you hear of midnight raids in a nursing home, don't be alarmed.

*

LILIAN MORTON

Lilian's 58-year-old husband Michael

died in a plane crash in 2012

I didn't return to work for eighteen months. While I was in Chicago for Michael's memorial service, a week after his death, I received a call from a man who was a small interest owner in our business, who informed me that I was no longer employed and no longer allowed in the business. He said I could also tell our oldest daughter that she was no longer employed. He told me he would have someone box up our things and Michael's things, and send them to us. I contacted an attorney and have fought with him for the last three years, but because of the way the company was set up, he was the only one who was able to make any decisions relative to the company, no matter how small his interest.

I started applying for jobs about three months after Michael's death but couldn't find anything suitable. I really wasn't ready but needed the income. A little over a year after his death, I sold the house and moved back to my hometown. I returned to work about six months after the move. It was hard to get an interview with anyone. They see a gap in your employment and you get tossed to the bottom of the stack. I ended up going to a temp agency and after a week had a full time job. It was hard going to work without Michael there. We had been working together for so many years.

*

LISA OWENS
Lisa's 50 year-old husband Greg
died of pancreatic cancer in 2014

I was Greg's caretaker, and when hospice said he needed round-the-clock care, I stayed home to care for him. I was blessed to have the job I have, and continued getting paid. I stayed home for one week after Greg's service, and then returned to work. I needed the distraction and needed to be with the people Greg loved so much. Yes, it was so hard because they don't understand death, and so they talk about him, but it was also healing to be able to talk about him.

*

MARY POTTER KENYON
Mary's 60-year-old husband David
died of heart failure in 2012

I had a workshop scheduled just two weeks after my husband's death, and I wasn't sure I would be able to do it. It was an extreme couponing workshop with a PowerPoint that consisted of photos of our shared shopping sprees. Our "dates" for several months before I'd begun doing workshops had consisted of power shopping sprees. Every single slide was going to be a reminder of my huge loss, and those shopping trips I'd done with my best friend and partner in life.

I asked my doctor if he thought I could do a workshop so soon after David's death, and he just shook his head and said "I don't know." Could I cancel something my husband had encouraged and been so proud of? My older sister Joan agreed to go to the workshop with me, and I think that saved me. Once I got through it without crying, I knew I could do it.

The insurance policy my husband had left was modest, but I knew it would cover the funeral and burial expenses, a newer vehicle, and there would still be enough left that I really wouldn't HAVE to work for almost two years. I remembered how much my husband hated me taking on work that I was less than thrilled with, just to make money. I decided that I would give myself fifteen months of grieving time before looking for work. I worked on a book project, did couponing and writing workshops, and spent many afternoons napping and sitting on the couch surrounded by piles of papers.

I worked: I wrote frantically a weekly coupon column for a newspaper, editing and finishing a couponing book, writing dozens of articles and essays, blogging, revising an older manuscript my husband had encouraged, all while working on a book about grief. But I didn't take on any projects I didn't want to. I said no a lot, but I don't regret those months. It seems very indulgent now, when I could have gotten a job and invested that money, but I had a lot of peaceful, quiet time, and my soul and heart needed it.

I never had so many quiet moments as I had during those months after David's death. I wrestled with the quiet sometimes, because the pain would come rushing in, and there was even a period when my frantic writing pace came to a crashing halt, and I had to learn to slow down and just be. That was difficult for me. I'd been so busy raising children, taking care of a home and a husband, homeschooling, and picking up odd jobs or running a home business, that I never took the time to just sit, and "be still."

I can actually look back and feel wistful about those months when I did whatever I wanted to do. It was during this time of writing, reading, and praying that I learned what it means to listen to God. When I got anxious or pulled down into darkness, I would hear "Be still and know that I am God." The words really didn't mean much before, but then became my mantra. You mean God can speak to me in the stillness? Who knew? I should have known that you can't have a relationship with someone without listening to them. I'd learned that with my husband during his cancer treatment in 2006. Once I'd learned it, we had the best marriage for a wonderful five years before he died from heart failure.

I was right. I needed to get a job by the end of 2013, and a perfect one came in the form of a library director position where I was allowed to bring my two homeschooled children to work with me. Less than two years later, I was offered a job writing for a newspaper. When I realized I would be paid to write and heard the words "health insurance" for me and my daughters during the interview, it felt like David was still watching out for me. As I transitioned from one job to the other, I was working ten-hour days with training my replacement. During that stressful period, one of my daughters said she felt like an orphan. That was hard to hear, but we do what we have to do, and now that I am down to one good job, along with my workshops, we are adjusting.

*

NANCY REDMOND
Nancy's 40-year-old husband Kevin
died of a heart attack in 2012

I felt so lonely when everyone went back to work and back to their own homes. I have said many times that their lives all went back to normal, but mine never did. I returned to work about three weeks after Kevin's death, and I was lucky enough to return to a group of people at work that I call my family. My direct supervisor had lost her husband about eighteen months earlier, so she understood completely the pain and being somewhere I needed to be, but didn't want to be. One of my oldest and dearest friends is a gal I worked at my first job with and who happened to help get me the job I have now. She met me at the door with a bouquet of flowers and walked me in to the office that first morning back, and then left me in the hands of our very thoughtful supervisor who walked with me around the office so I could say hello to my coworkers and do all the crying I needed to do as they welcomed me back with hugs and lots of love. To this day, I firmly believe that knowing what to do at work was my saving grace. I didn't know WHAT to do with this new life at home, but I did know what to do at work! I put myself on autopilot for many months and "faked it until I made it" through this dark tunnel.

*

MARY LEE ROBINSON
Mary Lee's 63-year-old husband Pat
died from a sudden stroke in 2013

When Pat died, I hadn't worked for a paycheck for several years, at his request. Before we moved to our new state, I was charged with overseeing the care of six octogenarian family members in three states, while Pat brought home the paycheck. I also did a lot of volunteer work, but at the time of his death, I was just wrapping up settling us in the home we built. I had not started volunteering anywhere, and between my age and the economy, there weren't many jobs for me. Fortunately, I really didn't need to work.

The initial weeks after Pat died, I was occupied with a flurry of administrative details. And the mail, the never-ending mail. Pat was widowed when we met. He was the executor for his wife and both of his parents. I was getting mail for four dead people and one errant stepson who claimed our previous address as his own. Daily mail that sometimes filled two tote bags continued for nearly a year.

Pat died in mid-February. That Easter Sunday, I found myself totally alone. I could barely get out of bed. Going to church was out of the question. None of my family telephoned. None of my new neighbors thought to ask me to join them at church or for a meal. One old friend called, but only one. One neighbor lost her husband exactly four weeks after I did. I delivered a meal, engaged her young son with some minor chores to give him a chance to be active, took over a couple books, called and checked on her. They were aware that I had very little family. That family, on the other hand, had a crowd for Easter. I could hear the music from their house across the way. Nobody thought to include me. A small handful of my other neighbors were solicitous in the first two weeks. After that, my time was up. I got a few invitations to go to lunch. Widows become the "lunch ladies." Nobody wants to invite us to dinner, and wives become funny about having us around their husbands. We learn real quick that a chill wind sweeps across a room we enter. My social life disappeared. Evenings alone became brutal.

In recent weeks, I'd submitted applications to volunteer at the hospital, at botanical gardens, and a museum. I never heard from any of them. It became clear to me, that Easter day, that I was going to have to build my own life raft, or I was going to join my husband. Many of my family members are gone now, but that Easter I thought quite a lot about them. I was blessed with wonderful memories of very loving grandparents, aunts and uncles and my dad. Out of eight of them, five had been widowed, two of them twice. If they could survive, so could I! I sat down at my laptop and searched for widows clubs. Every city I'd ever lived in had a widows club. Not this one! In Myrtle Beach, populated abundantly by retirees, nada, zip, zero. I could hear their collective voices, or maybe it was God saying, "Get up, get up, you have work to do!" I found an online platform for creating online clubs that met in person. I spent the rest of the day and the next day setting up a new club. It was to be open to both widows and widowers, but I had to make it clear that it wasn't a dating group. The purpose was to meet others who needed to build a new social life, safely. I wanted to operate it sort of like a rolling flash mob. "Here's the event, show up." The first two meetings were sparsely attended, with only two others showing up. The third meeting, held at a restaurant, had twenty-eight widows present. Within a year, membership grew to 178. I did have work to do!

*

CAROL SCIBELLI
Carol's 56-year-old husband Jimmy
died from lymphoma in 2006

I'm a freelance humor writer so I had the luxury to delay my re-entry into my work world. It was almost impossible for me to compose a cohesive sentence. My mind was jumbled. At least I knew not to take on any writing assignments or solicit projects for several months. I was relieved not to go back to a punch-a-clock type of job but maybe an enforced regiment might have helped me. I would have had to shake off the fog, clear my head and interact with coworkers. Instead, besides some time with friends and family, I was alone. Often I didn't answer the phone. Looking back, this may not have been the healthiest way to live and grieve. A routine might have been good for me.

On many occasions, to sell my husband's business, I did have to pull myself together to attend meetings with prospective buyers and ever present attorneys. All were kind and supportive and patient with the widow who was clueless about money. Whenever I had to be present, I was able to be and that surprised me. I learned about being human. We can be feeling one thing so strongly and project another. Over the years, I saw that this trait may have been one reason why so many people assume widows are okay when, in fact, we are close to losing it. We work so hard to hold it together that people believe us. And then we complain, they don't get it.

Each time I did venture out into the neighborhood I was fearful that I would run into someone who I knew or worse, someone who would ask, "How's Jimmy?" To fend off a long, suffocating hug, I was tempted to say, "Fine." I'm sure that at the same time my kids were tackling their own dreads. My daughter was a stay-at-mom with a two-year-old so she stayed busy with her family. This gave her focus and solace. My son, an accountant, went back to work almost immediately. I really don't know how he adjusted and felt, because he refused to talk about his pain. Whenever I coaxed him to tell me how he was feeling, he got annoyed with me and said, "I don't want to think about it. Now, you've made me think about it." He told me many years later that losing his father made him angry for a very long time.

Blogs were just becoming popular back then and I had been writing a blog about being a "grandma boomer" when Jimmy died. Now this subject seemed aimless. My friend Cathy, who was widowed a number of years earlier, encouraged me and told me to, "Write all your feelings and experiences down. You'll want to remember." I began to write the blog, *Poor Widow Me.* As all widows and widowers know, we experience a flurry of feelings. At any given moment we are bombarded with tears and fears and sadness. Triggers are everywhere. Writing forced me to pinpoint exactly what my emotion was at that moment. So many people commented that they understood what I was going through as a result of reading my blogs. This encouraged me to keep writing them. Writing became a release; it was cathartic. And the blogs served as notes when I decided to write a memoir.

Cathy was right. I never would have been able to capture the details of my experiences as accurately, as heartfelt, and even remember the funny if I hadn't busied myself writing about it fairly soon after Jimmy's death.

*

DIANNE WEST
Dianne's 69-year-old husband Vern
died from multiple myeloma in 2010

Vern died on a Wednesday, his service was on a Sunday, and I returned to work on Tuesday. I was responsible for an annual employee event coming up in a couple of weeks and felt it would be helpful to have something to concentrate on. It was. I went in early, stayed late, and brought work home. It filled my days and evenings with busy work to help keep my mind occupied on anything other than my loss.

When I returned to work, coworkers stopped by to offer condolences and I had some make those ridiculous comments we've all experienced. You know … "I know exactly how you feel," "He's in a better place," "God needed him." I know they meant well, but when two of them shared that putting their dog down made them know exactly how I felt, I really had no words. I was lucky that I had a private office and could shut the door whenever I needed to. During those first couple of weeks, I kept the door partially closed most of the time. I was working on that big project and didn't need the interruptions and I actually think it was a relief to my coworkers to not feel obligated to have to stop in and talk to me. I had worked at my company for over twenty-five years and had built up a lot of sick leave. I am grateful that I was allowed to take the time I needed during the cancer years….well, that was after my boss rather callously removed me from my position two weeks after the diagnosis, on my birthday, while my husband was still in ICU. As it turned out, she was right. The new position I was moved into allowed me much more freedom and far less stress. I could have taken more time than what I did for bereavement, but it was really very good for me to have a place to go each day. I don't think I would have done well staying home for an extended period of time. I needed to return to work where I could occasionally feel like the old Dianne. The one who had Vern to come home to, not the widow. But, of course, the reality hit me each day on the drive home.

In life, loss is inevitable. Everyone knows this, yet in the core of most people it remains deeply denied – "This should not happen to me." It is for this reason that loss is the most difficult challenge one has to face as a human being.
DAYANANDA SARASWATI

*

CHAPTER FIVE

THE QUESTION

Grievers use a very simple calendar. Before and after.
LYNDA CHELDELIN FELL

One day we have our dearly beloved. The next, we don't. So where does this leave us when others ask "Are you married?" How do we answer a question that appears simple to everyone but us?

*

TANYA CAMERON
Tanya's 43-year-old husband Ivor
died of a heart attack in 2013

That word "widow" was very hard to come to terms with. I didn't want my husband to pass away, I didn't want to be bringing up my boys alone. I felt embarrassed to be a widow, I was too young. My thinking was that you don't become a widow until you're much older, at least you have a lifetime together before anything like this would happen. The vows at our wedding, "Until death do us part," came much sooner than anybody could have imagined.

It's been two and a half years since my husband passed away. Not long ago someone referred to me as a "single mother." I felt labeled, I didn't choose to be a single mum. I very quickly put him straight, I was a widow. Yes, I said it, "widow." That was my turning point. I still refer to Ivor as my husband. Because he still is. We didn't separate or divorce. But I still find it hard to use either name. Everybody grieves differently and accepts things in different ways and in their own way. I think it is best if you just go with whatever feels right for you.

*

JONATHAN DEAN
Jonathan's 36-year-old wife Cara
died of double pneumonia in 2010

I have always said from the beginning that I am a widower. I have always, and will continue to reference Cara to people as my wife, because she ALWAYS will be. I tell people that we were common-law married, no children.

*

BONNIE FORSHEY
Bonnie's 43-year-old husband Carl
died in a car accident in 2005

When my husband died, I was devastated. I have been widowed twice, never kept it a secret. My husbands were big parts of my life, we shared children, and many years together. One does not simply forget.

*

STEPHEN HOCHHAUS
Stephen's 51-year-old wife Kathy
died of soft tissue sarcoma in 2011

I often say I'm married because I still feel married four and a half years later. I use the term widowed when it pertains to legal description.

*

DIANE MCKENZIE-SAPP
Diane's 65-year-old husband Ron
died from renal failure in 2006

I do not like being a widow. I do not like being invisible. I wanted a widow's ring and it didn't exist. I could wear a scarlet "W" on my forehead, but I would rather wear a widow's ring on my finger. There was no way to look at me and know I was a widow unless I TOLD you. When you looked at me when I was married, you could glance at my ring finger with its bands and know I was important to someone. Wearing a wedding ring shows that you are married. I am not married and I am painfully aware that the box I check off is widow. My income tax form is single. The only thing that wasn't taken from Mrs. Sapp is her husband's last name. I am a Ms. now. I had to take Ron's name off of the vehicle registration, the house, the bank account, the IRA, the insurance, the car, the phone, the water bill, the electric bill, the tax bill. Yes, rub my nose in it.… I am not a Mrs. I am losing him bit by bit.

When I was younger, on Mother's Day you would wear a white carnation if your mother had died and a pink carnation if she was alive. I remember the impression it made on me as a young girl to look across church and KNOW with just a glance what the status was with every single person in that room. No questions. No answers. Now wearing a wedding ring and saying, "I am a widow," I get a look that says I am an imposter, a fraud, a woman masquerading as a real married woman. A look that accuses, "How could you let me ask HOW is your husband? You should have warned me, I look like an idiot and it's your fault."

I wanted to make it known with just a look. I wanted a visible symbol, a death ring that showed I was exactly who I said I was, a widow. Why didn't the widows have a symbol like a widow's ring so that we would not have to explain? Why? Because nobody really gives widows a thought. I won't lose one more thing to death, especially my rings. The small business advisor, who finally gave up on me ever becoming a real business, asked, "What is it you want to do with your widow's ring?" I told him the story about the Mother's Day carnations story. I said that someday I would like our children to see a widow's ring on a woman's hand, and immediately know what is going on in her life. I would like them to empathize and be gentle with her soul, because she is now visible to you. So either I could invent the widow's ring or quietly disappear. And I have never been quiet. I was so darn tired of being invisible.

*

LILIAN MORTON
Lilian's 58-year-old husband Michael
died in a plane crash in 2012

It is still hard for me to answer that question. It took me at least a year to say the "W" word and now, depending on the way it comes up, I respond differently. Sometimes I say I'm a widow, especially on forms where I can just check a box. Sometimes I say that I am single or unmarried. I hate the looks and responses I get from people when I say I'm a widow. It is almost always followed by an, "Oh, I'm sorry." How do you respond to that???

*

LISA OWENS
Lisa's 50 year-old husband Greg
died of pancreatic cancer in 2014

The word widow is very hard to say. I hate to say it; it breaks my heart to say it. I am still a wife, I want to continue being his wife!

*

MARY POTTER KENYON
Mary's 60-year-old husband David
died of heart failure in 2012

Simple. I say, "I'm a widow." My answer is the same no matter what the situation. It is much harder for me to say I'm "single" than it is to say "widowed."

Removing the wedding ring was a difficult decision. I'd sit there twisting and twisting it, wondering what to do. I wasn't married anymore, but I still felt married. The decision was made for me. On the day I submitted my completed manuscript to the publisher I had signed with for my coupon book, I hit the send button and felt a sharp pain in my finger just as I heard a little "ping." My wedding ring cracked the minute I submitted the manuscript that my husband had encouraged and believed in! I was astonished at the timing, but it also felt like a sign from my husband.

*

NANCY REDMOND
Nancy's 40-year-old husband Kevin
died of a heart attack in 2012

Yes, eternally. If I feel safe enough to share the rest, I do. Otherwise, I leave it at that. The emotions range from the joy of remembering to the wistfulness and longing for that comfortable life that I once knew.

*

MARY LEE ROBINSON
Mary Lee's 63-year-old husband Pat
died from a sudden stroke in 2013

I seldom get the question directly, as I still wear my rings. That's another 5,000 word essay. I'll shorten it up some. Why the hell is it anybody else's business if I wear my rings or not? Why does anyone else care? I digress. When I do get the question, I'm honest but brief. I simply say something like, "I was widowed a couple of years ago," and then generally change the subject when I can. If my companion persists, I find those are the people who are often generally caring and not all that uncomfortable with discussing loss. Often, they have also experienced loss themselves. Either way, I try not to make a big deal about it. It was a difficult question to answer for about a year. It isn't anymore.

*

CAROL SCIBELLI
Carol's 56-year-old husband Jimmy
died from lymphoma in 2006

The first year I was a widow, I hesitated to tell strangers. The words, "I'm a widow," or "My husband passed away," seemed shocking for others to hear. And each time I heard myself say this out loud it was a jolt even to me, like a punch in the stomach. I winced to watch the surprise and pity on people's faces. Some wanted to know details. It was clear that they were concerned about their own husbands. I could practically read their mind, "If it could happen to her husband, so out of the blue, this dark shadow might creep into our happy home, too!" This was a turn off for me.

I remembered that my mother-in-law, a widow, constantly said, "It's a couples' world. I'm a fifth wheel." This was her mantra. Now here I was, not fitting in, being an extra, the odd one, after thirty-three years of being part of a pair. Sometimes, I'd feel the panic rising inside me just anticipating that "Are you married?" question. Most people responded, "But you're so young!" That part I liked. At fifty-five, at least I was young for something.

When possible, I'd scoot the question and change the subject. Often salespeople would say harmless things like, "I'll bet your husband would like how that looks on you." I'd cringe inside, but I'd just smile and nod. I wore my wedding band for two years so I could hardly blame a stranger if they assumed I was married. The first time I filled out a form that asked my marital status, I paused and looked around the doctor's office self-consciously and held my breath as I circled "widow." I had signed many papers as the executrix for the estate of James Scibelli, yet I think circling widow was a heart stopping moment because it was so public. When I had to bring the clipboard to the receptionist, I'd pray that she didn't read it carefully. If I got up the courage to look up into her eyes, I imagined there was knowingness behind her smile. When my name was called I was positive the nurse knew, too.

On my first birthday following Jimmy's death I was involved in a fender bender and it was the first and last time I volunteered that I was a widow. I wasn't using "the widow's card" to get away with something, at least I don't think I was. I was simply trying to explain that I was having a very bad day. In a heavy accent, the woman who owned the car I hit yelled at me, "Vat ver you dinking? Vat ver you dinking? Vat ver you dinking?" I blurted out, "My husband passed away three months ago, and today's my birthday!" She continued to copy down my information, and without looking up said, "I hear what you say. Your husband he passed away, but mine is going to kill me!" As luck would have it, I never heard from her. Either she did have a heart after all or her husband really did kill her...

By year three, I was much more at peace with my life and I could breezily say, "I'm a widow." I no longer cared or even noticed people's reaction. Possibly, they were more comfortable around me because time had passed and they assumed I was "over it." People also assumed I was divorced and when I said, "No, I'm a widow" they, men especially, seemed to warm up to me. That could be my imagination though.

*

KRISTI SMITH
Kristi's 48-year-old husband Michael died from cardiac arrest in 2011

Have you ever been reluctant to own a certain part of your identity or felt hesitant to step into a new reality? There is one area of my life where I have been having trouble making peace. You see I am a widow, but I don't want to be. I fight against owning this title for many reasons. First and foremost, because it means the love of my life has died; but second, because it is not who I want to be. "Widow" is not a sought after, coveted, prized title. No little girl dreams of one day growing up to be a widow. No one wants to be a widow. I know I don't want to be. For years, I have fought the facts but the test results are still the same. I am a widow and there is not one thing I can do about it. Try as I may, I cannot change the spots on this cougar. I feel like I have no choice. I can fight it or I can make peace with it. I can run from it or walk in the truth of it. I can deny who I am or accept it. Hmmm…denial sounds good. I have lived in denial before about other issues in my life. Denial is nothing new for me. I am honestly a pretty good dancer when it comes to skirting the truth. I lie to myself every day. Here are a couple of examples of how I twist the truth:

I am not chubby; I am curvy.
I am not arrogant; I am confident.
I am not materialistic; I just love to shop.
I am not a middle-aged woman; I am in the prime of life.

I don't have an issue with needing approval, but I sure hope you like me… See what I mean? Am I chubby or curvy? It depends on my perspective. If I like curves on a woman, I say I am "curvy." If I think all women should be thin, I call myself "chubby." I judge myself. I can rationalize my lies and make them sound sexier, but I know the real truth…I am reluctant to admit my weaknesses. Isn't that what denial is - lying to yourself? If I don't like who I am I can pretend to be something else. Can't I simply continue in my naked parade and have everyone tell me how marvelous I look in my golden-spun robe? Am I really only fooling myself? Yes, but a crafty fool I am. I find myself fussing with the facts and rearranging them to fit my fantasy. The real question is why?? Why do I hide from myself? What am I afraid of? Why can't I just blurt out the down and dirty details? I am a chubby, arrogant, materialistic, middle-aged woman who chronically needs approval!! I am also a curvy, confident, professional shopper in the prime of my life and I hope you like me.

Why do we put a twist on the truth? Let me be honest, the facts aren't always pretty and sometimes they are hard to accept. Most of the time it is not a matter of how you feel about a situation, it is literally a physical reality. You are either a widow or you are not. Being a widow is kind of like being pregnant; you are either a widow or you aren't. You can't be partially pregnant and you can't be partially a widow. Deep breath. I am a widow. There, I have said it. But admitting I am a widow is just acknowledging the facts of the situation; I still have a long way to go on admitting the reality of my condition. It has been four years since my husband's death and I still have a hard time identifying myself as a widow. So I just say that I am single and that is true, but it is not the full truth. I became single because my husband died. I don't have an ex-husband; I have a late husband. Side note: What does "late" husband even mean? Where did the term originate? Did someone decide it was easier to say my husband is late than to say he has died? And late… for what? Late for dinner? He is not late. He won't be home later. In fact, he won't be coming home…ever. He is not late from work; he is dead. I may get away with saying I am curvy when in reality I am chubby, but saying my husband is late is just a lie. He is not late. He is gone. Does it make it any less true if I don't admit it? Call me a reluctant widow, but a widow none the less. I am a wild widow writer.

*

DIANNE WEST
Dianne's 69-year-old husband Vern
died from multiple myeloma in 2010

I can't say that I've been asked about my marital status very often. But if specifically asked I would share that I am widowed. I don't love that word, but as I've worked within the widowed community I've come to respect it and all that it means. We are strong, resilient, caring people. And we were blessed to be able to love our spouse to their very last breath. Being widowed, however, doesn't mean I think of myself as single; I definitely do not. I still feel married to Vern and believe that I will always feel that way. I don't plan to date or remarry and I continued to wear his wedding band and my rings (a twenty-five-year anniversary band and a past-present-future ring he gave me after his diagnosis) for a long time.

I recall driving to work one day and realizing I hadn't put my rings back on after cleaning. I immediately turned the car around to go home and get them, even though it made me late to work. It was that important to me. I didn't think I would ever take my rings off, but when a coworker assumed I had remarried because of those rings, I decided it was time for change. Now I just wear Vern's band and a widow's ring on my left hand. I guess it's rather odd that I was offended by the remarriage comment, and yet it caused me to remove my rings. But it feels right. I also wear a pendant containing my husband's photo. Strangers often ask about it. I share that it's my husband and he passed away five years ago. Some react awkwardly (I suspect they think it holds his ashes), but most offer their condolences and remark how lovely the pendant is.

*

CHAPTER SIX

THE DATES

No matter what anyone says about grief and about time healing all wounds, the truth is, there are certain sorrows that never fade away until the heart stops beating and the last breath is taken. -UNKNOWN

Birthdays conjure memories of happier times. How do we honor the life that is no more? And how do we acknowledge the painful date that marks their death?

*

TANYA CAMERON
Tanya's 43-year-old husband Ivor
died of a heart attack in 2013

I try to keep myself busy and my mind occupied on other things, but it does not always work. I found the first year the hardest, getting through the "firsts" of all the anniversaries, birthdays, Christmas and Ivor's passing was very emotional on all occasions. On my husband's birthday, I was surrounded by all my family. It was a beautiful hot Australian summer's day which was also our Australia Day, January 26. We celebrated as we would every year, all the great foods including our pavlova (Ivor's favorite), everybody laughing, the boys were having a great time and then I looked around the room. Every one of my family was in the room, but one person was missing. I burst into tears. It wasn't fair, my sister had her husband, my brother had his wife, my parents had each other and I was alone. I hugged my boys and thanked them for being in my life.

I hated Saturdays, as that was the day of the week that Ivor passed away. Even when the first anniversary came around, I felt more emotional on the Saturday but by that date it had gone over to the Sunday. Reliving that whole horrible day, my parents took the boys and I out for lunch to keep us occupied.

I really struggled through my boys' birthday; it saddened me to think my husband wasn't by my side for their fourth and fifth birthdays. I tried to keep things as normal as I could for the sake of my boys. I still get emotional, thinking about what Ivor is missing out on. I don't like the boys seeing me fall apart, though I do shed tears with them now and then. I like to tell them it is okay to cry and boys are allowed to cry, as I am sure the superheroes cry sometimes.

*

JONATHAN DEAN
Jonathan's 36-year-old wife Cara
died of double pneumonia in 2010

Memories. Remembering all the happy times. The anniversary of her passing is more difficult as I am home ALONE and crying. No family participation at all.

*

BONNIE FORSHEY
Bonnie's 43-year-old husband Carl
died in a car accident in 2005

I always remember them on their birthdays, death anniversary, and our anniversary date. I remember on my children's birthdays. I will post an online tribute, and say a prayer.

*

STEPHEN HOCHHAUS
Stephen's 51-year-old wife Kathy
died of soft tissue sarcoma in 2011

I still go out to one of our favorite restaurants for Kathy's birthday. I usually go out of town for our anniversary, as I am in Hawaii right now for our day September 22, which is the day we first met. So I am spending that day at Kathy's favorite place on earth.

*

MARLISE MAGNA
Marlise's 36-year-old partner Blaine
died by suicide in 2010

I tell my close friends and family when his birthday and death anniversaries come up. Usually on his birthday I celebrate his life, but always feel a deep pang of sadness and empathy for his mom, seeing as he was her only child. His birthday I will always think about him, our past, what could've still been. It's a day I always am apprehensive about for weeks beforehand and I tend to stay-at-home and keep to myself. I always feel such guilt, and the questions pop up more than usual. These past two years it has been bittersweet as it's also my brother's wedding anniversary. At his wedding, I cried nonstop and people assumed it was due to joy for my brother.

*

DIANE MCKENZIE-SAPP
Diane's 65-year-old husband Ron
died from renal failure in 2006

Each birthday and each anniversary I review where I am now, how far I have come and how far I have to go. I look at what hurts? What needs healing? Is it my broken heart, the widows 3rd ring, stopping the tears, the loneliness, the fear of losing the connection, or not being strong enough to change and accept it? Or is it the loss of how Ron's voice sounded, the crinkle of his eyes or the goodness that filled him and the memory of him? I revisit my loss and, as a nurse, I compare his death with an amputation. To treat my pain and form a plan and a path for my journey, I seek remedies for the pains of death.

I view the loss of as an amputation.
I view my broken heart as an open gaping wound.
I view my pain as real and constant.
I view his death as a catastrophic void.
I view my loneliness as survivor's guilt.

By defining death as a disease with symptoms, I can treat and heal those symptoms. I will implement any rational to protect my heart and sanity. If your wound was visible to the rest of the world, if others understood that your pain is immense, if widows had a recovery plan, if we did not have to defend our grief maybe we would not be infected with a non-healing wound. Setting a time limit on grief is a hurtful condemnation of the widow's grief process, shared by those who have not lost a spouse but feel entitled to evaluate our progress. Widows have confided that no one understands their pain and loss. People say, "You should just move on," "You are stuck," "You have had enough time to deal with it." These words are judgmental and undermining. If you had lost a leg to amputation would these same people say the same words to you? If your loss was visible, would they say "Just deal with it?" No they would not. Your loss is an amputation of your heart and soul. Your "phantom pain" is real. Nobody can say when the expiration date on grief is supposed to be.

The Nursing Interventions for the Low Self Esteem resulting from an amputation are comparable to that of losing a spouse. Substitute "widow" for "amputee" to see for yourself that the feelings of loss, guilt, acceptance, grief are the significant, acceptable, usual and recognized symptoms of loss. Can you see the parallel?

Nursing Interventions Rationale:

- Consider patient's preparation and view of amputation.
- Amputation poses serious threats to patient's psychological and psychosocial adjustment.
- Help the amputee cope with his altered self-image. To accept the new self-more quickly.
- Encourage expression of fears, negative feelings, and grief over loss of body part. Venting emotions helps patient begin to deal with the fact and reality of life without a limb.
- Reinforce information including pain control and rehabilitation.
- Provides opportunity for patient to question and assimilate information and begin to deal with changes in body image and function, which can facilitate recovery.
- Assess degree of support available to patient. Sufficient support by friends can facilitate rehabilitation.
- Point out positive signs of healing. Integration of stump into body image can take months or even years.
- Encourage visits by another amputee. A peer who has been through a similar experience serves as a role model and can hope for recovery and a normal future.

Respect your grief. You know what you feel is real. If it takes years to recover from an amputation, why should you expect yourself to have a time limit? You will never be over the amputation of your heart and soul. Phantom pain will always be with you. You will heal with time, you will be different and you will accept your loss, but that does not mean you will ever get over it.

I designed rings to heal the pain. I created a visible and tangible remedy for each hurt. Each of these were created to heal a mourner's pain:

- Broken hearts to show on the outside what lives on the inside
- Rings made of tears
- A third ring to sit beside the still important wedding rings
- A simple black band with the serenity prayer inside
- A footprints rainbow ring of hope
- An antique-style black mourning ring
- A spinning prayer wheel ring

*

JULIE MJELVE
Julie's 42-year-old husband Cameron
died by suicide in 2011

Initially, acknowledging the birthday and anniversary of my husband's death was difficult. It was very emotional even just to decide what to do. My husband was buried in a different city than we live in, so that he could be in the family cemetery. So it's a bit of an outing to get there, and my children are still quite young. But, to my surprise, my young children have been my biggest help in figuring it all out, as well as coping with it.

It started on the first anniversary of Cameron's death. I wanted to take them to the grave site, but I didn't want it to be a terrible, sad day. I wanted to acknowledge Cameron's memory and acknowledge our grief, but mourning to me is more about remembering and honoring than it is about negative emotions. So, we took flowers to the gravesite (each child gets their own little flower arrangement, so they can each individually take part in the mourning ritual rather than just observing it). However after we had visited the gravesite we went to a lake for the afternoon.

The next year, we followed our grave visit with a lovely picnic at the local spray park. The kids initiated that we now also go on Father's Day, as well as on my husband's birthday. They have been able to approach it with a sense of importance instead of tragedy, and I think that really helps me deal with my emotions on those dates. It has also evolved as to who comes to the grave with us. My husband's parents live in a town very near by, so we have begun picking them up on the way and making it more of a family event. This helps to keep us connected, and helps us to remember we are all part of my husband's family. We never spend a long time in the cemetery. We put flowers on my husband's grave, as well as the other family members in that same cemetery. Then, we often go for dinner or dessert with his parents. It has become this nice time of connecting. There is still sadness over his loss, but the importance of remembering stands out overall and the sadness is more in the background.

*

LILIAN MORTON
Lilian's 58-year-old husband Michael
died in a plane crash in 2012

On Michael's birthday, I still wish him a happy birthday. I just do it in a prayer now because he was never one for big celebrations. On the first anniversary of Michael's death, I visited the airport and the crash site. That was hard. It was the first time that I had ever been to either place. The month leading up to the first anniversary was very difficult. It was as if I was starting the grieving process all over again. Sometimes I will open our journal and read it on that day. The days leading up to that day are still dark. I usually spend that day by myself reflecting on where my life is now versus what it would have been like if this never happened. On a day to day basis, I try not to let myself go there. At my job, I type the date every day repeatedly. If the anniversary date is a work day, every time I type the date, my heart skips a beat and it makes me sad.

*

LISA OWENS
Lisa's 50 year-old husband Greg
died of pancreatic cancer in 2014

I celebrate! Balloon release, dinner with Greg's family and friends, and change his flowers. It's all we have left.

*

MARY POTTER KENYON
Mary's 60-year-old husband David
died of heart failure in 2012

I visit the gravesite, bringing some birdseed, flowers, or a little "gift" to leave behind. It is usually me alone, but some of my children have visited with me. It makes my youngest girls really sad to visit their dad's grave, so I don't push it.

*

NANCY REDMOND
Nancy's 40-year-old husband Kevin
died of a heart attack in 2012

Each year on both Kevin's birthday and the anniversary of his death, I go to Lake Superior in Duluth, Minnesota, and hunt for agates which was "our" thing to do. On the first anniversary of his passing, my oldest son, daughter and grandson accompanied me to Lake Superior and my beautiful grandson put some "magic Grampa Kevin dust" into the lake where he would, in my grandson's words, "forever swim in the big lake." Out of the mouths of babes, indeed. My kids are very cognizant of the meaning of these two days and go out of their way to help me recognize those days.

*

MARY LEE ROBINSON
Mary Lee's 63-year-old husband Pat
died from a sudden stroke in 2013

Same answer for both questions. Pat's birthday is difficult and made more so by the fact that my late father's birthday is the day before. His death anniversary is a few days after Valentine's Day, and we marked that Valentine's in ICU. Same strategy for both occasions. I spend each of those days quietly, generally at home. I putter and do whatever I feel like doing and don't make big plans of any kind. Birthdays are a little sad, as birthdays in life were pretty sad. My folks and I were the only ones who celebrated my husband's birthday. Rarely did he get a phone call or a card from either of his kids. One year, even his mother neglected to remember it. Quiet is good.

*

CAROL SCIBELLI
Carol's 56-year-old husband Jimmy
died from lymphoma in 2006

Acknowledging Jimmy's birthday and death day has changed over the years. Certainly, the first anniversary of his death was the most painful and nervously anticipated. After several years I found that the days leading up to a specific date were far more stressful than the actual day. By the time the dreaded day arrived, it was almost anticlimactic. On the first anniversary of Jimmy's death my kids and I chose a photo from just a few months before he died. We put it in Newsday's memorial section, and underneath we wrote how much we loved and missed him. The second anniversary we ran the same photo with a similar sentiment. When the third anniversary came around, I said, (and I was serious) "We should use a more recent photo." Oh. Granted, that was a pretty stupid statement but, all in all, year three seemed to be the turning point for me. That's my excuse and I'm sticking to it!

My kids and I and my mother-in-law and very close friends all went out to dinner for Jimmy's first death anniversary. It was almost a celebration that we were all able to make it through the first year without him. My good friends paid the bill. I was extremely touched. I don't remember officially acknowledging the second year. Phone calls and emails were exchanged. I'm sure I spent extra time that day talking to Jimmy in the closet. My daughter tells me she and her oldest daughter, the only one of her three girls who knew Grandpa, send off a balloon each year to him but think after four years or so they stopped. Birthdays are quietly and privately remembered except for year two. My son and I just happened to be together on his dad's birthday and we clinked wine glasses and made a short toast.

As the years go by and more events happen, I silently nod to Jimmy. At the birth of each of our granddaughters, at the weddings of nieces and nephews and the birth of their kids I am still, ten years later, acutely aware that Jimmy is missing so much. It's mindboggling that the world continues to spin without him in it. Even when global situations arise, the inventions of smart phones, apps and social media, I think, Jimmy isn't here to see or know this. If he came back and heard I had people following me on Twitter, he'd call a cop! We've made lots of memories after Jimmy left us, and I shake my head knowing we are little by little leaving him behind. Often someone says, "Remember when we...?" Jimmy was already gone. It's still jarring.

*

DIANNE WEST
Dianne's 69-year-old husband Vern
died from multiple myeloma in 2010

I don't choose to honor the death anniversary. That day of the month, the twenty-second, stayed with me for quite a while, a monthly reminder of the passing of time since Vern was here with me. That day and those days leading up to it hold sacred memories that I find need to be held close. So I've chosen to not share the death anniversary or Vern's birthday with anyone other than our son. I've spent them mostly at home, but one year I drove Vern's Mustang convertible to Red Rock Canyon and had a lovely day of remembrance. Last year I was in Canada preparing for Camp Widow. This year I discovered Flying Wish Papers and our son and I wrote messages and sent them skyward.

I did start a new tradition for our wedding anniversary last year, my fourth without him, choosing to do random acts of kindness in his memory - the number of random acts to match the number of years we would have been married. Initially, that day was a hard one to get through; but spending that day thinking of others instead of myself has really made a difference. Last year our son and I did forty-five random acts on the surgical and oncology floors of the hospital we spent so much time in. That truly filled my heart with gratitude as we delivered flowers to patients, some completely alone and so very grateful to have someone stop by. This year, perhaps because it was a milestone five years, I didn't feel strong enough to have face-to-face conversations with the recipients so I chose to place the flowers randomly in grocery and big box stores and at the library, to be found unexpectedly. Now that I've passed the five-year mark, I may expand this tradition to include Vern's birthday and the death anniversary.

*

It's okay to cry.
I always feel better after a good cry,
like I've released a small bit of the agony.
When you're in the middle of the "moment," when you
can't stop crying, there is fear that the pain will never end.
But allowing yourself those moments are an important part of the
healing as we process the deep anguish mixed with the
profound love we have for our loved one.

LYNDA CHELDELIN FELL

*

CHAPTER SEVEN

THE HOLIDAYS

The only predictable thing about grief is that it's unpredictable. -LYNDA CHELDELIN FELL

The holiday season comes around like clockwork, and for those in mourning, this time of year brings a kaleidoscope of emotions. If the grief is still fresh, the holidays can be downright raw. How do we navigate the invitations, decorations, and festivities without our dearly beloved?

*

TANYA CAMERON
Tanya's 43-year-old husband Ivor
died of a heart attack in 2013

Ivor and I were Mr. & Mrs. Christmas. We both loved Christmas so much, it was just that special time of year. Decorating the house was the fun of it, Ivor would place lights all around the roof of our home and I would organize the inside and the garden. We had a lovely tree and all our names on the baubles, even one for our dog. The first Christmas was very hard to get through, just like the birthdays, Mother's Day and Father's Day. I tried to keep positive as much as I could for the boys' sake. I decorated our new home with lots of lights on the outside, as much as I could do, and the inside. Putting up the tree was very hard, remembering all the wonderful Christmases we had, all the baubles had memories attached. Christmas Day we set an extra place for Ivor; I really felt his presence at the table. Family get-togethers and the boys' birthdays are still hard to deal with. As I look around the room at all my family, they all have their loved ones but Ivor is still missing. At times I just have to walk out of the room to pull myself together and sometimes I would just sit there with tears rolling down my face for all to see.

*

BONNIE FORSHEY
Bonnie's 43-year-old husband Carl
died in a car accident in 2005

I have lost almost everyone I have ever loved, so the holidays are excruciating for me. I hate to go out because I see happy people, shopping and buying gifts. I see decorations everywhere, all reminders of how my life used to be. I try to turn off my feelings and sleep through the holidays. They used to be happy days, we all ate together and had a life. Now, I have nothing but bittersweet memories of the family that I no longer have.

*

STEPHEN HOCHHAUS
Stephen's 51-year-old wife Kathy
died of soft tissue sarcoma in 2011

Always a difficult time, as the first one alone was sad at best. We always made such a "do" of Christmas. I put up the decorations as before, just with a lot less passion.

*

MARLISE MAGNA
Marlise's 36-year-old partner Blaine
died by suicide in 2010

Since the passing of my partner I don't really celebrate any holidays anymore. I tend to avoid all family gatherings and friends' parties. I've become very much an introvert, although I'm good at wearing my extrovert mask when needed. I find it awkward going alone and even when taking a partner, the looks and what I think their perceptions are just eats me. Christmas I would say is the holiday that stands out, as well as Easter. I've become "reliably unreliable" in attending celebrations. I find all outings and holidays a time of extreme anxiety for myself.

*

DIANE MCKENZIE-SAPP
Diane's 65-year-old husband Ron
died from renal failure in 2006

Holidays are so tough. Thanksgiving is hard. Christmas is lonely now. My world is less bright and emptier. Could I design a ring that would get me through the holidays? You feel guilty if you laugh or relax. I was told over and over, "It just takes time." Those words felt to my heart as if I was supposed to FORGET. Forgetting was not an option. If I laughed, if I stopped crying would that be a betrayal of the promise I made to always remember? We have guilt for being here when they are not. And deep inside, you feel that if you stop being sad and start having a life without them that you have betrayed their memory. What is a person supposed to do? Be happy or sad? Be guilty or move on? What if there was a magical way to laugh with a grandchild and share that moment with your love? What if you could send your love to them anytime and anywhere you wanted? What if you could let them know that you would never forget and you are together always?

The Tibetan prayer wheels have prayers written all over the wheel. When that wheel spins the prayers are spun into the air. Those prayers rise and go to heaven. This is magical.

I designed two "Prayer Wheel" rings. The "Always in My Heart & Soul" lives on fingers and chains all over the world. After wearing this ring and spinning it daily, a man in Scotland wrote, "Thank you Diane. You have given me peace." My ring with a miniature prayer wheel has the words "Always in my heart & soul" burned into the stainless steel. Each time you want to send a message to your love that you will never forget, that you will always love, even in a crowded room, you can. It is your little secret way to say the words in your heart, ease your guilt and begin to move into that room with a smile that reaches your eyes. The second prayer wheel has the serenity prayer. It is a powerful affirmation to spin to heaven.

On Christmas, I gift myself with a present from Ron. It never has to be returned because the color and size is perfect. I thank him and wear (usually a newly designed ring) with pride. On Valentine's Day I wear a Red Broken Heart and eat a box of chocolate covered cherries. You can make these difficult days important to yourself with intimate conversation, a small glass of wine, a special video, a written letter expressing what you forgot to say or songs that you both enjoyed. It hurts to live without your partner. Remake "you" with anything that brings a smile. My salvation was the rings. It is mine, as not everyone thinks as I do. Finding yourself isn't easy.

*

LILIAN MORTON
Lilian's 58-year-old husband Michael
died in a plane crash in 2012

Every holiday that first year was unbearable. It was the first Christmas, birthday, anniversary, etc. AD (after death). The first Christmas, I bought all new decorations. I couldn't bear going through all of the memories yet. The hardest holiday of all for me is Valentine's Day. Michael died just a few days before Valentine's Day. He had already bought me and the kids cards. I found them in his nightstand drawer. I would be perfectly okay if everyone just decided to no longer celebrate that day, I guess because it's so close to the anniversary of his death and what the holiday represents. I just feel like it's twisting the knife. That holiday has not gotten any easier to bear. It's still just as painful today as ever.

*

LISA OWENS
Lisa's 50 year-old husband Greg
died of pancreatic cancer in 2014

Christmas is hard because I am off work for the week. I have too much time to feel alone, too much time to think. All of the holidays are hard, but Greg was simple and we never went all-out for any holiday. That's good now, because there were no rituals, traditions to work through.

*

MARY POTTER KENYON
Mary's 60-year-old husband David
died of heart failure in 2012

None of the holidays are much fun now, but Christmas is awful. I used to be the "Queen of Christmas," planning so far ahead that I was done shopping by July. Now I barely care, and that is sad, especially for the youngest members of our family. My daughter Abby was just eight when her dad died. It was two years before I could make myself get out the old decorations for the tree. Even then, I only did it for Abby because she wanted to. My heart wasn't in it. I have grandchildren who still enjoy the magic of Christmas but it just isn't the same without my husband. I can hardly bear to go to extended family celebrations because they all still have their spouses. I feel so alone among them. I get through the holidays whatever way works.

111

The second Christmas without my husband we were also missing my grandson, who had died of cancer. The only way we could get through it was to have a contest to see who could come up with the most hideous gift. Seriously. It was the first time I'd seen my daughter smile in a long time. I do feel very blessed to be surrounded by my children on the holidays, but the "stuff" and the "food" just doesn't seem to matter so much anymore.

*

NANCY REDMOND
Nancy's 40-year-old husband Kevin
died of a heart attack in 2012

All of the holidays are filled with that longing of "if only," but as time has gone on, I try to honor Kevin's memory by celebrating those with whom I am still on this journey. At Christmastime, I always make a Scandinavian ice candle and light it at my front door and keep it burning from dusk on Christmas Eve until dawn on December 26. I miss Kevin the most on our three anniversaries -- the anniversary of our meeting, the anniversary of our reconciliation (another story for another day!) and our wedding anniversary.

*

MARY LEE ROBINSON
Mary Lee's 63-year-old husband Pat
died from a sudden stroke in 2013

I've been single many more years than I've been married. I married late, and then was divorced a while. The holidays have always been tough for me, except for the ones spent with my husband. At the same time, growing up my mother worked odd shifts as a nurse. We celebrated Thanksgiving and Christmas when we could, and often on a different day. It was fine. I sort of take the same approach now. I have good friends who help me with my tree, and we make an evening of it. Two families realized my plight, once

112

I was newly alone, and I've spent very pleasant holidays with them. Is it jolly? Well, maybe for a little while, and it certainly beats sitting home the whole day alone. I'm very thankful for their kindness. I try to focus on the real meaning of each holiday, and I'm especially grateful to see New Year's Day. As a result, I've developed a campaign called the "Set an Extra Plate" Initiative. The idea is to plant the idea in the heads of families all over the country to do just that, set an extra plate and invite someone who is alone to join them for a holiday meal. The concept also works for families who have lost a key family member. Old traditions can be sad with an empty place at the table. Do me a favor and help spread the word. Better yet....activate the "Set an Extra Plate" initiative in your own family.

*

CAROL SCIBELLI
Carol's 56-year-old husband Jimmy
died from lymphoma in 2006

The first Thanksgiving was a no brainer. My immediate family and I drove to New Jersey to be with my best friend and her family. They are the friends we consider family, so everyone around the table was missing Jimmy. It felt right to be together. Before Jimmy's death, we spent Thanksgiving with his two brothers and their kids, usually with Jimmy and me hosting. We had many disagreements after Jimmy died, and our relationship was strained at Thanksgiving and later fractured. My bereavement therapist explained that when an in-law relationship is on the fence before a death, after a death it falls off like Humpty Dumpty, never to be put back together again.

Our big holiday was Christmas Eve, though. It rolled around eight months after Jimmy died. Since he was only sick for a few weeks, our last Christmas Eve was our decades old tradition of Jimmy planning and preparing an elaborate fish dinner. But, my husband didn't just cook fish and serve it. He designed platters of shrimp and calamari and eels to mimic a theme every year. Once I found him at the kitchen table working on "a volcano of clams and mussels for Christmas Eve." It was August. His proudest project was blue foil paper to simulate water, teeny boats from oyster shells filled with shrimp "swimming" on the foil to "land" where they "docked" to find crab legs. Friends and family (twenty-five plus) would gather around and Jimmy announced in a booming voice, "Abbondanza!" which meant abundance in Italian. Grownups would squeal like children. The children would jump and clap and then ask for macaroni and cheese. This was our Christmas Eve. It was perfect.

As Christmas Eve 2006 loomed closer our family grew more bewildered. They looked to me. If their dad was King Christmas, I was the Queen. They waited for my ruling. Okay, maybe I'm being too dramatic here, but they were expecting me to figure out how to celebrate this first year. I had decided not to put up our tree or any decorations this first holiday in my house. Ironically the cemetery mailed me an ornament in the shape of a wreath (I'll bet very few people know that Pine Lawn gives out Christmas presents). In the center, in gold, it read: James Scibelli, 1950-2006. My kids thought it was morbid. So did I. I didn't display it. There was nothing to hang it on, anyway. There was no way we could stay home and no self-respecting Italian family dines out on Christmas Eve. Since I'm Jewish, in the end, out won out and we all went to a restaurant with our heads down.

After so many years of entertaining a house full, we were a pathetically small group; my daughter and her husband at the time, their daughter, Skylar who was two and a half, my mother-in-law, my son and me. Feeling that we needed a dose of Christmas spirit I inadvertently chose a restaurant that was so off the charts with holiday cheer we may as well have been dining at the North Pole. People were actually wearing red sweaters with reindeer on the front and some women had blinking snowmen for earrings. We opted for a table in the corner. The carolers found us, though. Their cheeks were so rosy they begged for a slap, but before I could reach out they began to sing. I rolled my eyes and reached for a steak knife pretending to plunge it into them or me. Then, Skylar squealed with joy. I put the knife down. Her sweet little innocent face reminded us all that this was new to her. It was only her third Christmas. For the rest of the night, we struggled to stay in the moment for Skylar, to make this lightweight Christmas Eve memory as festive as possible. She will never know her grandfather's abbondanza Christmas, but the following year I put up a tree and I made some fish and some mac and cheese.

Over the years, we've varied our celebrations. I sold my house two seasons ago and now I live in an apartment, so mostly these last few have been at my daughter's house with her new husband and more kids, friends and other relatives. We tell ourselves that Christmas is for kids anyway, but in the old days, with Jimmy at the helm, that time of year we were all children. It was magical.

*

DIANNE WEST
Dianne's 69-year-old husband Vern
died from multiple myeloma in 2010

We started a new tradition for Thanksgiving the very first year, since it was just two months after Vern died. Our son isn't a huge fan of the traditional Thanksgiving meal, so he and I decided to try going out for dinner that day. We chose a Mexican restaurant in a casino that was a favorite of Vern's, and we have returned there each year. One year our son invited a classmate who was alone to join us – and then his mom and aunt surprised him by arriving that day, so they joined us too. This year my Soaring Spirits widow group coleader will join us. This feels like a really good tradition.

I desperately felt the need to get away from all of the office holiday parties that first year, just a few months after Vern died. It was hard seeing people decorating the office and discussing all of their holiday plans, plans that I would have also been making if Vern was still alive. So I made a rather spur-of-the-moment decision to head off to Key West, Florida, in December – a place I had never been to before. Our son decided to go with me, but he enjoyed the nightlife and slept most of the day. I took tours, explored the city, spent time reading on the beach during the day and slept at night. We'd have dinner together each evening and then he'd head off to Duvall Street and I'd walk back to the peaceful quiet of the hotel. It really was perfect and gave me the confidence to know I could travel alone in the future.

I used to love the Christmas holidays and dressed the entire house up with all sorts of holiday cheer. But after Vern died, I no longer had a desire to decorate and that has continued to this five-year point. It just seems such a monumental waste of time to do it for just me. And my single adult son says he doesn't care one way or the other. Our ornaments have been collected over our forty-one years together and that box of memories has just been too hard for me to deal with. So I just haven't opened it.

I attended Brave Girl Camp in November 2012, and shared my story of losing my Christmas spirit. At the end of camp, they presented me with all of the glittery, colorful ornaments they had used to decorate the retreat. Their wonderful gift touched my heart and pushed me to put up a new, smaller tree that year. It helped that those ornaments were so very different in style and colors from my normal decorations. And when I looked at them I was reminded of the love and kindness shown to me by my Brave Girl family. However, when 2013 rolled around I once again fell back into my "no decorations" attitude.

I'm not sure the holidays are any harder than the birthday or death day but since they involve decorating, that has most certainly been impacted in my household. I think if I were to get to a point that the decorating was something I wanted to do … for me … then it would once again be worth the effort. I haven't gotten to that point yet, but perhaps this will be the year to open up that box of memories.

*

CHAPTER EIGHT

THE BELONGINGS

Of all possessions, a friend is the most precious.

HERODOTUS

Our spouse's belongings are a direct connection to what once was and what we desperately want back. They *are* what is left of our spouse until one day the smell has dissipated, the threads are bare, or we discover a need greater than our own. When does the time come to address the painful task of sorting through the memory-laden belongings, and how does one begin?

*

TANYA CAMERON
Tanya's 43-year-old husband Ivor
died of a heart attack in 2013

This is one of the hardest things to do. Everyone needs to deal with this in their own time and don't let anybody tell you different. When you are ready! With four weeks' notice, we had moved from our home in Adelaide to a country town three hours away to take up a new job. I had no time to go through our things, so just decided to let the removalist company pack all our belongings up. We decided to rent a house for twelve months, which would give us time to look around the area and see where we would purchase our next home. We had only been renting for eight months when Ivor passed away. I didn't want to be in that house any longer, the quicker I could get the boys and I out of there the better.

I asked my mum to come over on this particular day so I could start to clean out Ivor's clothes, it was four weeks after he passed away. Every item had a memory, every memory made floods of tears happen. I could laugh and cry all at the same time. Some of his clothing went to charity, others went to my dad, brother and brother-in-law (they were all the same size) and I kept a few things for me. I cleared out the whole side of his clothing in our wardrobe. I cried, I couldn't open that side again. It was bare, as if he no longer existed. He left suddenly, he took nothing with him, and he left everything behind.

The boys and I moved into my parents' place until the settlement of my new home was ready. I hated going back to our home, but I needed to pack up the rest of our belongings. We moved into our new home, and I brought a large glass corner unit. I got it so I could place some of Ivor's favorite items on display for all of us to see. He loved his wooden ship "The Bounty," which his parents had given him. The other ship "The Victory," I had bought him. I didn't want those items stuffed in a box like his favorite mug, the one the boys gave him on his first Father's Day.

Ivor has been gone now for two and a half years, and I love looking through the glass door and remembering all the great times we had together. I have Ivor's boxes in the shed. I haven't touched them since moving from our original home, I can't touch them. I know they are there. In my time I will open them up and look through them, but it has to be in my time.

*

JONATHAN DEAN
Jonathan's 36-year-old wife Cara
died of double pneumonia in 2010

It took a while, but I managed to bring three bags of clothing to Value Village with my sister-in-law. I still, to this day, have a fourth bag which I can't and will not part with.

*

BONNIE FORSHEY
Bonnie's 43-year-old husband Carl
died in a car accident in 2005

When my husband died, I boxed everything up and gave his clothing to his brother. They wore the same size and his brother was happy to get them. I also sold Carl's truck to his brother, because I could not possibly make the payments and take care of everything alone. I know people handle things in different ways. I waited for about a month before I could actually let things go. It hurt too much for me to open my closet and see Carl's clothes hanging there. I knew that he would never be back and they could benefit someone else. It was hard to let go, but even harder to hang on. I kept a few things that were sentimental, a couple of his big T-shirts, his cologne, and jewelry.

*

STEPHEN HOCHHAUS
Stephen's 51-year-old wife Kathy
died of soft tissue sarcoma in 2011

I donated many of Kathy's clothes to a hospice resale facility who helped me with counseling and support, so I felt good helping such an organization and I know she would too. I kept some of her clothes which mean a lot to me, such as her wedding dress and the dress she was wearing the day I met her. Her jewelry remains with me, and I wear a special piece around my neck at all times.

*

MARLISE MAGNA
Marlise's 36-year-old partner Blaine
died by suicide in 2010

I had nothing to do with packing up Blaine's belongings. In fact, I have nothing of his sadly. All I have is a ring I gave him and necklaces of mine that he wore. I currently wear the chain around my neck with a cross pendant. His mom and close family friends almost immediately packed up his belongings. His mom had his computer hacked to delete all social media and email accounts and had me deleted off our online music pages on which we published songs. I felt anger at first - but now I realize to them it would've probably been a constant reminder of what happened.

*

DIANE MCKENZIE-SAPP
Diane's 65-year-old husband Ron
died from renal failure in 2006

The question, "Have you packed up their belongings?" is a sore subject to me. It grates and plucks nerves I didn't know existed. What's the hurry? Why do people ask that question? What difference does it make? How does it affect anything now? Where do things go? BACK OFF and shut up about it already. I will do what I will do when I am good and ready. Why is it on anyone's checkoff list that things that belonged to the decreased must now be categorized, erased, demolished, listed and filed? Haven't I lost enough already without others demanding that I scrape off the last bits and pieces of him?

Anything Ron had mentioned that he wanted to give someone was done. His tools and clothes were given away. Gifts and family photos were returned to their respective donors. Walkers and hospital equipment were returned, donated or given away. It took me five years to remove the evidence of medical malpractice. Ron asked me not to ruin the doctors' lives. What he wanted was not what I wanted. I sat with x-rays, reports and statements for five years before I gave it up. My son dutifully offered to help with the cleanup; he said we could get a dumpster and just throw stuff in. I said I would call when I was ready. It has been ten years, I haven't called yet. But what I did do was buy antiques, coins and collectables. I told my son his inheritance was valuable trinkets and when I died, if he brought over a dumpster and threw everything in it, he would be tossing away his inheritance. Good luck with the treasure hunt. The Catholic Church can take bits and pieces of a saint's body and call them holy relics. They have sent slivers of bone and clothing and toes and heads to church alters around the world. Honor and prayers remember the good deed of the saint. If those relics are a part of the signature of a saint, who is to say that I cannot keep the pieces of Ron's life that were important to him and call them a relics? Archeologists find pottery shards and carved wooden idols and weave an entire culture's history around those finds. These artifacts go into museums where patrons wander the marble halls and appreciate the history of old mementos from the past. Why can't I keep my shards from the past without judgment?

I keep Ron's history with me. Relics I have kept, but not limited to, are his music, his softball glove, his newspapers and their headlines stating "Baltimore Colts Leave Baltimore," and "Cal Ripken's Iron Man" status, his tie tacks and cufflinks, his driver's license and unused passport. I wear Ron's old sweatshirts, sweatpants and old flannel pajamas. I spray his cologne on the pillows. I don't know why I kept all Ron's keys but maybe someday I will make a wind chime with them. These things are a signature, a sum and substance of who Ron was and is. And I do not disturb relics. I cherish his history.

You may not agree and may think I am stuck or a hoarder or morbid. I usually say humm when I am asked a question about the circumstances that surround my husband's death. Anyone who queries me with, "What are/did you do about Ron's -----?" will get a head slightly cocked to one side, eyes hooded, and a long, low slightly dangerous hummmmm. Best not ask.

*

JULIE MJELVE
Julie's 42-year-old husband Cameron
died by suicide in 2011

I packed up my loved one's stuff primarily by myself, but there were a few instances where different friends came to help me. It's a difficult job, and there were things I wish I had done differently. Everyone has their own opinion of what to keep and what not to keep. There were items that friends encouraged me to give away that I wish I had kept. On the flip side, there were other items that friends encouraged me to keep that I now look back on and think, "What in the world did I keep that for?" So, it is a difficult task, but I think better to keep too much than not enough. You can always go back later and give things away, but you can't get them back once they're gone. It did bring a lot of emotions. I think it's very important to have the right people help you. People who can be patient and understanding with the emotions you are experiencing, and the difficulty you will have giving away an object that seems absolutely mundane and ridiculous to keep in their eyes, but holds incredible memories for you.

I cried, a lot, while I packed my husband's things. If felt as though I was packing away not just his things, but my dreams of our life together. It wasn't just packing random physical items, it was packing away everything I'd hoped for since childhood. Even now, four years later, I find it very difficult to go through Cameron's things. Some things are easy to give away at this point, some will even bring a smile to my face as I remember the event they are associated with (something I definitely did not experience in the original packing!). Some things still bring tears to my eyes, as I relive the pain of his loss, and the pain of my lost dreams and goals for our life together. But I do find that allowing myself to experience the pain all over again has its healing moments. I have to be careful about how much I do at one time, as it can still overwhelm me. But, in small pieces, I also continue to heal.

*

LISA OWENS
Lisa's 50 year-old husband Greg
died of pancreatic cancer in 2014

I didn't touch Greg's stuff for months, but slowly I have moved some things. Personal hygiene things are still in the bathroom drawers, and clothes are still in his drawers. His shampoo bottle is still in shower. It's comforting to see that he was alive and not a dream.

*

MARY POTTER KENYON
Mary's 60-year-old husband David
died of heart failure in 2012

I immediately got rid of my husband's socks, underwear and pajamas; things that seemed too intimate to hang onto. His favorite T-shirts were clung to at night by my three youngest daughters and myself. We each slept with one. Most telling was what I got rid of that was mine; I threw away my lovely nighties that my husband liked to see me wear, shoving them into the bottom of a garbage bag. Within a week or two I had my sons choose whether they wanted their dad's shoes, and one son also took a pair of brand new jeans. The rest of my husband's clothes sat in the closet for eight months before I tackled going through them. His drawer remained filled in the dresser for a year. It was nearly eighteen months after his death that I tackled going through everything once again, and putting away a single box of favorite shirts, some cologne, his billfold, a comb; things that had been on our dresser, in his drawer, or in the closet.

The impetus for really cleaning out was when I moved into a bedroom across the hall, and my youngest took over my bedroom, and the bed I had shared with her father. It made sense, since she was climbing into my bed every night after her father died anyway. I just gave her the bed! I do remember with that final packing up sobbing into a sweatshirt that still retained his smell.

*

NANCY REDMOND
Nancy's 40-year-old husband Kevin
died of a heart attack in 2012

I tried many times before I was able to pack up a few of Kevin's belongings. As occasions come up and as I am influenced by what I believe to be Kevin's spirit, I have shared his belongings with those to whom he would want them given. Initially it was really difficult to let go of any part of Kevin's physical life manifested in these belongings, but as time has gone on (now three-plus years), the happiness that has come from sharing these things with others has far outweighed the sadness.

*

MARY LEE ROBINSON
Mary Lee's 63-year-old husband Pat
died from a sudden stroke in 2013

In the immediate aftermath of discovering that my husband changed the beneficiary designations on all of our income producing assets, I was devastated at the betrayal. We'd had an agreement. I married him, leaving my family and friends and a job and a good job market, in order to be with him in another state so that we could care for his folks. He was going to be the breadwinner; I was going to be the caretaker. He would provide for me, and if he preceded me, I was to use the income from these assets to live on and, if his sons had matured sufficiently, leave the capital to them. If they had not improved, I was to leave it where it would do some good. As both of us are veterans, Wounded Warrior was at the top of the list.

I won't enumerate all the indicators that surfaced, in time, but they were numerous. Pat had been having small strokes for six months before he died. In short, he wasn't in his right mind. I didn't know that for many, many months. I do now. Medical professionals, his best friend and the family agree. They were just as stunned as I was. In my fury at what felt like a devastating betrayal, I got rid of all but one T-shirt pretty early on. A neighbor helped me box them up and she took them to her church. I welcomed her help, as I don't know if I physically had the energy to do it alone.

I went to sell his car, but found I couldn't do it. Pat was a smoker, and never smoked around me, but he did smoke in his car. I would go and sit in it or drive it, just to experience the aroma of the smoke. It took me a little over a year to get rid of it. Since it was paid for, there wasn't much rush. His personal effects and photos were more of a challenge. I knew his sons would want to have something of their father, something personal. The problem is that I didn't have any addresses for them. There were none in Pat's records. I don't think he knew them. I found my oldest stepson with some easy internet searches. The youngest took three months to find. He finally surfaced on Facebook.

I packed up watches, army commendations, retirement awards, jewelry, and all the knickknacks acquired in a life. With the help of my friend, we sorted through all the photos and put them into albums. The boys got all the photos from their childhoods, all the photos of their mother, all of their grandparents, all from their dad's life before me. I kept all the pictures of Pat's life with me. I also included a portion of Pat's ashes, suggesting that the boys might want to conduct a memorial of their own, possibly with their mother's ashes in their possession.

Sobbing all the while, I sat down and wrote a letter to the boys, writing words as kindly as I could. I explained a little about the circumstances of Pat's death. I also explained that with their father gone, there was no reason for us to have a relationship, as we really never had one before. We did not share values about much of anything. The only thing we had in common was that we all loved their dad. With that, I closed with goodbye. I read it to a friend as a "kindness check." It passed, in her opinion, so I enclosed the letter, sealed and addressed the box and that was that.

I still have photographs around, some greeting cards and special gifts from Pat, a T-shirt I wear now and then. And I have visits. Boy, do I have visits. Pat comes around fairly often and manifests in several familiar ways. My Rottweiler, who adopted me after Pat was gone, starts growling, barking and wagging her tail most evenings about the same time. There is nothing visible there, and she looks up. Pat was six-foot two-inches. I had a houseguest last week. She did it in the presence of my guest, while I was out of the house. He shows up in other ways, as well. He's my favorite memorial. It always makes me smile.

*

CAROL SCIBELLI
Carol's 56-year-old husband Jimmy
died from lymphoma in 2006

Instead of visiting my husband in the cemetery, I'd sit in our closet and talk to his shirts and pants and loafers. No worries I'd get lost and no need to stop on the way to pick up flowers. I could stay in my pajamas although I suspected that Jimmy preferred me nude, just like in real life. There in the closet, our conversations were similar to real life, too. I'd be yapping and he'd be napping.

I held on to his clothes for about eighteen months. Every so often a friend would volunteer to help me go through Jimmy's things. I'd shake my head and say I wasn't ready. This was true, but more true was that I wanted to quietly, maybe with a glass of red wine by my side, or the bottle with a straw in it, look at each piece of clothing and be alone to hug them and reminisce about them privately. When pressed, I'd joke, "It's not that I'm so sentimental. I just don't need the closet space." This was partially the case, but once I did have the closet all to myself it miraculously filled up. I hesitated doing the closet because I knew it would be painful. I relaxed a bit once I heard about and decided to have a memory quilt, sometimes called a memorial quilt, made from my husband's clothes for each of my kids. Squares of familiar shirts and pants would forever be on the foot of my son's bed, or the arm of my daughter's couch. I could visit them/him whenever I visited the kids. Not my bed or couch, though. I hadn't started dating yet, but knew at some point I would. No way could I imagine getting cozy with someone on the couch, having my late husband's wardrobe sitting next to us. And, even more disturbing, what if "new guy" was wearing the exact same shirt as one of those little squares?

I kept Jimmy's tuxedo because to me it symbolized happiness and celebration and elegance. Whenever we were dressed up, we danced and laughed. Life felt special. I held onto the tuxedo accessories too including the bow ties, tuxedo shirts, his patent leather shoes. My son, Doug, isn't as big as his dad was, so he had his own tux, but he wanted his father's suspenders. He's been my plus-one for several black tie events and is proud to wear them along with his dad's dressy gold watch. I gave that to him, too. I think I may have given Doug a pair or two of cufflinks. My son-in-law, at the time, asked for and I gave him Jimmy's Breitling watch. He had often admired it. My good friend Teri only wanted Jimmy's reading glasses. She explained that she remembers walking into the kitchen in the morning and seeing him doing the crossword puzzle with his glasses on the edge of his nose. Personal belongings are precious to keep, but they can get lost or stolen or broken. My memories will always stay close...until I'm old and senile and don't remember I was ever married. "Jimmy who?"

*

KRISTI SMITH
Kristi's 48-year-old husband Michael
died from cardiac arrest in 2011

One of the hardest jobs for me to do, emotionally, was to clean out Mike's clothes from my closet. I put it off for the longest time, but it was hard to walk into my closet and still see his clothes hanging there. It made me miss him more and was actually hurting my heart instead of healing it. I knew I needed to do it, but who could help me with this? I thought of my sister-in-law, Melissa. She has done professional cleaning and organizing for years — she was perfect. Not only was she professional, but I knew she would be able to help me emotionally with this task. She is a small woman, but she is strong both physically and emotionally. On the morning she showed up, we hugged and cried and sorted through shirts and jeans and uniforms. We made three piles: things to keep, things to give away, and things I was not sure what to do with yet. We moved the things we were keeping out of my closet and downstairs to a spare bedroom closet. Then she helped me bag up the things to give away and we put them in her car. The remaining piles of things I was not sure what to do with were bagged and put downstairs to be dealt with later. It was a hard day, but I was so thankful for her willingness to help me do what I could not bear to do by myself. Later that day, I received a picture from one of Melissa's boys. He was wearing Mike's sweater. The look on his face said it all - the sweater was transferring Mike's love to his nephew.

The next area to tackle was the storage room in our basement. You know - the dumping ground for everything! Rachel, Cheryl, and Jen came over and helped me by sorting through piles of stuff accumulated over the years. They helped me determine what I needed to keep to build my new life. My workroom was full of items that were appropriate for our household before my husband died. Our goal was to pare down to the items I would need to move forward after death entered our home. It was quite an undertaking and they helped with their positive attitudes and willingness to do whatever I needed them to do. They organized shelves, carted out unwanted items to their cars, and removed the clutter so that I could breathe again. Visual clutter clutters the mind, and I needed clarity. I needed to eliminate unnecessary things from my workroom, which was a symbol of my life, and be left with only what I needed to go on into the future God had for me. At the end of the day, I waved goodbye to my faithful friends, and two van loads of items were on their way to Goodwill.

On to Mike's workshop. For this, I called in my handyman buddy, Lynn. He was able to help me put together a pared down toolbox and other items I would need. Once we had done that, we set aside the nicer tools to give to family, friends and neighbors - socket sets, drills, rakes, etc. We cleared out old paint cans, tossed broken pieces and parts, sorted through fishing gear, and organized supplies that belonged with the house like flooring and paint. Another area to be sorted was the camping gear. Mike was a backpacker and hiker. I decided to let our two daughters keep what they wanted, and then they could pass along the rest of the gear to family members.

Mike was also a pilot. Over the years, he had gathered plaques, trophies, and airline uniforms. Some of these items were very meaningful. We kept two of his white shirts with epaulets, his flight jacket with pins, his captain's hat with wings, and his leather jacket. These would be timeless treasures. After sorting through all of Mike's stuff, the two most meaningful items to me were his Bible and his journal. Mike was a pastor. He had used his Bible to marry, bury, and carry people through the hard times. It was his life source, and now it would carry me. Mike started a leather-bound journal about a year and a half before he died. Addressed to our daughters, it is filled with Mike's words of encouragement and wisdom. I keep the journal in the fireproof box, and it is our most prized possession of the man we love so dearly.

*

DIANNE WEST
Dianne's 69-year-old husband Vern
died from multiple myeloma in 2010

This is an area that has been an issue for me – well, I should say that others seem to think it's an issue. It's been five years and nearly all of my husband's things are still in the house. His clothes are in the closet, his things in drawers, his Ohio State memorabilia still on display, his car in the driveway. I've had offers of help for me to get rid of things, but I've just not felt compelled to do it. They've also reminded me that others could benefit from Vern's clothing and I do understand that - but I'm not going to let that guilt me into doing this before I'm ready. I get some real comfort seeing Vern's things in the places they have been in for so long. It feels right. I truly don't understand the push to remove a loved one's presence from the home within a set period of time. If I were moving, then of course I would need to go through things to decide what to keep or give away. But since I'm staying in our home, there just seems to be no rush for me to strip his presence from our home. I will do it eventually, perhaps soon. But I will do it when I'm ready to do it.

I'm not stuck in my grief. I'm living my life fairly well at this point. I'm traveling, taking classes, co-leading a local Soaring Spirits regional group, and I have made new friends. And since I don't plan to date or remarry, there's no need for me to clear things out to make room for anyone else.

*

CHAPTER NINE

THE DARKNESS

Walking with a friend in the dark is better than walking alone in the light. -HELEN KELLER

Suicidal thoughts occur for some in the immediate aftermath of profound loss, yet few readily admit it for fear of being judged or condemned. While there would be no rainbow without the rain, where do we find the energy to weather the storm?

*

TANYA CAMERON
Tanya's 43-year-old husband Ivor
died of a heart attack in 2013

I didn't think I would ever admit to having these feelings of taking my own life. Would I have done it if I didn't have my kids? I am not sure. Could I actually go through with it? I don't really know. A few times on a Sunday morning when the boys have jumped into bed with me for their family hug, I have often wondered, "Would I take them with me if I did decide that's the way we were going to go? How would I do it? What would the boys do without me? Who is going to look after them when I am gone?" I lie in bed and many times have thought I could just drug the three of us and then we would all go together. Who gets my home? Which family member have to clean it out? I couldn't put that burden on my parents. They keep a close eye on the boys and me. They help me with the school runs. What would they do without us? Thankfully, I have never felt that low to actually be able to go through with it. I think too much about the consequences of what would happen if I did do it. If I got really depressed, no doubt I would do it and I wouldn't be thinking about the aftermath. All the questions, I can only answer this honestly. No, I wouldn't take my life, not for the world. I love my boys, family and friends. I know what the heartache feels like in losing a husband, a sibling and friends. I have seen and felt the pain of losing these loved ones. I know the feeling of being the one left behind. If I could protect the world from hurt and grief, I would. I know I cannot stop any of it, but I can start by not taking my own or my boys' lives.

*

JONATHAN DEAN
Jonathan's 36-year-old wife Cara
died of double pneumonia in 2010

Only in the beginning. I told my psychologist, but said to her that nothing will be done. To this day, I still think of how to finish my life, but still nothing is done.

*

BONNIE FORSHEY
Bonnie's 43-year-old husband Carl
died in a car accident in 2005

No, I never thought of suicide. I became extremely depressed and had to take an antidepressant, but I knew I had to continue on because of my daughter. Life is difficult though, and everywhere I go there are constant reminders of Carl and places that we went together. I still grieve for the life that we could have had.

132

*

STEPHEN HOCHHAUS
Stephen's 51-year-old wife Kathy
died of soft tissue sarcoma in 2011

In the first months, I wanted death in the worst way. I felt I needed to go right then or I might not find her. I just couldn't do that to my sons and grandchildren, and the desire left me by the third month.

*

MARLISE MAGNA
Marlise's 36-year-old partner Blaine
died by suicide in 2010

Yes. In fact I have been admitted to hospital and ended up on life support quite a few times after his passing. At one point, the ER knew me on a first name basis, I was there so often. I am a very open person and I wear my heart on my sleeve, and people did suspect I would attempt suicide. Eventually, after prolonged intensive psychotherapy, I realized it just wasn't my time and was not fair to the people I would leave behind. A friend asked me one day whether I want to be remembered as "the girl who killed herself" or would I rather leave a legacy. After that I never tried again. I still have deep sorrow and despair, but I also have faith and that keeps me going.

*

DIANE MCKENZIE-SAPP
Diane's 65-year-old husband Ron
died from renal failure in 2006

Every night I prayed not to awake in the morning. I did not have the will to take my own life. I did not want to make a mess that someone would have to clean up. I didn't care enough. I tried to neglect myself to death. If I only ate sugar, cola, candy bars, smoked like a chimney, didn't take my medications, got no sleep, skipped most meals, and if I did not take care of myself, then by all odds I should suffer the medical consequences of my bad choices. Turns out, it is rather hard for a zombie to die. The only thing that got me up off the floor was I needed to help other widows with my rings so they would not feel the pain that I felt. Once I had my purpose and direction I would continue one breath at a time and one minute at a time.

*

JULIE MJELVE
Julie's 42-year-old husband Cameron
died by suicide in 2011

I have had thoughts of suicide since my spouse passed away. My life has been very difficult. I'm raising three very young children alone. At the time of my husband's passing, my children were three and a half years old, two years old, and five months old. My youngest daughter has Down syndrome, and it has been difficult at times coping with the extent of her disability as well as all the appointments. Furthermore, my oldest child is now eight years old, and was diagnosed with Tourette's syndrome six months ago, adding to the challenges our household faces. Three months ago my middle child, now six years old, was diagnosed with an anxiety disorder. This has all been a lot to handle, especially without a spouse to talk to, debrief with, and to make decisions together. There have been many, many appointments and therapies and as a result I am not working, which creates an extra financial strain. My family does not live in the same city as I do, except for my dad who is here only for a few months of the year, and so family support is minimal at best. So, yes, thoughts of suicide do occur to me when I'm overwhelmed. Fortunately though, I am able to focus on my children and how much they need me, and what would happen to them if I too were gone. It is a strong motivator for me. Also, I have learned significantly how to pray. I used to pray for God to take away the difficult situations, and struggled to understand why he did not lighten my load so it was not so overwhelming. But over time, I have learned to take a different focus. Now I pray for God to give me the strength to deal with the situations that arise. I pray for God to provide through finances as well as people who can help support me. And now he answers. Well, he answered before too, he just said no. The answers may not come in a way I expected or preferred, especially the timelines I would prefer, but if I pay attention, the strength to survive another day comes, and he provides. We have a roof over our head, food on our table, and new friends who help us through the tough times.

*

NANCY REDMOND
Nancy's 40-year-old husband Kevin
died of a heart attack in 2012

I absolutely adore my children, grandson and family, so suicide was never a thought in my mind, but I wanted to "die" in those first painful months. I wanted to be with Kevin, but I thankfully realized that I had children and grandchildren who still need me here. The most insightful thing I heard from one of my children was, "When Kevin died (he was their stepfather), we not only lost him, but we almost lost YOU." I owe it to my kids, my grandson, the legacy of love I share with Kevin, to me, and to God to live the life I am supposed to live here!

*

CAROL SCIBELLI
Carol's 56-year-old husband Jimmy
died from lymphoma in 2006

I never thought or considered suicide. That said, early on each day was a struggle. I was blindsided and confused. I spent a crazy amount of time the first year and even the second babbling to Jimmy out loud and in my head. While I was with someone else, I imagined he was right next to me taking it all in. Being alone was overwhelming, but there were joyful times too with family and friends. Throughout our thirty-three years of marriage, Jimmy protected me from the hard decisions. In time, I managed to grasp all the things Jimmy took care of that I had cleverly managed to avoid for decades. Now, here I was learning to take care of the bills, the house, the car, etc. It was an eye opener for me. After a while, I adapted and actually enjoyed being responsible. It may sound odd, but I finally felt like a grownup. Sadly, I think Jimmy would prefer the new take-charge me. He carried many burdens alone. So far, I've lived ten more years than Jimmy did. During this decade, when life was unkind, I envied Jimmy not being here to feel the pain. Overall though, I am grateful to be alive to experience another loving relationship with a man and to be a matriarch for my kids and granddaughters.

*

DIANNE WEST
Dianne's 69-year-old husband Vern
died from multiple myeloma in 2010

In those very early months after Vern died, I was very apathetic about my life in general, although I did not have actual thoughts of suicide. The pain of my loss did not allow me to place much value on my own life at that point. I continued to act publicly as others expected, but I didn't take good care of myself at all. I was exhausted physically from the heavy caregiving and emotionally from my loss. I rarely slept. I didn't eat regular meals, only snacking on junk food late at night. I subconsciously thought that this was good, as it might just hasten my death. I could not envision a worthwhile future without Vern and was just waiting for it to all be over. Luckily, I was able to climb out of that pit fairly quickly. My faith, God, helped me see that I could still have a good life, albeit a very different life than we had planned. It started with a gratitude journal, writing down three things at the end of each day that I was grateful for. In the beginning, I could only come up with basic things. I took a shower and got dressed today. I didn't cry on the way to work. The sun was shining today. By forcing myself to find something positive in each day, truly brought me back to living.

CHAPTER TEN

THE FRIENDS

Remember, you don't need a certain number of friends,
just a number of friends you can be certain of.

UNKNOWN

When we are mourning, some of our friendships undergo transitions. Some bonds remain steady, dependable and faithful. Some we sever by choice. And, perhaps unexpectedly, new friends enter our life. Did you experience a shift in your friendships after your spouse's passing?

*

TANYA CAMERON
Tanya's 43-year-old husband Ivor
died of a heart attack in 2013

I do find it strange when I have gone out for dinner or socialized that everyone has a partner or husband, and I am on my own. Though I find myself so busy in putting all my time and energy in with my boys that I don't go out all that much. Being the sole parent, it is hard to have time to myself and at times it does get lonely. I live quite a distance from my friends, but they are only a phone call away. When we moved into a country town I found it hard to even meet with people as I was working fulltime, and on weekends people are more inclined to spend time with their families. I have started having one day a week off and now being able to socialize with some mums from the school. None of them are in my situation but it's great to just sit and chat. They reassure me that anytime I need any kind of help, I only have to ask. That's really all I could ask for, a great lot of friends.

*

JONATHAN DEAN
Jonathan's 36-year-old wife Cara
died of double pneumonia in 2010

I have no friends. The four friends we had when my wife was alive want nothing to do with me. Five years seven months later and no contact at all.

*

BONNIE FORSHEY
Bonnie's 43-year-old husband Carl
died in a car accident in 2005

They were all there for me during Carl's funeral and for about a month afterwards, and that was it. I understand that they have their lives and families. My in-laws all moved out of state, and I never hear from any of them. It feels like it was all just a dream. Carl is no longer here, the family is gone, and so are our friends. I am left to deal with my ghosts on my own.

*

STEPHEN HOCHHAUS
Stephen's 51-year-old wife Kathy
died of soft tissue sarcoma in 2011

Everyone mourns at first, yet they move past it. I don't feel the same so I have learned to keep my feelings to myself because frankly, most of my friends don't want to hear about it any longer. They would even change the subject when I would start to tell them how I was feeling. A few friends and family "get it" and for them, I am grateful.

*

MARLISE MAGNA
Marlise's 36-year-old partner Blaine
died by suicide in 2010

My circle of friends has pretty much slowly but surely changed since Blaine died. The friends who have stayed behind still treat me the same. I think the fact that I've always been open about my feelings has helped them understand and not feel they need to wear kid gloves around me.

*

DIANE MCKENZIE-SAPP
Diane's 65-year-old husband Ron
died from renal failure in 2006

How I Turned Into a Witch. We lived in Mainstream, America just down the road from Stepford. As a couple, Ron and I had a few lifelong friends. We celebrated life events, shared vacations, summer barbeques, and fireworks on the fourth of July. Christmas gatherings preceded the New Year with each other. They were at the bedside the night Ron died. Comforting words were given as I began my life as a widow. However, they saw me differently now; maybe they felt the widow thing was contagious. I didn't belong anymore. I imagine that shunning would feel the same. Left out of the gatherings but invited to the weddings and baby showers, and received notifications of graduations and new births. Maybe I did not grieve fast enough for them. Discontented, I spoke peculiarly about rings and new customs. I was adamant that there should be a widow's ring. They were married, so did not see it. When I crafted rings for other widows, maybe my friends felt I was choosing that aspect of my life over their lives. Although to be brutally honest, words and feelings about death and widowhood scare the crap out of anyone that is not there. Our sadness brings them down, and so they avoid the subject and anyone close to it. They would not choose to hurt on purpose.

Before I found myself on this island, I did not know any better either. I choose not to educate them because I don't want them to feel badly about something they didn't do. I love them still. I no longer have a clan. What was I going to be? I had to build a new and different life for the new me. I have lost my husband, my friends, a good bit of my monetary and social support. Will I die because of it? No.

Since I was building this new bionic woman, I will let her do all the things that a clan member doesn't do. I will let the child in me play unfettered. I will take classes and learn about things that have been taboo. I would evolve into a witch! It went against all that my parents, husband and faith decreed. But they were gone and I was alone. Who was left to say no? So I said, "Why not?" I wanted to make a connection with my dead husband, communicate within the netherworld, and I was willing to explore any dimension possible. How could I do it? When should I do it? What did I need to do? What talisman should I carry? How would I come back? Could I walk in the valley of death and fear no evil? Why not? I went to the only place that might know the way. I took classes in witchcraft. It was one year long. After that year, you could join into a coven or a group of like-minded individuals. Then I learned that there are solitary witches, a wondrous revelation, they choose to walk their path alone willingly and with purpose. I walked alongside the most enchanting people for a year. Then we parted ways. I have not looked back; I travel the Road Less Traveled. My Journey is mine alone. I studied Wicca, tarot cards, herbs, religion, crystals, meditation, mythology, ascended masters, horoscopes, spells and potions, protection magic, circles and more. I learned to hear whispers, notice signs, and say thank you for green lights. I learned you had to believe in yourself and what you were doing, think it through and then do it. No doubts and no naysayers.

I learned to never do something you can't undo, and a curse will bounce back upon the curser with thrice the venom, I was a cautious witch, a doer of good. I learned to be within myself. I learned to ground myself, and to expect inner peace when asked. I found that I am a green witch, I heal and I am empathic. I learned creating my rings is a gift from the gods, and I thank them. I learned that being spiritual is my way of life and I can do that without calling myself a witch.

And if they thought of me at all, my friends most probably thought I was running sky clad in moonlit fields and living a Midnight Summers Dream. I once told a friend that on the first Saturday of each month for the next year, I would be attending a school for witches. We had gone to Catholic elementary school and high school together. She said, "Oh, my. What would Ron have said about that?" I replied in a deep manly voice, "Not while I'm alive," or "Over my dead body." Dear friends, do you wonder where witches come from? Well, I guess you make them.

*

JULIE MJELVE
Julie's 42-year-old husband Cameron
died by suicide in 2011

The interactions with my husband's friends have decreased significantly. However, I have maintained an excellent relationship with his parents. I was surprised by this originally; I wasn't sure how they would want to interact with me. After all their son, the reason they know me, is now gone. However, they have embraced me fully as a daughter and have strove to ensure that my children and I are taken care of. They have completely taken on the role of grandparents. We even pick them up and visit Cameron's gravesite together. Our bond continues to increase, probably more so than if my husband had still been alive.

*

LISA OWENS
Lisa's 50 year-old husband Greg
died of pancreatic cancer in 2014

Being with the friends we had together has changed. It's hard to be with them; they are couples, I am alone, the third wheel. It's also hard to be with his family, alone.

*

MARY POTTER KENYON
Mary's 60-year-old husband David
died of heart failure in 2012

I have a close friend, Mary, who somehow knew what I needed after David's death. I'm not sure how she knew. She hasn't lost a parent, sibling, or spouse, and yet she knew to ask me questions no one else was asking like, "How can you stand it?" She also took me out to eat once a month, treating me to lunch, and letting me talk. That really strengthened our friendship and we ended up co-writing a book about female friendship.

I wish friends and family knew how lonely I am. Despite all my workshops and classes, and now, a job with a newspaper, interviewing people, large groups are difficult for me. But I love an afternoon visit with a couple or would like to be invited out for coffee, lunch or a movie.

*

NANCY REDMOND
Nancy's 40-year-old husband Kevin
died of a heart attack in 2012

I have had many friendships end along this journey but I have had an equal amount of new friendships created, many of which are stronger and more meaningful than those I lost along the way. I have several friends who have never left my side, and I never forget to thank them for the role they play in the puzzle of my life.

*

MARY LEE ROBINSON
Mary Lee's 63-year-old husband Pat
died from a sudden stroke in 2013

Most of my neighbors immediately distanced themselves from me. It was as though widowhood was catching. My longest friendships did not survive. My best friend of forty-five years, my matron of honor, sent a sympathy card. Then she called me. That was four months later, and she proceeded to tell me that she was all alone too. She had her husband, her stepson, a sister, and a brother, but she was all alone. She hadn't called because she had been busy. Pat used to work for them at tax season. But she was busy. For four months. My other best friend of forty-five years was a little better about calling, but being male, didn't bestow tea and sympathy. But he called. I asked him repeatedly to make plans to visit with his girlfriend; I could put them up in a condo to themselves. I live in a beach town. I'd asked that when we lived in West Virginia also. He's retired. He had time. He announced that he was coming to my state and would be staying with his navy buddy, about an hour away. He then called to say that an hour was too far away. They wouldn't be able to squeeze me in. Then I remembered that neither of them attended my dad's memorial, and they both knew Dad very well. That was local for them. I decided then and there that I had no place in their lives, and so they no longer had a place in mine. Since that time, I have been blessed by several wonderful people who walked in when everyone else was walking out. Those new friends are front and center in my life now.

*

CAROL SCIBELLI
Carol's 56-year-old husband Jimmy
died from lymphoma in 2006

I was the first in my crowd to get married, the first to have children, and the first to lose my husband. No one awarded me a blue ribbon or a trophy. I never won a prize. Somehow, in a mixed-up crazy way, I felt and still do feel entitled. After all, I had no example to follow. Romantic comedies and Dr. Spock were my references. As friends married, I handed out marital advice and when they had children, it was hand-me-downs. And then came the big one: widowhood. I wanted to wear my widowhood well. What does that even mean? Well, I stood tall and independent, and began life on my own with a sense of adventure. I may have surprised my friends by my resilience. I know I surprised myself. Part of me wanted to show by example that when we lose our spouse, we don't have to lose ourselves. Mostly, I was just trying desperately to get through each day. My good friends called me every day. When I didn't pick up or if I wanted to hang up quickly, they said they understood. I knew they didn't. How could they? I'd go out to dinner with my girlfriends and I'd be antsy before the main course arrived. They'd see it on my face and gently say, "You've had it, haven't you?" This was the first-year stage when making plans was almost impossible for me. I'd look forward to an event and when the day came I'd panic. "I can't do that," I'd say. They treated me like I was a delicate teacup. I was.

Many weekends my couple friends invited me to join them. Often I'd go feeling self-conscious. I was convinced that everyone in the restaurant was staring at me, knowing I was the odd one at the table, the one to be pitied. I even avoided eye contact with the waiter. A year or so later couples stopped asking me. Ironically, now I'd be fine dining out alone on a Saturday night with couples. The next day they would tell me what they did and where they went and who they went with. I don't think it dawned on them to say, "Why don't you come along?" My intense grieving time was over and I didn't need babysitting anymore. I didn't particularly want to go with them. I casually noted their behavior and wondered if they were responding to a vibe I was sending. For the first two years I trotted next door to my friends Sheri and Fred, and we watched The Sopranos and other TV shows together. This was comfortable. It felt safe and familiar. My friend Jade and I became much closer after Jimmy died. She was there for me without question twenty-four hours a day if I needed her. It was a happy surprise and today we are still very close. This bonded us. My nephew Roby said to me early on, "Most people mean well." Some might argue with that, but I agree with him. His small reminder helped me to understand that even my friends who weren't in touch regularly may be thinking of me. We are all guilty of being too lazy to reach out.

*

DIANNE WEST
Dianne's 69-year-old husband Vern
died from multiple myeloma in 2010

Interactions with friends changed drastically after Vern died. Well, there were some pretty dramatic changes while he was ill and it continued to change after. I think I probably need to take some responsibility for the changes, although it took me awhile to recognize that. The way I behaved in public certainly gave the impression that I was doing well, and perhaps some felt I no longer needed their support, so they disappeared. They didn't realize my public performance was all an act. Or maybe they did and they just didn't want to have to be cautious about what they said for fear I would break down. And since I was "cocooning" on the weekends, I wasn't opening myself up to socializing with anyone anyway.

The couples pretty much left first. I was no longer included in activities that we would have been included in as a couple. They apparently didn't even think about including me as a single. Perhaps they were doing it to be kind, thinking it would be hard for me to be a single amongst couples, but they never asked. I just learned about the various events afterward, and it hurt to be forgotten, to be excluded.

At five years I've found a pretty good life balance that fits my personality. I have some very good friends I socialize with regularly, mostly all widowed and new friends post-loss. I've always been a people person and enjoy socializing, but it can really wear me out. So I need to allow myself some dedicated alone time to recharge.

It saddens me that long-time friends walked away and, in one instance, I was the one who had to walk away. I've finally come to terms with those losses and try to view it like that quote "People come into your life for a reason, a season or a lifetime …."

*

CHAPTER ELEVEN

THE RELATIONSHIPS

I have found the paradox that if you love until it hurts,
there can be no more hurt, only more love.

-MOTHER TERESA

For many of us, familial relationships are the cornerstones that help us stay sane; they keep us laughing, learning, and loving. We speak one another's language and finish one another's sentences. Sometimes, however, loss touches us in different ways. What family relations, if any, were impacted by the loss of your spouse?

*

JONATHAN DEAN
Jonathan's 36-year-old wife Cara
died of double pneumonia in 2010

The friendship we had for nine years eight months came to a complete halt when my wife passed away and five years seven months later. The four friends want nothing to do with me.

*

BONNIE FORSHEY
Bonnie's 43-year-old husband Carl
died in a car accident in 2005

I can't say that I honestly lost any relationships, other than my in-laws. My husband had been through so much in his life. After he fell 110 feet at work, he came close to death. He was in severe pain all of the time. He lost the ability to work, and that made him feel like less of a man. He then was in a number of car accidents, and the last one claimed his life. After his death, the family no longer speaks to me.

*

STEPHEN HOCHHAUS
Stephen's 51-year-old wife Kathy
died of soft tissue sarcoma in 2011

My relationship with my sister-in-law has been the most impacted out of all the individuals in my life. I had always enjoyed a good and friendly relationship with my wife's sister until hours after my wife's death. It began when I was asked about a will and property we owned. This behavior continued which I could not deal with, as I was devastated by the loss, and she appeared so unaffected. My stepmom passed a year after my wife, and I went to the funeral and remained close to my stepdad. I spent time with him as we both were grieving, and I tried to give him comfort. My wife would have wanted that. A month later was Father's Day and my sister-in-law left for vacation for five weeks, leaving him alone. I travelled to be with him since I had lost my own father four months after my wife passed. I never got over the callousness of that woman and now we no longer speak, for my father-in-law passed four months after that visit. My sister-in-law had hurt my wife's feelings and made my wife cry more than once, yet my wife would always say, "But she's my sister," and forgive. I just can't do it even though I tried.

My last connection with Canada ended and I am better off being among friends and family who still may ask how I am and speak lovingly of my bride. The one thing that sticks in my mind was how my sister-in-law told me that she promised my wife that she would look out for me, but never once offered to help. Within months of my wife's passing, my own brother said, "Yeah, I know. You told us that before," when I was speaking about something my wife had said or did. He was tired of hearing about her. Since my dad died, he and I have not spoken; it has been more than three years. It is interesting that my brother and my sister-in-law share the same birthday, one which today has no meaning to me.

*

MARLISE MAGNA
Marlise's 36-year-old partner Blaine
died by suicide in 2010

Blaine's death caused a temporary disconnect which slowly turned into a permanent disconnect with my gran. I used to see my gran at least once a week when I'd take her shopping and for a meal, and we'd speak via telephone often. After Blaine died, I just withdrew and the contact became more and more infrequent. I kind of figured that she'd given up on me as she never phoned me on my birthday for the first time ever. I kept thinking I would call and then go see her, but she passed away one day out of the blue. At least she had an awesome day with family; they were all there when she died. To this day I have severe regret over my social paralysis after Blaine's death and not seeing my beloved gran.

*

DIANE MCKENZIE-SAPP
Diane's 65-year-old husband Ron
died from renal failure in 2006

Loss and family. I am fanatical, obsessed, and passionate about my business, Widows Rings. It should be no surprise that my vision

149

to create a widow's ring would push away some (most) family and friends. My unwavering insistence was that there should be a widow's ring and, if it didn't exist, that was not a good reason to think that it could not exist.

From the beginning of my widowhood I was obsessed with the idea of a widow's ring. The vision came in a dream and I had to make it real. If you asked, "How are you doing?" I would give you an update on my latest design idea. I know you feared for my sanity and my pension, but a turtle can't swim without sticking out its neck, and I believed this was what I was born to do. My family and closest friends felt the idea would run its course and fall along the wayside and die. This passion persisted against all odds. My sister asked what a widow's ring looked like in my artistic vision. I said I didn't know but even if I had a signature ring, that there could not be one ring for all widows as each of us has a different journey.

I persisted in spending time and money on researching mourning jewelry. Queen Victoria had decreed that those who attended court would be in full mourning attire complete with mourning jewelry. This practice endured for over twenty years and influenced worldwide fashion including our Civil War. Impressed, I vowed if one woman, even if she was a Queen, could make that type of change happen for her man, I would strive to do the same for my man. One day my oldest daughter was deeply troubled as I wore my new solitaire of a huge black tear shaped diamond. I felt it was the almost right ring for me now. She expressed her dismay at my removing my wedding rings and replacing them with something that her dad had not given me. She asked if I wanted to appear single. No. She asked if I didn't love him anymore. NO. "Why are you removing the wedding rings? You should leave them there for a least a year." Explaining that I was no longer married; until death does you part was real and severed ties. I was nowhere, and felt invisible, as if I was pretending to be married and it was all a lie, although I realized that removing my rings had affected me as much as her. That night I put them back on. It still wasn't right. I wouldn't cut his pictures from our family album; he still was part of me, and he was still part of our family forever. And I refused to lose one more thing that day. Taking off my rings was a decision that would not be made by time but rather by my heart. I would take them off when it felt right. If that took years, so be it. I was still a widow and I still needed to change the story told on my finger.

What if I added a ring that would sit next to my rings? A third ring, a widow's ring, would make all the difference to how I saw myself; one that continued the story, one that included the past, present and possibly my future. At first I had a small inexpensive ring and was accepted immediately. The plating wore off after several months and I knew that for some of us, a ring that lasted for as long as we needed it had been conceived. The first black-stoned channel-set ring in stainless steel was the result of women who wore their ring every day. It is called the Forever Ring and is the first ring a widow should try. I get notes thanking me for this ring; it has made a difference in the world. And that is all each of us aspire to, making a difference. A skeptical widowed woman asked, "What is your return policy?" This new idea of a widow's ring is met with skepticism and dismissed frequently. I told her, "My return policy is when you get your ring and place it on your finger, if you do not sigh 'aaahhh,' and you do not say to yourself, "This feels right," then you can return the ring and I will refund your entire purchase except for postage." I have sent hundreds of rings around the world to hug the fingers of broken-hearted wounded souls, and maybe two have been returned. Because my daughter called me out, the third ring, the widow's ring, came into the light.

*

LISA OWENS
Lisa's 50 year-old husband Greg
died of pancreatic cancer in 2014

I was never close to Greg's family until the end, but now it's so hard to be around them without Greg. That was what we did together, and I can't go alone. We message each other, but even that is getting less and less.

*

MARY POTTER KENYON
Mary's 60-year-old husband David
died of heart failure in 2012

I can't help but feel a little disconnected from siblings and friends in that I have experienced a loss that they have not. Can they truly understand this cloak of sadness that covers me at all times? Of course, I would never want them to experience the loss just so they can understand. I avoid group events where everyone is paired up with their spouse, and I'm not sure they understand that, either. People who love us want us to be okay, they want us to move on, and so I tend to hide some of what I am feeling, not sharing my true thoughts and feelings because it would be too hard to explain. I do have siblings and friends who seem to know how difficult this loss has been for me, and that helps.

*

NANCY REDMOND
Nancy's 40-year-old husband Kevin
died of a heart attack in 2012

My relationships with my mom, my children, my grandson, and my mother-in-law have all become so much stronger in the three-plus years since Kevin crossed over. We have all learned that tomorrow is not promised to any of us, and that we need to enjoy and love each other while we are together.

My relationships with many of my friends have become nonexistent. I don't know if it is the fear of death, the inability to express their feelings toward me, or if it was Kevin who held us all together. I have several lifelong friends who have stayed with me through all phases of this journey -- good, bad, and ugly -- but there are those who have fallen off this train, never to be heard from again. I used to mourn the loss of those friendships, yet now I realize that no matter how big or small, everyone who comes into my life provides a "piece of the puzzle." I am grateful for those pieces and have moved on with my head held high and hopefully my heart in the right place. I have also had a permanent "disconnect" with Kevin's daughter. She has much regret when it comes to how she treated her dad, and I truly can't help her with that. When I used to gently remind her before Kevin died that "next times" don't always come, she used to get very irritated with me. Well, I hate to say it, but I told her so. She is angry on many levels about her dad's passing, and I truly am not qualified to help her with those regrets and feelings, so I have let her go with nothing but the best wishes for a great life.

*

MARY LEE ROBINSON
Mary Lee's 63-year-old husband Pat
died from a sudden stroke in 2013

Undoubtedly, losing my two longest friendships has to top that list. The rupture is permanent. My choice.

*

CAROL SCIBELLI
Carol's 56-year-old husband Jimmy
died from lymphoma in 2006

My bereavement shrink told me that if a widow has a good relationship with her in-laws before her husband's death, then they would remain close. If it's not so great before, count on it to crumble afterwards. From the moment Jimmy brought me home to meet his mom, we clicked and fell right in step with each other. Throughout the forty something years as a family, we had our small, icky moments but mostly we laughed and teased and cared deeply for each other. Until her death last year at ninety-six, we sustained a loving relationship. Soon after Jimmy passed away she encouraged me to "find someone." She was widowed at sixty-five and she never dated. "Don't do what I did," she'd caution me. "It's a couple's world. Be part of a couple." Nothing made me feel more loved than hearing her say this. I'd tell my friends, "If my son was married and he died, I doubt I'd be cheering on my daughter-in-law to be with someone else."

Throughout our marriage, we were tight with Jimmy's two older brothers and their wives. We enjoyed celebrating holidays, playing card games and singing karaoke. We spent countless weekends playing Trivial Pursuit. For several Thanksgivings, Jimmy and I took the entire family to upstate New York to the Inn at Lake Joseph where we rented an old mansion for several nights. Each family had two kids and it was important to us that all the cousins spend time together. Our goal was that they would build memories they'd carry with them always. We hoped these weekends away would cement their "cousinhood" and as adults they'd stay connected. At some point though, Jimmy and I realized that if not for him and me planning an event, we wouldn't get together. We stopped initiating and our family began to unravel.

When Jimmy passed away, my relationship with my two brothers-law wasn't broken, but it was damaged. Over the first few months, I was hurt and disappointed that they never called or visited my children. Mama Bear kicked in and words were exchanged. Now, years later, I have a cordial relationship with one brother. As for the other brother, his wife and their children, we don't speak to one another. Naturally, there's much more to it than this, but while I'm usually "an open book," I don't feel it's fair to them or to me to write more about it in this one.

Losing the family who played and laughed and seemed to care about me and my kids has left me not only sad, but also part of me doubts the genuineness of "the good old days." At least I learned to value and cherish those who step up to be kind and loving and caring when life throws us a curve ball.

*

DIANNE WEST
Dianne's 69-year-old husband Vern
died from multiple myeloma in 2010

None of my siblings came out to support me during the long, hard cancer years. None of them came to the funeral. I wouldn't be honest if I didn't acknowledge this impacted me greatly. I've felt some pretty deep hurt and anger as I've tried to work through this, and I still don't understand it – but finally God gave me the grace to just accept that it is what it is. I'd like to say that this situation has given me a reason to not feel obligated to go back for any of their or their spouses' funerals, but I'm not sure I could do that. I obviously don't think the way they do and won't know what I'll do until that time arrives.

I had to walk away from a long friendship, and I'm still working my way through it three years later. She was there for me during the final months of Vern's illness and helped me greatly with the funeral. We did some things together and she sent me wonderful, uplifting messages for the first year or so. But then the friendship changed. She felt I had found new friends with my Brave Girls and Widowed Village communities (those are online friendships). The emails slowed; I wasn't included in their couple activities; I wasn't included in any activities. It felt like she thought her job was done, and she was no longer obligated to be my friend. When she forgot to pick me up at the airport it felt like that was a huge indication of where I fit into her life. I decided it was best for me to walk away rather than feel I was a burden or an afterthought. As the years pass, there have been a few times I've almost called her to see if we could salvage the friendship. But each time that little voice in my head tells me no, it would not be best for me.

I should say,
one of the things about being a widow or a widower,
you really, really need a sense of humor,
because everything's going to fall apart.
JOYCE CAROL OATES

*

CHAPTER TWELVE

THE FAITH

Love is the only law capable of transforming grief into hope. -LYNDA CHELDELIN FELL

Grief affects most areas of our life, including faith. For some, faith deepens as it becomes a safe haven for our sorrow. For others, it can be a source of disappointment, leading to fractured beliefs. Has your beliefs or faith been impacted by your loss?

*

TANYA CAMERON
Tanya's 43-year-old husband Ivor
died of a heart attack in 2013

I am not a religious person and neither was my husband. I do believe that things happen for a reason.

*

JONATHAN DEAN
Jonathan's 36-year-old wife Cara
died of double pneumonia in 2010

I respect all religions, but I am atheist. I believe happiness comes within and not going to a church or synagogue to bring happiness to oneself. But like I said, I respect all religions.

*

BONNIE FORSHEY
Bonnie's 43-year-old husband Carl
died in a car accident in 2005

I no longer attend church. I have incurred too much pain and too many losses.

*

STEPHEN HOCHHAUS
Stephen's 51-year-old wife Kathy
died of soft tissue sarcoma in 2011

My wife and I were not at all religious. We did believe in a higher power. I was raised in a very religious family, but my heart took me somewhere else. I don't ever wonder why God made things happen. Bad things just happen to good people. I enjoy being with others who do have a strong faith if they don't use it to judge others and, find comfort for themselves.

*

MARLISE MAGNA
Marlise's 36-year-old partner Blaine
died by suicide in 2010

Yes! In a positive way! When Blaine passed away, I was not really a believer, for lack of a better word. I was more spiritual and just said yes, there is a God, but that's that. Blaine's mom had arranged a Christian memorial service for him, but I don't believe he was a Christian upon his passing. When I was in the hospital after his death, pastors tried to reach out to me but I literally would not even see them and got very irritated by their concern for a stranger. About two years later, I started dating a pastor and he never forced the issue. One day we just got to discussing Jesus and bam - his statements made sense and he could back them up with hard evidence (I query everything!). Subsequently, I got saved, enrolled to study theology, and have since stepped into ministry and counseling.

I wish my faith could show others that there IS hope and life after a loss. Also that it would give people more strength after their loss, because we will see our loved ones again. My faith has been my strength ever since.

*

DIANE MCKENZIE-SAPP
Diane's 65-year-old husband Ron
died from renal failure in 2006

There was a time when I thought "The next person that says my husband's death was God's will, will have their mouth padlocked with crazy glue." Thankfully it remained only a thought since neither my husband nor God would have found it justified. I cannot find belief in any religious institution that has waged a crusade, a jihad, employed a religious assassin, a caste system, blind cult obedience or witch hunts. That eliminates most major religions. As a mother, it infuriates me when my children are spiteful to each other. How would I feel if they were trying to kill each other? Only God knows.

After my husband died, I sought wisdom in the older, purer religions. I explored the Kabbalah religion, the Hematites, the Dead Sea Scrolls, the Old Testament, Ascended Masters, nature-based paganism, druidism, Edgar Cayce and the earliest Christian religions and gnostic religion bordered on what believed. None were a perfect match for my questions.

I asked God, "Did you have to take my mother, my father, and my husband, for me to truly understand grief?" I don't question his plan; I questioned my role as the surviving swan. I asked Him for help and found these words: God give me the strength to accept what I cannot change. The courage to change what I can and the wisdom to know the difference. These words became a mantra that I prayed and breathed when there were no other words that made sense to me. The courage to change what I can eventually became more meaningful than acceptance. Those words were burned into the first ring I designed.

After seeking God's presence in a temple, I found more solace in my garden. Winged creatures are the ambassadors of heaven. Butterflies tease my nose and a praying mantis will sit on my finger. Robins sit patiently during gardening and pounce on uncovered worms. A hospice nurse sees death every day. Impending death has its physical signs and there are other signs as well. Birds gather outside when the time is near. While driving to my hospice patient, I would see the shadow of a bird cross my windshield and wonder if I would arrive in time. Blackbirds perch on dead limbs outside the nursing homes. I saw these stopovers as signs that each soul was guided home with iridescent wings. Seeing a giant woodpecker being harassed by a mocking bird, I felt a profound sadness and soon a gracious man died alone because of his stepson's selfish motives. An untimely flock of robins landed in my Maryland yard during a January snowstorm, and a sweet but sassy lady died a peaceful death that day.

Peregrine falcons live on high rise buildings and soaring metal bridge spans. When one landed in my neighbors tree and stared into my eyes I knew why he was there. The nurse said my husband was "on deaths door," and to come as soon as possible. I shouted at the falcon," Go away! I am not ready for you!" He ruffled his feathers and flew away in the opposite direction of my poor sick husband. We had another three months.

While I was content that a falcon would be his ambassador, I felt this beautiful bird was sacrificed. To explain my fanciful discontent, I will share a fable that exists in my head. As a child I never saw a dead bird. I really had no idea if or how birds died. But as the world grew older and machines began to hum, I noticed the bird body count escalating. I speculated that each bird aspires to guide a human soul to heaven and, with its dying breath, is received into the sunlit hall of the mighty kingdom. This mission is the final journey of each worthy aerial creature. The book is opened, the soul is designated; the bird is carefully chosen and charged with the holy mission to return with only this one soul. The flight path is tracked and the bird is flying toward its GPS destination to await the imminent glorious outcome. All is well that ends well. But what would happen if their assigned soul did not leave? What would happen if a surgeon in shock trauma, or a midwife, or a first responder arrived in time, or a woman shouted "Go away!" and denied death? That bird, be it a falcon or sparrow or blackbird or dove, failed its sacred mission. Without their assigned soul there was no passage through heaven's door. The bird, a fallen angel, must remain here in this world. One chance to soar before God is all that is given. Modern miracles saved one life and doomed another.

*

JULIE MJELVE

Julie's 42-year-old husband Cameron

died by suicide in 2011

My faith has indeed been impacted by my loss. Fortunately, I can say that it has been deepened. It has caused me to question my beliefs in God, especially why God would allow this to happen, why he didn't save my husband, find him the help he needed. I make my guesses. My husband was hurting, and perhaps God allowed it as a way to set him free from his pain. At his funeral I had them play the song "Amazing grace, my chains are gone, I've been set free." I could see that my husband's mental illness was destroying him. So at least now he's in a place where there is no more pain. I still hurt, but God can also help me through that pain and give me the strength to make it through another day. His tombstone says "Earth has no sorrow that heaven cannot heal." There is another song that has helped me find meaning. It's called "Blessings" by Laura Story. The whole song has wonderful lyrics, but some of the most impactful for me are "What if your blessings come through rain drops? What if your healing comes through tears? What if a thousand sleepless nights are what it takes to know you're near? What if trials of this life are your mercies in disguise?" This has been a very difficult time for me. But I have found that I am a different person. I think I'm stronger in many different ways.

I stand up more for myself. I speak out for others more. I've learned that instead of praying for God to take away the pain and the difficulties I now experience as a result of the loss of my husband (which He never answers!), I now pray that God would provide for me whatever the resources I need for the particular difficulty, whether it be finances, a meal, a shoulder to cry on, words of comfort. These He does answer. And as a result, I've learned how to trust in God more. What I wish Christians would do more of in their approach and support of the bereaved is to act more. Words, cards are nice, but the best way to show your love, and God's love for others, is to serve them. It's quite traditional to make a meal and it is absolutely appreciated, but I would recommend to go a step further. Do some dishes. Do some laundry. Help with groceries. I just read about a family from a farming community that experienced a loss, and the news report stated how the whole family community is coming together to make sure the crops get harvested. To me, this shows God's love far more than patting me on the shoulder and telling me my husband is heaven now.

*

LISA OWENS
Lisa's 50 year-old husband Greg
died of pancreatic cancer in 2014

My faith has gotten stronger! Greg was so strong in his faith, and mine grew stronger watching him! He touched so many lives with his positive outlook, fighting until his last breath.

*

MARY POTTER KENYON
Mary's 60-year-old husband David
died of heart failure in 2012

Extremely. I have become a different, more faith-filled person through loss. In those dark nights of the soul, when I felt so alone, I turned to a God who became my fortress. I learned to listen when

I pray, and not just call out in anguish. I feel blessed that I have been able to develop a real relationship with Jesus Christ, and in the process, with his followers. My world is so much bigger now, with many brothers and sisters in Christ. My Catholic church failed miserably with no heartfelt praying (other than rote prayers) nor Bible studies available, when I needed both. The priest didn't reach out to me, and other than a card or two, neither did anyone from a bereavement committee. I had to find my own answers and rather than leave the church, I brought the answers I needed into my own parish, beginning a Bible study, and eventually, this year, a widow-widowers support group. Even that group met with some resistance from the current priest, who didn't think a "dating service" was appropriate for our parish. I don't blame an entire church for this, however. In fact, this single priest's reaction made me all the more certain that there needed to be other answers for widows and widowers in our area.

*

NANCY REDMOND
Nancy's 40-year-old husband Kevin
died of a heart attack in 2012

My spiritual faith has been strengthened immeasurably by Kevin's passing. There is not one day that I don't dream of Kevin, "soul travel" with him at night, or have countless signs from this man who carried the other half of my heart with him Home to the other side. I hear, see, and feel him with my heart and soul, and for those great gifts, I thank God. My spiritually has been strengthened in ways that I feel it would not otherwise have been made stronger but through the loss of Kevin.

*

MARY LEE ROBINSON
Mary Lee's 63-year-old husband Pat
died from a sudden stroke in 2013

I am a little surprised, but my faith has grown stronger. It has grown a lot stronger. Initially, I clung to my Bible and scriptural readings to try and sort it all out. I also had the example of my family members, some of whom had severe losses and yet never lost their own faith. I never ever blamed God for taking my husband from me. While I've been angry occasionally that we didn't get to have the time together that we expected, take the trips we planned, live out the dreams we had, from the beginning I accepted that it was just Pat's time.

I also believe that God called me to work with widows and widowers and, more importantly, the non-grieving community to improve how grievers are treated. The book I wrote with other widows and widowers was intended to help non-grievers know how to better prepare and how to treat the widowed in their own communities.

*

CAROL SCIBELLI
Carol's 56-year-old husband Jimmy
died from lymphoma in 2006

I was born to Jewish parents. We were reform, the least observant Jews. Our family only went to temple for bar mitzvahs or weddings. I never attended Hebrew school. I did not have a bat mitzvah. Jimmy was Catholic and we laughed when in 1972, the year we wed, the priest referred to our marriage as a "mixed union." To us, we were the same because religion wasn't emphasized in his family, either. His parents never went to church. Sunday morning meant we could sleep late and feast on pasta with meatballs and more pasta. If we were visiting my cousins, it was matzo ball soup and brisket. Different food was the extent of our differences. We raised our daughter and son with no organized religion. We celebrated all the holidays until one year when I couldn't find the menorah for Hanukkah, Christmas won out. Faith to me always meant believing in God, or a higher power, but that's being spiritual, not being part of an organized religion. I've always believed that things happen for a reason, even negative episodes. I tell my kids (based on the fact that I am forever getting lost) that wherever we are, that's where we're supposed to be. This may be why I wasn't bitter and angry when Jimmy died. I was able to be resilient because I am convinced that I am living the life and taking the path that I was intended to travel. I guess that's faith.

*

KRISTI SMITH
Kristi's 48-year-old husband Michael
died from cardiac arrest in 2011

As women, we feel like we should be able to carry the weight of everyone else around us, but when we get tired or need a turn being carried, we are the first to shame ourselves for it. We do a lot of the carrying, so wouldn't it make sense that we should be able to take a turn at being carried and not feel guilty about it? No. It's like we should never need to be carried, because we are the carriers.

"Lean On Me" was the last song my husband learned to play on the piano for me. Little did I know how important this concept would become just months later. Everything changed when my husband died. His death happened so fast, and the pain of loss was so crippling, that I was unable to absorb it. I could not stand the sight of my husband lying lifeless on the driveway. I could not bear the burden of my shattering heart and the weight of my two daughters' terror-filled eyes. I remember standing in the driveway and feeling like I would surely be swept away in this tornado of grief. My mind was swirling and my emotions were imploding. I felt like I would suffocate under the weight of it all and be crushed like a bug. I was outsized by the mammoth of emotions driving toward me. An avalanche was heading straight for my little family. I was afraid we were all going to be buried alive. The shear shock of my husband's death was enough to take my breath.

Suddenly I was falling, not falling physically, but emotionally falling apart. I was about to lose it when God swooped in and caught me. Instantly, I was in the firm but gentle grip of something bigger. At first I didn't know who or what it was that had scooped me up and I will be honest with you, I didn't care. I just needed to be held, protected, and sustained while everything I held dear to me was hanging in the balance between life and death. What is bigger than death? The heart of God. I knew God was a soft place to land, but I was not landing... I was falling. I had not aimed for the safety net of my Savior. In my moment of weakness, I had not targeted anything at all, but there He was. I would like to say that I leaned into God, but it was more like my knees buckled and I fell into Him. God Himself gathered me in His arms and held me against His chest. I could tell by the way that He was holding me that He would never let me go. In that moment, God allowed me to lean on Him like never before.

Maybe as women we carry the burdens of everyone else, but I am grateful to a God who cradled me when I needed it most. God was the safety net that gently caught me in mid-air. Compared to crashing to my emotional death I would much rather be carried. Not only did He hold me that pivotal evening, but He continues to hold me up. In the first few months it was as if God had some sort of stabilizing rod running through my spine that held me up. I did not stand of my own power, I can tell you that!!!

During the coming seasons of grief, God also taught me who else I could lean on. Not all the people who I had expected to be strong were able to help me stand. Maybe they were overcome by their own brokenness, struggling in their own season of life, or perhaps they just had an inability to know how to handle something so severe. I am not sure. There were those who could not handle it at all, but there were also others. Seasoned warriors who had built up incredible muscles and stamina and were true angels to me. I could lean on them with my whole weight of fear, anger, disappointment, or sorrow and they could take it. They were stronger than me and they allowed me, even encouraged me, to fall back into them. I am forever changed by their willingness to help me stand when I had no strength of my own. And then there were those precious friends and family members who were able to stand together with me. Neither one of us were placing more weight than the other. We simply fell forward onto each other and that was enough to keep us both standing. Like a suspension bridge we stayed above the water by leaning onto each other. Their strength became mine and mine theirs. We learned how to lean on each other.

*

DIANNE WEST
Dianne's 69-year-old husband Vern
died from multiple myeloma in 2010

My faith is what held me up during my husband's illness and death. But when I say faith, I'm not referring to my church community. They let me down at the diagnosis and were not there for me at all. I stopped attending church and have not yet returned. Perhaps I will one day. I've received great comfort, however, from my deep faith in God/Jesus/Holy Spirit. He has been here with me through every single heartbreaking thing that has happened. I've not ever thought "Why me?" or been angry at God. He has given me the peace I've needed to accept that death is a part of life, and to be grateful for those final hours I was able to spend with Vern. I don't believe that God gives me these trials, or that He was punishing me for some deed. I just know that He is here with me always, helping me survive whatever life happens to throw at me.

I'm not Jewish, but I do love their custom of sitting shiva with the bereaved. To just have those who care about you sit with you silently until you initiate a conversation, and then share stories about the person you lost and not try to fix you by saying those standard phrases: "He's in a better place," "He's no longer suffering," etc. What a difference that would make.

*

CHAPTER THIRTEEN

OUR HEALTH

Health is a state of complete physical, mental, and social well-being, and not merely the absence of disease or infirmity. -WORLD HEALTH ORGANIZATION

As our anatomical and physiological systems work in tandem with our emotional well-being, when one part of our body is stressed, other parts become compromised. Has your grief affected your physical health?

*

TANYA CAMERON
Tanya's 43-year-old husband Ivor
died of a heart attack in 2013

Overall I have lost ten kilos, not that I ever had been a big person, but my husband was a chef. It was always his good cooking. I have found myself not eating as much, it has been such a stressful time to go through and still is two and a half years on. I am running around after the boys so much and working that I keep moving all the time. I have never gone to the gym; I don't really think that is for me. I would rather walk up to the shops but still find myself trying to find that time. The boys start complaining that they have sore legs. I can never win.

I have noticed that I do seem to get sick and catch a lot of colds. It is probably due to me being run down and perhaps I should slow down. Easier said than done when I am the only parent my boys have. There is always something to do around the house, whether it is inside or out, I have to work to keep the income coming in. My whole life has changed, the dynamics are now different.

*

JONATHAN DEAN
Jonathan's 36-year-old wife Cara
died of double pneumonia in 2010

My eating has gone down the drain. I am not eating healthy. I have gained weight.

*

BONNIE FORSHEY
Bonnie's 43-year-old husband Carl
died in a car accident in 2005

My health has declined due to the loss. Carl was a big part of my life, and the loss caused me to become depressed and anxious. Later I developed many autoimmune diseases that I can't bounce back from.

*

STEPHEN HOCHHAUS
Stephen's 51-year-old wife Kathy
died of soft tissue sarcoma in 2011

I find myself aging so much more rapidly. In the early months and years, I became ill more easily with colds, bronchitis and the like. I knew deep inside that I was worn down by sorrow itself, and had very little reason to live. I gained a lot of weight as well and after four years, I began to start turning that around.

When my wife was dying, I had a toothache which went unattended. After she passed, I tried to ignore it until the physical pain outweighed the emotional one. I ended up fighting that infection for months before completing a root canal. I think the loss of a will to live can do these things to you. I believe I still have a ways to go, but have no doubt that I am going in the right direction, approaching my fifth year widowed.

*

MARLISE MAGNA
Marlise's 36-year-old partner Blaine
died by suicide in 2010

It has affected my health as well as appearance in a major way. Appearance-wise, after Blaine died, I lost a lot of weight and kept changing my look. I went from short hair to long, to shaving it all off and getting many piercings. Now I am a bit more "normal" and no more piercings and bald head for me. I guess I was trying to find myself or the authentic me. My identity was always defined by my partner, so I felt adrift and lost in the world. Health-wise, I did have pre-existing conditions before his passing but they increased substantially after my loss. I developed a blood sugar problem causing me to gain weight again. My chronic pain disorder sent my pain levels through the roof. I am constantly ill with something. The biggest problem I've had since Blaine's passing is that I suffer from severe insomnia. I cannot take sleeping tablets as I sleepwalk and drink more pills in my sleep. They also paralyze my breathing. Nighttime is terror time for me. I have this saying that 4 a.m. knows all my secrets....

*

DIANE MCKENZIE-SAPP
Diane's 65-year-old husband Ron
died from renal failure in 2006

A hospice nurse treats all manner of pain. Pain is a symptom of an underlying issue. When I state that I have pain, I should be heard. Not all pain can be found under a microscope. After my husband died, I visited the doctor. I had aches and pains, could not stop crying and I could not sleep. My grief was as apparent as my lab tests. I was treated with tiny pills but fragments of me remained invisible and hurting. My pain was called depression, I was advised that it will get better with time, speak with a counselor, focus on the future and not live in the past. I was sick with grief. No tests measured my angst; it wasn't real, and the doctor believed it must be all in my head. The doctor only needed to acknowledge my pain, tell me it was normal during grieving and that most likely I would not die of it. The pain subsides with time because either the pain lessened or we learned to live with the pain. He could say that he had nothing to offer to relieve the pain. All he needed to say was "I believe you will carry this pain for some time, and I am sorry for your loss."

Pain comes with many names and each is treated a bit differently. I compare the pain of death to the pain of amputation.

- Psychosocial pain: Factors such as boredom, loneliness, depression, and death of significant others contributes to the pain. Psychosocial pain is associated with depression and manifests with painful physical symptoms such as headache, backache, stomach ache, joint ache, and muscle ache. Depression and pain share common neurochemical pathways.

- Somatic symptom disorder pain: Somatoform pain disorder is pain that is severe enough to disrupt a person's everyday life. The pain is like that of a physical disorder, but no physical cause is found. The pain is thought to be due to psychological problems. The pain that people with this disorder feel is real. It is not created or faked on purpose (malingering). Some experience a decline in health leading to further health issues, while others use their loss as a catalyst to improve their health.

- Neuropathic pain is a complex, chronic pain state that usually is accompanied by tissue injury. With neuropathic pain, the nerve fibers themselves might be damaged, dysfunctional, or injured. These damaged nerve fibers send incorrect signals to other pain centers.

- Amputation and phantom pain: Phantom limb pain is the feeling of pain in an absent limb or a portion of a limb. The pain sensation varies from individual to individual. Phantom limb sensation is the term given to any sensory phenomenon (except pain) which is felt at an absent limb or a portion of the limb. It has been known that at least eighty percent of amputees experience phantom sensations at some point in their lives. Some experience some level of this phantom pain and feeling in the missing limb for the rest of their lives. A woman had severe pain in her leg due to claudication, a condition in which leg pain is caused by obstruction of the arteries. For years she was treated for the vascular condition. Her circulation became so bad that the doctors amputated her leg. Her pain continued. She still had pain in her missing leg that was agonizing and persistent. Her pain was exactly where it had pained her prior to the amputation and not where the leg was amputated. Doctors call this "phantom pain," a neurological pain for which there is no long-term treatment. Because the syndrome of phantom pain has been recognized since the 1600s, no one said she was crazy, did not tell her it will get better with time, did not tell her to "get over it," to speak with a counselor, or that she needs to change focus. Nobody would say those things to an amputee even though the pain is in a place they can't see. Why can't a widow's phantom pain be as real? The best pain relief for her has been acupuncture.

Accepting that there is no treatment was the first step in my healing, acupuncture was a major factor in freeing this invisible blockage. Reiki has soothed the pain. My rings helped me heal and each one that helps another widow eases my journey as well. Just because you can't see it doesn't mean it does not exist. If phantom pain is real for an amputee then why would anyone tell a widow that her pain is not real? The loss of your other half is an amputation of your heart and soul. When after-death pain is acknowledged as real and not a mood motivated by loneliness and grief, widows and widowers can learn to live with half a heart and understand that pain is part of healing, and healing takes as long as it takes.

*

LISA OWENS
Lisa's 50 year-old husband Greg
died of pancreatic cancer in 2014

Yes, I have lost about thirty pounds, and I'm not complaining. I'm trying to be healthy. Emotionally, I feel stronger. I have my days, but I have to keep Greg's faith in humanity and God alive!

*

NANCY REDMOND
Nancy's 40-year-old husband Kevin
died of a heart attack in 2012

I have lost a good deal of weight since Kevin's passing. I suspect most of it is trying to figure out a "new normal" for my eating patterns. Food is a "chore" now and I eat to exist rather than enjoying consuming food. I know it's an unhealthy attitude (I have two children who are nurses and they remind me constantly!!), but for now, it is what it is. My family physician has told me that as long as I don't keep on losing weight and agree to take vitamins, she's okay with things the way they are. I have had bouts of severe anxiety since Kevin died. The two things that bother me the most are (1) being stuck in traffic (I feel like jumping out of the car and doing the "Ricky Bobby" thing and walking!), and (2) waiting in line. I think they are similar in many ways -- I just don't have the patience to "sit" any longer. My family physician has offered me medications to quell the really bad bouts of anxiety or panic attacks, but I tend to take a more holistic approach to medicine and try to work through these episodes on my own by using meditation, aromatherapy and acupressure.

*

MARY LEE ROBINSON
Mary Lee's 63-year-old husband Pat
died from a sudden stroke in 2013

The cumulative stress of losing my husband, along with untangling some very messy financial affairs, some neighborhood shunning, as well as war, famine and pestilence (it really felt like that when a large tree fell on my roof, then a hurricane flooded my yard) has taken its toll. Especially in the first year, it seemed as though there was a major disaster once a month. I learned of another one five minutes ago. It seems I have a leak in my water line, the part I'm responsible for. The house is three years old. About eighteen months after Pat was gone, I started experiencing gastrointestinal problems. I have IBS, which is closely tied to stress and, once acquired, does not go away. It is simply managed. I now have a very restrictive list of foods that are safe for me. That could have some bonuses, but everything I learned from Weight Watchers about losing weight is invalid for what I need to eat now. Rice, pasta, potatoes and bread are now a mainstay for me. Oh my, if it's not one thing, it's another, and it could be worse. God promised me he would not desert me, and I believe it.

*

CAROL SCIBELLI
Carol's 56-year-old husband Jimmy
died from lymphoma in 2006

For the first few months, I was exhausted all day. At least this helped me to sleep well at night. Nothing kept me awake, not even Saturday Night Live. To this day, there are only a few nights a year that I lay in bed with my mind racing. I must bore myself so I conk out. Jimmy and I both were fairly cavalier about illness. We believed that many symptoms were mind over matter. "Shake it off," we would say to others and ourselves. Obviously, Jimmy's cancer was not something he could just shake off. Since he died, I am far more cognizant of every sensation in my body. I told my doctor early on that I wanted to have a full body scan. She discouraged me. "At any given moment," she said, "our bodies might be harboring a foreign something, even cancer, but a healthy immune system rids it from our system. If we find something, we'll have to deal with it. Don't put yourself through that." So since 2006, I've walked the line between awareness and paranoia. Since I am acutely aware that I am the last grandparent standing, I try not to give in to "feeling my age" of sixty-five. Lately, when I play with my granddaughters, I've noticed it's harder to get up from the floor, and my little five-month-old granddaughter somehow feels much heavier to me than the older kids felt at that age. I'd like to, but I can't blame every ache and pain on loss. A decade is a decade.

*

DIANNE WEST
Dianne's 69-year-old husband Vern
died from multiple myeloma in 2010

While many lose weight after their loss, I gained. I rarely ate a regular meal and existed on coffee and snacks, sometimes stopping for fast food on the way home from work to have my first meal of the day. My age, my metabolism, and my extremely poor eating habits caused the pounds to pile on. Ice cream was my comfort food and my sleep aid. I didn't waste time with a bowl; I just grabbed the container and a spoon and sat down in front of my laptop. If I got sleepy and went to bed, I could get a few hours of sleep. Vern had wanted me to do two things for myself that I didn't do until a few months after he died. One was to go to a hairdresser. Just writing that makes me smile, because I recall asking him if I looked that terrible. But he knew I was coloring and cutting my hair myself during those cancer years, and this was a treat he thought I deserved. The other was to have a complete physical. I've never been good at keeping up with those scheduled female exams and it had been seven years since my last doctor visit. So five months after Vern died, I scheduled a physical. Mammogram, pap, chest x-ray, first time colonoscopy, blood work – the whole shebang. I remember commenting in my online bereavement group that if I were to develop cancer, I would not do any treatments because I wouldn't want to prolong my life – and I truly believed that. However, when faced with a medical scare during these exams, I learned that my will to live was stronger than I had believed. I've not become overly health-conscious after this scare and have kept some of my bad habits, but I'm more aware now that I do want to live. I still have things I need to do.

Faith is taking the first step
even when you don't see the whole staircase.
MARTIN LUTHER KING, JR.

*

CHAPTER FOURTEEN

THE QUIET

Heavy hearts, like heavy clouds in the sky, are best relieved by letting go of a little water. ANTOINE RIVAROL

The endless void left in our spouse's absence remains day and night. When our minds are free from distractions is the moment when sorrow fills the void, threatening to overtake us, unleashing the torrent of tears. For some, that moment happens during the day, for others it comes at night. What time is hardest for you?

*

TANYA CAMERON
Tanya's 43-year-old husband Ivor
died of a heart attack in 2013

I find that nighttime is the hardest. You can fill in the days, but the nights are so lonely. When the kids go to bed, that's the time I want to chat about my day. It's the loneliness, needing that adult chat, to talk to someone about what the kids did, what happened at work. A few times something good has happened at work and I think I can't wait to go home and tell Ivor, and then reality hits. Ivor passed away on a Saturday morning. For the first year I hated Saturday mornings. In my mind I was reliving the whole terrible morning, but that has gotten a little easier as time has passed.

*

JONATHAN DEAN
Jonathan's 36-year-old wife Cara
died of double pneumonia in 2010

I wake up positive every morning but throughout the day, many reminders trigger tears. Going to bed at the time we used to each night is very hard. There has been no change. I still cry myself to sleep.

*

BONNIE FORSHEY
Bonnie's 43-year-old husband Carl
died in a car accident in 2005

Evenings are hardest. We would have supper, talk about our days, and spend quality time together. Things were not always bad between us, there were lots of good times. I try to remember the good and forget the bad. Carl's accident changed everything in our relationship. He has been gone for a while, but I still miss him and always will. I have learned to adapt, but it will never be the same.

*

STEPHEN HOCHHAUS
Stephen's 51-year-old wife Kathy
died of soft tissue sarcoma in 2011

Evening is the most difficult because that is when I am alone and all of the distractions are gone. It peaks at bedtime, when I get into bed and just think about my wife and my life without her. After more than four years, I still would give anything to have her beside me. When you had a life that always included going to bed together, you will miss always those last conversations of the day with the content feeling of loving and being loved. You sleep so much better when all is right with the world. Most evenings are content without undue worries yet when life would throw trouble your way, it was a comfort to hear Kathy telling me not to worry, things will work out. These days, I never feel so secure.

*

MARLISE MAGNA
Marlise's 36-year-old partner Blaine
died by suicide in 2010

Definitely the evenings. I never battled sleeping but since the loss I have become an insomniac. Sometimes I'm awake seventy-two hours on end before a few hours of fitful, nightmare-filled sleep. I can't really say why although I suspect its posttraumatic stress disorder as diagnosed. It's sadly has only gotten worse and worse. The worst of the worst for me is usually between 2 a.m. and 4 a.m. They say night is always darkest before the daylight breaks, and that's exactly how I experience it - a pitch black void filled with deafening silence.

*

DIANE MCKENZIE-SAPP
Diane's 65-year-old husband Ron
died from renal failure in 2006

The worst time of the day was when the dark overcame the light. Evening was the opening act, and night was a solo performance. Evenings was when we shared the best of our day. Sharing is impossible now. Now I talk back to TV commentaries. I control the remote and I immerse myself in mind-numbing fiction. One way to live with the grief is by substituting the rewarding and loving union that once existed with a pattern of mind-numbing, unrewarding, senseless actions. Sticking your head in the sand works too, but it leaves your butt sticking out. Finding what will work for you takes time, and trial and error. I found my rings and I shared them. It was the single most important thing that got me up off that floor. I owe my sanity to those rings.

With night comes the BED. Our bed is my personal hell; it reminds me nightly of how alone I am. A queen-sized bed is much too roomy for the fetal position. Night was a sleepless, sobbing nightmare or a drug-induced coma. Some widows re-do their bedroom, and change the décor to remove the reminders. I still sleep with Ron's pillow, and on his side of the bed. I bought a crate-trained dog and made her sleep on the bed. The TV drones all night as I can't endure the void. I stalked sleep. Acupuncture was the only treatment to help in many ways. While waiting for my appointment, I happened upon a hematite ring. I was drawn to it. I bought it for under thirty dollars. It was the least expensive sleeping potion I tried. After three days of wearing this hematite ring I slept. I really slept, woke rested and revived for the first time in months. When I wore any hematite like rings, necklaces and bracelets, I slept. Exploring the properties and qualities of hematite, I found that according to legend it absorbs grief. I also learned when hematite has absorbed as much grief as it can hold, it shatters. My daughter went through at least three rings. I was asked by an eBay customer, "How do I know when to take it off?" You will know.

It is during the night we know a pain so devastating, you question if you can survive. I questioned: Does anyone survive unscathed? Does everyone feel this pain? Is this the ultimate pain? Who grieves the most?

I have three children, all of them beautiful and inquisitive. Separately, they would come to me, cuddle close, look into my eyes and ask; "Who do you love the most?" I would answer, "All of you the same." "The same." How was this possible, their raised eyebrows asked. I explained, "If you had three glasses of water and you filled them all to the tiptop so that if even a tiny drop more would be too much, which one has the most water? The love I have for you is a big glass filled to the tiptop with love and there is a glass filled to the tiptop for each one of you." When suffering the death of our spouse, we are grieving with a full glass of grief, sometimes it spills over and yet it never empties. Who grieves the most? Is it the married woman, the unmarried or is it the young woman with children or the older woman with no support? Is it widower, the orphan child, or same sex partners? Is it the Christian, Jew, Hindu, Shinto? Do the followers of Taoism, Buddhism, Catholicism or Muslim grieve as much as I do?

Grief is not a contest. Never think your glass holds more grief. Each of us has our full cup of heartache and not a drop more. All glasses are filled to the brim with sorrow. Respect their grief as you would have yours respected.

It is the darkest just before dawn. According to a bitter widow friend, I was told this is the time when visits are made. She told me around 4:30 a.m., her husband visited her and showed her those repairs needed in their home and even suggested a likely repairman. I asked her to send him over the next time he called, as I needed some help in that area. Her husband didn't come, but for a single time my husband did. I had begged for a visit each night. In the spring, surrounded in light he came to me. He spoke not a word and I knew it was him. That ethereal visitation exceeded all hopes and was the most satisfying night of my life. Instinct said that this was the first and last time for a visit. I sobbed as thankfulness and desolation comingled until the dawning of a new day.

*

JULIE MJELVE
Julie's 42-year-old husband Cameron
died by suicide in 2011

Bedtime is the hardest time of day for me. The kids keep me quite busy during the day and evening, but when everything has settled and it's time to head to that lonely, empty bed, that's where I struggle. I look at the duvet cover, which we picked out as a wedding present, and it's just such a reminder that not only is he gone, but I am alone. My dreams for our future together is gone. I would like to buy a new one and start over, decorate the bedroom fresh, but since he's been gone, money has been tight and I just can't afford it. Plus, it upsets me to think that I "need" to give it away, as we chose it because we both really loved it. I still love the design of it, and it makes me angry to feel like I can't enjoy it, the way I should be able to. So, bedtime is my hardest time of day.

*

LISA OWENS
Lisa's 50 year-old husband Greg
died of pancreatic cancer in 2014

Night is the hardest...when the day is over and wish I had Greg to come home too. I miss our talks, our giggles, and just being in the same room together.

*

NANCY REDMOND
Nancy's 40-year-old husband Kevin
died of a heart attack in 2012

What time isn't a hard time? I miss Kevin with every breath I breathe. I miss him when I wake in the morning and when I leave for work each day. I miss his text messages during my day at work, looking down and smiling at his words of love and thoughtfulness. I miss coming home to his car in the driveway and the hugs at the front door. I miss chatting with Kev as we go about our daily routines. I miss eating dinner with him. I miss discussing our days at work or issues that concern our world. I miss the snuggles before bed and the kisses goodnight.

And the next day? It begins again....

*

MARY LEE ROBINSON
Mary Lee's 63-year-old husband Pat
died from a sudden stroke in 2013

We made a point of having dinner together every night. My husband was most insistent about that. While dinner was cooking, about 5 p.m. we would sit and enjoy a glass of wine together. We talked and shared our day. Pat always had stories to tell me about his clients, or about his pool player buddies. I told him about my latest project and he encouraged me. He told me several times that it was his favorite part of the day too, and his best reason for coming home. I miss his company and that custom deeply. Now that hour passes and I don't always notice, but I still miss the ritual. Of course, I always miss him when I wake up and remember he isn't next to me. I do that still, two and a half years later.

*

CAROL SCIBELLI
Carol's 56-year-old husband Jimmy
died from lymphoma in 2006

Waking up alone the first few months was hard. Each morning I'd open my eyes and I'd forget that Jimmy was gone. That short-lived grogginess was the best part of my day. Instantly, I'd feel the sharp pain of reality. I'd try not to look over at the empty space besides me. Just making the bed was jarring because Jimmy's smooth sheets and unused pillow didn't need to be touched. I considered changing sides, sleeping on his side, but never did. I didn't have a nine-to-five job or a routine to follow, and often thought that if I did it might have forced me to jump out of bed faster and get on with my day. Over time, it became more natural to wake up alone. The first time a man slept in my bed, it was eerie to see that "lump" under the blanket. I remember fantasizing that it was Jimmy back where he belonged. Fantasizing that Jimmy was the "stranger" in my bed didn't stop there – if you know what I mean.

*

KRISTI SMITH
Kristi's 48-year-old husband Michael
died from cardiac arrest in 2011

Bedtime is the absolute hardest for me. I miss my husband the most at night. My heart literally aches for him. The sheets feel cold and the bed is empty. Sleeping single in a double bed sucks after twenty-five years of marriage. Some women have a hard time

185

staying in the house at night after their husbands die, because they are scared of nighttime noises and afraid someone could break in. I don't mind being alone, but I understand there is a difference between being alone and being lonely. I am lonely.

This big old bed gets lonely at night. I miss feeling Michael's arms around me, his feet wrapped up in mine, and his breath on the back of my neck. I miss whispering our love and falling asleep together. I miss the smell of campfire still on his skin. To be honest, it's not just the snuggle time that I miss. I also miss the excitement and fun of making love. No one ever talks about that (and when I say no one, I mean NO ONE!!!). It is difficult to go from being sexually active for decades and then stop cold turkey when your spouse dies. The fact that no one talks about it makes it even worse. The silence creates some sort of shame around it. This shouldn't be. It's a rough enough transition without feeling shamed. We need to be able to talk about it. I don't need to tell someone the details of my past sex life, but there should at least be some acknowledgment that it has suddenly stopped. It would be great for someone to say to me that it must be heart breaking to miss your lover.

I miss my husband's hugs and kisses (he always was a fantastic kisser and he was known for his warm hugs), but I miss a whole lot more than that about him. We met on my fifteenth birthday and were high school sweethearts. It was true love and we married after college. There was a physical attraction to him that I never have had to anyone else. He was a great lover and we definitely had an active sex life together. It was electric. Magical. We both poured out our hearts and souls into each other and we had a passionate relationship. Some people lose the magic after a few years. We kept the fire burning strong. We enjoyed our time together as a couple and made it a priority to protect that time.

When Michael died suddenly at age forty-eight, it was traumatic. I went through emotional and physical withdrawal. My heart was broken and my body was in shock. Among the other thoughts swirling in my head was the thought that we will never make love again. Making love was so much more than physical, it was emotional and spiritual. My whole being cried out for him. We were used to intimacy. Now there was nothing. I feel like I went from being a bride on an extended honeymoon to being a nun in a convent overnight. I think people wanted me to be some kind of asexual being now. To make matters worse, they expected this transition to happen suddenly and completely. The expectation was for me to go to bed a bride one day and wake up a widow the next with absolutely no feelings of sexuality whatsoever. No yearnings. No longings. Sexuality is not a light switch that you leave on for years and then one morning you just turn it off. That is just not reality. Friends encouraged me to go out and find someone else. There was no way I could replace the kind of connection my husband and I had by just hooking up with someone new. There is no comparison. I did not even want anyone else to touch me. Making love is not the same thing as having sex. Anyone can have sex. Making love is special. When there was no substitute for love and no way to scratch that itch, I just had to live with the itch.

Nighttime is still the hardest time of the day for me. Oh, I have gotten more used to him not being here, but I still miss him. I know someday I will find someone who will love me with that special love and I will love him with my whole heart. Until then, I will live with the fond memories of a deep and passionate love affair that I was able to call marriage.

*

DIANNE WEST
Dianne's 69-year-old husband Vern
died from multiple myeloma in 2010

Early on it was all hard. I cried in the car during the drive into work, and again on the drive home. I think walking into our home after work was the hardest time of day for me. Vern wasn't here, and that simple act of opening the front door seemed to emphasize my aloneness. No one here to share my day with, no one who cared how I was feeling, no one here....

After about four months I found Widowed Village, an online community, and then began to look forward to coming home and spending time in the chat room with my new friends. We had little in common – ranging in age from twenties to seventies, no kids, grown kids, little kids, pregnant; long marriage, newly married, engaged – but the loss of our person was all that we needed to form a strong bond. That was my therapy.

Now, at five years, evenings seem to be when I most often find myself especially missing Vern. I rarely have the TV on, so the house is quiet (unlike the nonstop sports-related programs that filled the house when he was here). And it seems to be the time when my heart feels his absence most.

*

CHAPTER FIFTEEN

OUR FEAR

The oldest and strongest emotion of mankind is fear, and the oldest and strongest kind of fear is fear of the unknown.   -H. P. LOVECRAFT

Fear can cut like a knife and immobilize us like a straitjacket. It whispers to us that our lives will never be the same, our misfortunes will manifest themselves again, and that we are helpless. How do we control our fear, so it doesn't control us?

*

TANYA CAMERON
Tanya's 43-year-old husband Ivor
died of a heart attack in 2013

I am most afraid of not seeing my boys grow up. Also, if something happens to me, what is going to happen to them? They already have lost their dad at such a young age. It is still my fear today, I think it will always be in the back of my mind. You don't think of these things until you have gone through what we are going through.

*

JONATHAN DEAN
Jonathan's 36-year-old wife Cara
died of double pneumonia in 2010

I am most afraid of when my brother passes. He is seven years older than me.

*

BONNIE FORSHEY
Bonnie's 43-year-old husband Carl
died in a car accident in 2005

I am afraid of drug addictions. My husband was doing drugs and I had no idea. I found out when it was too late, and after $180,000 disappeared from my bank account.

*

STEPHEN HOCHHAUS
Stephen's 51-year-old wife Kathy
died of soft tissue sarcoma in 2011

My wife was an accountant by trade and always handled the finances, both with our business and at home. After she died, I was forced to deal with those matters, and my biggest fear is messing up taxes and bills. Making decisions on what to do about household issues, even shopping, causes anxiety in my head. I'm always afraid of messing up, while she had total confidence.

*

MARLISE MAGNA
Marlise's 36-year-old partner Blaine
died by suicide in 2010

I cannot say I fear anything besides bugs. I guess the only real fear I have would be another loss, especially of my parents. Lately, I lie awake thinking about this. I'd be utterly lost. I don't fear my own death though. I just fear not living my life before my end.

*

DIANE MCKENZIE-SAPP
Diane's 65-year-old husband Ron
died from renal failure in 2006

I am not afraid to die, I am afraid that the art I have created will not live past me. My rings have made a difference in the world. They were heaven inspired, and I feel that I am doing what I was born to do. I want them to continue to heal broken hearts long past my time. With my death, I imagine the rings being sold for scrap metal and tossed into the garbage. I envision those who would never know the relief of these heaven-sent rings.

Early in 2014, I said that the collection of rings I had designed was complete. In November 2014, I was diagnosed with a rare relentless cancer. The doctor had a helpless look when he said, "You have angiosarcoma. It is rare and not much is known about it, and the usual prognosis is three months. I am sorry." My children and family rallied to research cancer doctors, treatments, herbals, diets, and healers. They asked what they could do. To their dismay my only future concern was, "How are the rings going to continue after me?" My children filled orders while I could not, but I had no long-term solution.

I had surgery in December 2014. I face reoccurrence at any time. I was led to a world renowned doctor at the Texas Medical Center. I am in remission with a scan every three months, watching for metastasis and suspicious symptoms. I was desperate for a solution to the question, "What will happen with the rings?" I voiced my concern to a higher being. "This was your idea, I was your tool. If it is time for me to go, if the designs are completed, if you have a plan for their continued existence, so be it. It is in your hands."

Help is not a coincidence. Mike was selected when I printed all the Maryland patent agents, filling up both sides of forty pages. I spread them out and stabbed randomly with a pen. I stabbed Mike. I called and asked if he would agent my design patent. He didn't do design patents and didn't know anyone who did. I suggested if he started doing them he would have the entire field to himself. He began the process with no fees and no guarantees, and won my patent.

Help is not a coincidence. Another godsend was Mary Lee Robinson, author of *The Widow or Widower Next Door*. When she came into my life, I found a solution and a kindred spirit. She is a ray of light, outgoing, pragmatic, and the savior for my rings. She promised she would continue the rings after I died. I breathed a breath of fresh air. We would merge our strengths. She is my maven. A maven is a trusted expert in a particular field who seeks to pass knowledge on to others. The word maven comes from Hebrew meaning "one who understands," based on an accumulation of knowledge. Without Mary Lee, the newest rings would not have left the drawing board.

Apparently my creative calling is renewed on a trimonthly cycle. God's wake-up message says, "Act as if today is the rest of your life, tomorrow is not guaranteed." Thinking that a remarkable collection of remembrance rings was completed, I was divinely corrected and this bargain was an ingenious approach to gain my attention. Motivated with a ticking-time extension, I designed several new rings.

1. Broken Heart Legacy: The patented broken heart with a duet of eternity rings fitting the special curves of the broken heart design.
2. Wind Below My Wings: Footprints on a rainbow is a hopeful promise. After every storm there is a rainbow. Never-ending footprints tread the endless journey. The words inside say, "When you only saw one set of footprints…it was then that I carried you."
3. Sterling Silver Eternity: Widow's third ring bands to replace the plated one. A Claddagh broken heart inside an intricate puzzle ring, so beautiful.

4. Fallen Heroes Ring. This has been an elusive project. I could not find a symbol to honor all our military, firemen and police who served our country. I have been asked by several service groups to design a ring that would honor their fallen hero. Until my gaze fell upon a flag at Half-Staff, this was the single symbol that enveloped all services.

5. Broken Heart Pendant: It is a broken heart sculpted and cut out in a silhouette in a silver frame. One side of the heart is gold and reverses to silver.

Dear Lord,

Within the last nine months I designed five new rings and a pendant. I need to live for two to four more years to get more designs done. The odds are one in one-hundred-thousand. Are YOU renewing?

*

JULIE MJELVE
Julie's 42-year-old husband Cameron
died by suicide in 2011

I'm most afraid of what if something happens to me, what will then become of my children. We don't have family that is close to us, either geographically or emotionally. They've already lost their father, so now I'm all they have left.

What.if.something.happens.to.me.

*

LISA OWENS
Lisa's 50 year-old husband Greg
died of pancreatic cancer in 2014

I fear never feeling love again. I am fifty-one, and so afraid I will live the rest of my life alone. I know I cannot, nor do I want to, replace Greg, but I miss male companionship.

*

MARY POTTER KENYON
Mary's 60-year-old husband David
died of heart failure in 2012

I'm afraid that I am making a mess of mothering, and not being there enough for my girls. I'm afraid my children are going to be scarred for life because they lost their dad. And I'm afraid I will never be loved again. I had true love once, and shouldn't be selfish or greedy, or expect to have it twice in one lifetime, but David knew how much I loved holding hands and hugging. He once said that if he ever died, he would want me to find someone so I could have that. I would have wanted that for him, too. But no sex! That was a joke between us. "I'd want you to find love, and have someone to hold your hand, and hug you and kiss you, but no sex!" And we'd laugh.

*

NANCY REDMOND
Nancy's 40-year-old husband Kevin
died of a heart attack in 2012

I am afraid of forgetting Kevin. I am afraid of forgetting his looks. I had a panic attack recently because I couldn't remember what his feet looked like! I fear forgetting his voice, I fear forgetting our inside jokes, I fear that those around me will forget him. I fear the new life that God has in store for me. I fear never knowing love like I had with Kevin again. I fear little things that never used to cause me anxiety like driving in traffic or going places I've never been before. I am starting to work through many of these fears and share many of them with my family members who reassure me when I am anxious and ground me when I need to find my footing again. Over time, I truly feel my fears have become much less intense, heart-wrenching, adrenaline-producing fears but more deep-seated, quiet fears which are not so visible to those around me anymore. Most times, they aren't even aware of my feelings, and I've gotten good at hiding them from even those closest to me.

*

MARY LEE ROBINSON
Mary Lee's 63-year-old husband Pat
died from a sudden stroke in 2013

I am in sheer terror of growing old, feeble, addled, dependent and alone. I fervently hope that I'm not here long enough for that to happen. I have no close family left, other than my half cousin who is older than I am and lives four states away. She's very dear and an inspiration, but we are too far away. I've always been fiercely independent. The idea of losing that is maddening. I couldn't stand it.

*

CAROL SCIBELLI
Carol's 56-year-old husband Jimmy
died from lymphoma in 2006

This may sound odd and all-encompassing, but my husband handled everything. So after he died, I felt helpless in the category of life. In the beginning, I was most afraid of tackling my own existence without him. Weeks before Jimmy passed away, I sobbed to him, "I don't know how to do anything!" I can still feel that panic. Immediately, I knew that this was a selfish reaction, but I was ridiculously ill-equipped and unprepared to face day-to-day responsibility. I had raised two kids who were twenty-nine and twenty-five when their dad died, and I was a grandmother of a two-year-old, but I had never rented a car, bought a stock, paid a bill, made a hotel reservation or a mortgage payment. Throughout our marriage, I had gloated that I was smart enough to have a smart husband but, in looking back, I see how playing the role of the "little woman" kept me ignorant and immature. Jimmy would laugh and tell our friends, "Carol assumes she has money in her checking account if she still has checks left." Of course, this was an exaggeration, but at the time we both thought it was funny. We'd tease that I was clueless about money. I would ask jokingly, "Does a spreadsheet have a thread count? Is a hedge fund in the chipmunk family? Do homeless people live in tax shelters?" Suddenly, Jimmy dies and I am left husbandless and helpless. Life whacked me on the head and now, at fifty-five years of age, I was forced to use it. Over time, I became aware and whole. I was finally functioning as a grown-up. It felt wonderful. I'd often think, "This is really not a big deal to do. Why did it seem like such a mystery to me?" I'm ashamed that I didn't strive to shake up our "dance" and be an equal partner for Jimmy. Ironically, he respected strong, capable, independent women. I know it would have been a huge relief for him if I were his helpmate. I so much regret that he couldn't count on me to share major decisions. If he is watching me, I'll bet he is shaking his head, "Who is this capable woman?" I often look back and wonder, "How could I have been so dependent? Sure, I'm adorable, but that's no excuse!"

*

DIANNE WEST
Dianne's 69-year-old husband Vern
died from multiple myeloma in 2010

The thought of needing medical care without having someone by my side as an advocate is quite frightening. My husband could have died on several occasions had I not been there to inform them of an issue, ask questions, take care of his needs, call 9-1-1. One of my sisters is widowed, has dementia and is now left alone in a nursing home. Our son says he will be there for me, but he did not handle his father's illness well, and I'm not confident he would be able to do any better with me, nor would I want to burden him with that responsibility. I've said this out loud and prayed that those terribly hard caregiving years will have earned me a quick and pain-free death when it's my time. And if I'm totally honest, I also fear having a stroke or heart attack in my home and not being found for days. Right now that wouldn't be a concern because our son has moved back in for a while. But when he leaves and I'm alone again, it's a concern. I've jokingly said I'll need to get one of those "I've fallen and I can't get up" things, but as I get older that's actually not sounding like something to joke about. It may be my only option.

CHAPTER SIXTEEN

OUR COMFORT

Life is made up, not of great sacrifices or duties, but of little things, in which smiles and kindness, and small obligations given habitually, are what preserve the heart and secure comfort.   -HUMPHRY DAVY

Transition sometimes feels as if we have embarked on a foreign journey with no compass or light. Rather than fill our bag with necessities, we often seek to fill it with emotional items that bring us comfort as we find our way through the storm. What items or rituals bring you the most comfort?

*

TANYA CAMERON
Tanya's 43-year-old husband Ivor
died of a heart attack in 2013

Being with my kids give me the most comfort. I love when they talk about their daddy and they like to ask questions. I have to be thankful that Ivor passed away in his chair, at home with his family. It could have been a lot worse.

*

JONATHAN DEAN
Jonathan's 36-year-old wife Cara
died of double pneumonia in 2010

Driving the elderly. What my job is. People telling me the words, "Move forward."

*

BONNIE FORSHEY
Bonnie's 43-year-old husband Carl
died in a car accident in 2005

My memories bring me comfort, along with the photographs of him.

*

STEPHEN HOCHHAUS
Stephen's 51-year-old wife Kathy
died of soft tissue sarcoma in 2011

My grandchildren give me the most comfort. I have triplet granddaughters and a grandson within walking distance of my home. Often when I am at my lowest and have had a bad day, I know I can go over for a happy fix. Having them spend the night at my house distracts me from all the pain and loneliness. Just watching them play brings great comfort to me. Having them cuddle up to me warms my very soul and helps fill the need for the tactile touch I lost with my wife's death.

*

MARLISE MAGNA
Marlise's 36-year-old partner Blaine
died by suicide in 2010

Just after Blaine died, I was so afraid of forgetting all our memories, so I obsessively started writing them down in a notebook. Every now and then I will take it out and read through it, and die a thousand little deaths. I also sometimes wear a ring of mine Blaine used to wear. Also, knowing he's at peace now brings me comfort.

*

DIANE MCKENZIE-SAPP
Diane's 65-year-old husband Ron
died from renal failure in 2006

I had to drive to Myrtle Beach, South Carolina, for a widows conference. The drive was very long and I needed to be indoors by dark. I took my dog, my rings and a suitcase. I started out early and without a GPS system. I invited three men to be backseat drivers, they were St. Christopher (the patron saint of travelers), my departed father and my late husband who was a truck driver (Knight of the Road). I selected CD music for them and began the journey with high hopes. I followed the road signs to Myrtle Beach. Darkness fell in a blanket. I was on a dual lane highway with no houses and no street lights. I had no idea where I was or if the road would curve into a swamp or ravine. A car passed me going very fast even for a moonshiner. I followed the taillights afraid to look at the speedometer as far as I could until he disappeared.

Praying for divine intervention, I spun my newest ring, the Prayer Wheel Ring, and said "God help me." I cried to the backseat, "You guys have to take over now, I am done." Somehow they got me off the highway onto a small one lane road. The only light was a gas station/ roadhouse/ liquor store with burly men in pickup trucks. "Whatcha gonna do?" theme song played in my head as I warily approached the cashier and asked for directions and a coffee. I feared the directions would a Rocky Horror Picture Show rerun. However those men turned into bearded angel agents, giving me directions and leading me to a lighted road with reasonable speed limits. I made it to the conference, and the widows loved the new rings. Their favorite was the FOREVER, a widow's third ring but the ALWAYS IN MY HEART & SOUL, the prayer wheel ring I had spun to protect myself, was the runner up.

"All's well that ends well," works if you travel with your own guardian angels. Please invest in a GPS driving directions device. There is nothing more terrifying than being alone, lost in the dark.

I am comforted each time I design a new ring. Each ring has its purpose. To design a ring and define its purpose, I relive the fear and pain someplace in my grief that was a quagmire. Those painful moments are brought under the microscope. By envisioning the pain to be a visible wound with symptoms, I examine the aching sore to see why it hurts. When I can SEE the wound, I dissect it then I nurse and treat the wound by eliminating and weakening the power it has over me. If I see a broken heart tearing me apart, I make that heart visible to the sunlight by wearing the Broken Heart Ring. If I see uncertainty, I wear assurance with the Always in My Heart & Soul ring. If it is despair, words of strength are found in the serenity prayer. If I feel alone and invisible, I make a ring only for widows, then she returns visible to stand with other widows.

Grief has many layers and penetrates our soul much deeper than anticipated; it has no expiration date, and will fester as any untreated wound will do if it is left in the dark. Whenever you can bring the darkness into the light, it loses its power over you. Our questions are similar but our answers are not. It is true that each of us has our own path to walk.

My first question started the entire concept of Widow Rings. What do I do about my rings? I didn't accept any of the usual answers. My ring finger once told the story of my life, and now it told lies. Torn between leaving my rings in place and masquerading as a married woman, or removing my rings therefore denying our history, was not a solution. I needed a different and creative answer. I needed a widow's ring. A ring that finished the story told on my finger, honored the memory of our commitment, that fit next to my wedding rings and spoke to the person I was today, a widow.

My solution was the widow's third ring. It was the answer for me and many others around the world. My mail thanks me, "The ring is perfect," "It's a comfort and it feels right," and "I treasure this." How does it comfort? First you notice the weight lifted from your heart. As it encircles your finger, you feel it hugging. You exhale, you sigh and say "ahhhh." It's the first time you have breathed in a very long time. You smile with the knowledge that it feels right. I am comforted, and my journey is lightened when I minister to another.

*

JULIE MJELVE
Julie's 42-year-old husband Cameron
died by suicide in 2011

The thing that brings me the most comfort is to acknowledge that I hurt, that I grieve, that I'm sad. Trying to hide all that just makes it hurt worse. I feel better when I don't have to hide it. And so, as a means of comfort, I made myself a few different variations of a mourning symbol to wear. It started out with a piece of black craft ribbon that I wrapped around my wedding band. I ended up wearing it for a year, it became a kind of ritual. After the year I was able to get a silicone bracelet with mourning symbols on it, and I wore that for about another year. It's hard to find the words to describe how they bring me comfort, but they really do. Somehow they allow me to express those deep emotions that I can't find words for, and they make me feel like I've stopped hiding, and have acknowledged the pain I'm in. That's what brings me comfort.

*

LISA OWENS
Lisa's 50 year-old husband Greg
died of pancreatic cancer in 2014

I put Greg's T-shirts on my pillows so I can sleep holding on to his favorite shirts. I haven't moved his things; seeing his razor and shampoo are comforting as I start and end my day. Every once in a while, I'll spray Greg's cologne on just so I can smell him throughout the day.

*

MARY POTTER KENYON
Mary's 60-year-old husband David
died of heart failure in 2012

For several weeks after David died, I wore his watch everywhere. Something about the heaviness of it on my wrist brought me comfort, knowing he had worn it every day. Reading books by others who had lost their spouse helped me too. My faith has been a lifeline for me: reading the Bible, praying, spending time with a devotional. Journaling and writing was also very healing. What brings me the most comfort, however, are the tangible signs I have been given: a Neil Diamond CD appearing from nowhere, pennies and dimes everywhere when they weren't there moments before, things like that. I have had so many signs from heaven.

*

NANCY REDMOND
Nancy's 40-year-old husband Kevin
died of a heart attack in 2012

Wearing Kevin's wedding ring is a sure-fire way to bring peace to my heart, as does wearing any of his clothing or sleeping with his "memorial urn" in my hand at night. I find comfort in walking along the Mississippi River (our spot) or looking at photos of happy times, and especially love looking through my wedding photos. I also find comfort in talking about Kevin, and talking to Kevin's spirit which I'm sure has never left my side.

*

MARY LEE ROBINSON
Mary Lee's 63-year-old husband Pat
died from a sudden stroke in 2013

Meditative prayer is almost a daily routine now, and it helps. Reading devotionals and meditations does too. Writing in my journal helped immensely in the beginning and still does, although I don't do it daily any more.

I have a pendant with some charms on it that I wear all the time. It has a cross with a serenity prayer on the back, a tiny woodpecker (they were Pat's favorites), a calla lily with a mustard seed stamen (a gift from my cousin), and both of our birthstones. I also still wear my wedding band and diamond that my dad gave to my mother, guarded top and bottom by two black stone bands. I'm a big believer in mourning jewelry. I think it's a custom that should come back. It calms me quite a lot. I don't feel so alone when I look at it.

*

CAROL SCIBELLI
Carol's 56-year-old husband Jimmy
died from lymphoma in 2006

Right from the beginning I found comfort being amongst Jimmy's clothes, so I parked myself in our closet for long stretches of time. As I sat with his shirts, ties and pants, I babbled to him. I told him what I was going to do that day. I complained about the people who never called, and I praised those who did. This was similar to our real life gossiping, except that my alive husband had no patience for my long drawn out stories. He'd shout in frustration, "Get to the point already!" In our closet I was free to carry on. Sometimes I cried and wore myself out. I dozed off wrapped in his Giants sweatshirt and we both rested in peace. It was preposterous to me that his life had ended and I was alive experiencing the pain of losing him. I couldn't get my head around the fact that he no longer existed. It was actually ridiculous to me that he was gone, and I'd tell him this. I used the word "ridiculous." For at least the first year my mantra was, "How could this happen?"

Staying in the house in Merrick, Long Island where we raised the kids and lived together for twenty-five years was a comfort to me for many years after Jimmy passed away. I expected to die in that house. I never planned to move. I loved having my kids and granddaughter come over to familiar surroundings. I began to host holidays there again and I had a backyard and a finished basement for Skylar, my granddaughter, to play in. I spent three or four days a week in the city and didn't mind the hour-long drive. Long Island was my home, our home. Suddenly, all that changed. Maybe it was sudden, but the catalyst was Hurricane Sandy. The day after the hurricane, the neighbors milled around outside assessing the damage and it jumped out at me that I was the only single woman. Everyone else was either couples or families. I didn't belong there anymore. I started dating at year three, and I never felt one hundred percent comfortable "entertaining" men in the same house I had shared with my husband. In January 2014, I sold the house and moved into Manhattan. It was the best thing I could have done, but I guess the timing was right. Eight years had passed. The same surroundings that brought me comfort all that time felt stale. I needed to breathe new air, even polluted city air.

I took some furniture and keepsakes and knickknacks from the house with me. Each item that Jimmy and I bought together has its own story, a story that now only I remember. It's a lonely feeling to not be able to nod and laugh and slap five about why we bought that lamp. Each piece looks different in my apartment, and I'm glad. Starting fresh was the point. And, now, mostly new mixed with a little old gives me comfort.

*

DIANNE WEST
Dianne's 69-year-old husband Vern
died from multiple myeloma in 2010

I purchased a locket with my husband's photo in it, and I wear it every day. When I travel to new places or I'm attending a concert or a show I know Vern would have loved, I hold that locket in my hand and bring it up to my heart or just rub the smooth surface. I also find heart shaped stones or shells or see heart shaped clouds whenever I travel. These things make me feel that he is right there enjoying the moment with me and are very comforting. I use Vern's shirts as sleepshirts, and I carry his driver's license in my wallet. I love opening up my wallet and seeing it there. He was so happy to be well enough to get his license renewed during the cancer years and his happiness shows in that photo. Vern's ashes are in a beautiful wooden box that I keep on a stand in our family room, along with a few mementos and photos. I had originally thought I would spread his ashes in places that were special to us, but that just hasn't felt right. So he's staying here with me in our home and I've asked our son to mix our ashes together when my time comes. He can then decide whether he wants to spread them, hold onto them, or place them in a cemetery or mausoleum.

Time for me to go now
I won't say goodbye
Look for me in rainbows
Way up in the sky

In the morning sunrise
When all the world is new
Just look for me and love me
As you know I loved you

Time for me to leave you
I won't say goodbye
Look for me in rainbows
High up in the sky

In the evening sunset
When all the world is through,
Just look for me and love me
And I'll be close to you

It won't be forever
The day will come and then
My loving arms will hold you
When we meet again

Time for us to part now
we won't say goodbye
Look for me in rainbows
shining in the sky.

Every waking moment
and all your whole life through
Just look for me and love me
as you know I loved you.

Just wish me to be near you,
And I'll be there with you.

CONN BERNARD

*

CHAPTER SEVENTEEN

OUR SILVER LINING

Even a small star shines in darkness. -FINNISH PROVERB

In the earliest days following loss, the thought that anything good can come from our experience is beyond comprehension. Yet some say there are blessings in everything. Have you discovered a silver lining in your loss?

*

TANYA CAMERON
Tanya's 43-year-old husband Ivor
died of a heart attack in 2013

This doesn't take the pain away, but I am thankful that Ivor passed away at home. It could have been a lot different if he suffered his heart attack behind the wheel of our car with our children in the car, or any other innocent lives that could have been taken away.

*

BONNIE FORSHEY
Bonnie's 43-year-old husband Carl
died in a car accident in 2005

When I lost my husband, I lost my best friend. I had to learn to do things on my own, because he always took care of everything. I had to learn how to survive on my own and I found out just how strong I really was. I had always relied on him for everything; now I do everything on my own.

*

STEPHEN HOCHHAUS
Stephen's 51-year-old wife Kathy
died of soft tissue sarcoma in 2011

The silver lining to my loss has to be when I became aware of who I had become. I realized I could be content living on with the memory and thoughts of my wife still existing inside my very soul. I understood that I could find happiness exploring everything around me as I travel and try new experiences. Early in my grief's journey, I thought I could not live without her. I now realize that I don't have to live without her. Who I am today had become a combination of two people. All that I do and enjoy is a product of the couple I used to be part of. And now when I make decisions about changes in my life, I realize that those decisions are made up of a man who chose things with another person's perspective which had truly evolved into "my" perspective. My tastes have changed. While I was afraid to try new things before I met my wife, I was coaxed into being adventurous because she was. Today, I realize that I am not afraid to fly.

*

MARLISE MAGNA
Marlise's 36-year-old partner Blaine
died by suicide in 2010

A silver lining is that Blaine is at peace now. It has made me a stronger person, and I found my faith and calling in the process.

*

DIANE MCKENZIE-SAPP
Diane's 65-year-old husband Ron
died from renal failure in 2006

My rainbow has been the rings I design for widows. The rings touch and weave their healing magic. The rings are pieces of art with a story to tell. They are my salvation, my journey and the rings are my gift. The rings honor and remember the man who was a part of me. The rings live only because of him. Through these rings. I give to the community of widows and widowers.

Death delivers isolation on an island of darkness. Grief sickens us and we don't know how to heal. In biblical times, lepers had to retreat into the desert and caves to be with their own kind. Until recently everyone with leprosy was forcibly required to live on an island. As a widow I have often felt isolated and quarantined like the lepers of old. The times are changing; in the last ten years lepers are treated with antibiotics, and growing communities of widows combat grief as the monster it is. My Heart of Steel ring pays homage to the inner strength and resolve the young widow must have to raise children and mourn at the same time.

The unexpected blessing is not my rings. The silver lining is the growing internet community supporting widows, extraordinary people who offer hope. Behind each website, widows camp, Facebook page, grief counseling, the pamphlets, books and their authors, the widows rings that are committed to helping widows, there is a strong, determined woman who began as a solitary woman crushed by death. Each battled her demon grief and

*

LISA OWENS
Lisa's 50 year-old husband Greg
died of pancreatic cancer in 2014

I am a better person because of having been loved by such as wonderful man! Greg fought so hard to live; he wanted to live a life that we all take for granted. I appreciate the little things and try really hard to live a positive life, and I don't waste time on negative things. Though some days I fail, I haven't let it break me. I want him to be proud!

*

MARY POTTER KENYON
Mary's 60-year-old husband David
died of heart failure in 2012

I look back to just four years ago, before my husband passed away, and I was a different person. My husband's death was the impetus for a lot of change in my life. The biggest thing was that I got closer to God. That had begun a year before when my mother died, but losing my spouse threw me into a very dark place, and I knew the only way out was through the light that God can bring. I learned how to listen and discern HIS plans for me. I realized I'd never developed a real relationship with Jesus Christ. I was fifty-two years-old and had never studied the Bible.

I was very much an introvert for most of my adult life, but had begun doing workshops and teaching writing classes right before David died. He loved seeing me that way, and told me I was flying. It wasn't easy, but I made a decision to continue flying, even without the wind beneath my wings, in his honor. Now, I speak in churches, hospices, and libraries, and conduct writing classes and workshops. When someone stops me after a speech to tell me what a gifted speaker I am, I want to say, "It isn't me. This gift was given to me." I signed four book contracts in the three years after my husband's death. It feels like he is still watching over me, and saying, "Fly, Mary, fly."

*

NANCY REDMOND
Nancy's 40-year-old husband Kevin
died of a heart attack in 2012

The biggest blessing for me has been the increased spiritual awareness of Kevin's continued presence, not only in my life, but in the lives of my children as well. Other blessings include loving more deeply, cherishing little moments that are, in all actuality the big moments of our lives, and understanding that the last words I ever spoke to my husband -- "I love you" -- are truly my saving grace. The last words I heard him say to me were, "I love you, too." Those words have provided solace and peace to an anxious heart so very many times along this three-plus year journey, and I cherish them and give thanks to God for them always. I have learned that although I don't like this journey all the time (most of the time!), I can and will do this by the grace of God, and when all is said and done, and Kevin meets me at those Gates of Heaven, I pray he says, "Well done, my love!"

*

MARY LEE ROBINSON
Mary Lee's 63-year-old husband Pat
died from a sudden stroke in 2013

My faith has deepened three-fold. I've struggled all my life to find my faithful way, but now I am more certain about it. It has become a crucial part of me. Through it, I found a strength and bravery and talents I never knew I possessed. I'm not at all certain that I had them before, and I know that they are gifts from my higher power. I've culled friends who were not such good friends, as it turns out. In their place, I've made new friends who are worth their weight in gold. I've discovered a life purpose, helping the widowed, and a vision I had no idea about, before Pat's death. All of these kind of bloomed over time. Pat has been gone about two and a half years, at this writing. Each of these gifts arrived soon after, but each continues to take shape and clarity each day.

*

CAROL SCIBELLI
Carol's 56-year-old husband Jimmy
died from lymphoma in 2006

I discovered that I'm capable. I published a memoir called *Poor Widow Me*. This helped launch me as a speaker at widow groups and grief conferences. I call myself the funniest widow on earth, but that's not really a big statement, after all, most widows are grumpy. My self-esteem soars each time I engage widows and make them laugh. I believe I earned the respect of my kids and Skylar, my granddaughter. They see I'm strong and independent. This may influence them to embrace an emotionally healthy attitude, too.

After Jimmy died, my relationship with my nephew Carlo Scibelli became the silver lining to beat all others. He passed away on January 9, 2015. This a shortened blog I wrote.

NOT EVERYONE HAS A CHUCKLES

Fifty years ago Jimmy strutted into our eighth grade homeroom and announced, "I'm an uncle!" Five years later little Chuckie was a perfect specimen to practice our parenting skills on. He wasn't fully formed and we weren't fully invested. We would take Chuckie to amusement parks and boat rides and back to my tiny apartment in Queens to let him chase around my poor pet rabbit.

We married, had a daughter and a son and because Chuckie looked so much like Jimmy, both Jacki and Dougie as babies were easily soothed by him. They snuggled into his pillow-top tummy and cooed as this chubby teenager rocked them and sang "When the moon hits your eye like a big pizza pie, it's amour." Pizza was a big event in Chuck's life, along with White Castle belly bombs and Carvel ice cream. Not a tidy sort of guy, it was easy to tell what he had for lunch because he was wearing it. Food and family, in that order, was most important to him until he fell in love with singing. He chose opera, although he would say, "Opera chose me." We made fun of how pretentious that was, especially from a man with marinara sauce on his shirt.

Our family fell into calling him Chuckles. He was funny and loud and silly - a Chuckles. Professionally he changed his name to Carlo figuring a tenor called Chuckles Pavarotti might not be taken seriously. He married, had a son, got divorced and traveled the world singing to huge audiences. In between gigs when he wasn't on the West Coast with his son and his mom, he stayed with us. He literally sang for his supper and he made it, too. His specialties were anything heavy and Italian that could be sopped up with bread. We had barbeques with friends, and everyone knew Chuck. Every gathering with him was a party. Life was good, until it wasn't.

In April 2006, Jimmy died. Chuckie swooped in and we became locked together in grief. My house was his home. We ate muffin tops for breakfast and read our horoscopes aloud. He came up with funny quips, and I stole them to post on Facebook. I joked that when he sang in the shower, I should open the window and charge admission. When I ventured out, Chuckie was my plus one. At home he helped me with my computer and scream "How could you not remember your password?" Then, he made me dinner. He'd see Jimmy. I'd come home to "You just missed him. He doesn't like the color you painted the kitchen." I'd tell him "That's because you don't."

He sang Nessun Dorma at my sixtieth birthday party, and that night my friends and family called him Carlo. He nicknamed my dog Tony Baloney, and promised that if anything happened to me, he would take care of him. We stayed at the house during Hurricane Sandy even though we were ordered to evacuate. After a houseboat landed in my backyard, we took off for Atlantic City. After that, I didn't feel I belonged in the suburbs anymore. He said "It's like eating leftovers." I sold the house. We each got our own place in Manhattan. Chuckie and I un-clung, if that's a word, to a healthy emotional dependency, if that's such a thing.

I was with my boyfriend, Mickey, now and they played golf and smoked cigars...a new chapter. Chuck was with me and my kids and granddaughters for most holidays, but this Christmas he went to California to be with his mom, his son, and nieces. My daughter called him for his lasagna recipe. Back in New York, right after the New Year, Chuck had stomach pains and brought himself to the emergency room. It was pancreatitis. He turned fifty on January 5, 2015, and died four days later. He was surrounded by love, but only a fraction of the love he gave.

Today I remembered what my granddaughter Skylar used to say, "We're lucky. Not everyone has a Chuckles."

*

DIANNE WEST
Dianne's 69-year-old husband Vern
died from multiple myeloma in 2010

I feel I have found my life's purpose because of my loss – at least for this last stage of my life. I would never have needed to find Widowed Village if not for Vern's death. I would never have been searching for a place to fill the void in my life and in my heart that Brave Girls Club has given me, if not for Vern's death. Finding those two amazing online communities not only saved me from being consumed by my grief, they have opened up a whole new path of service for me. Helping others navigate this difficult widowed road has served as therapy for me. I've found that if I am listening, hearing, assisting others it helps me to shift the focus off myself and my loss. It doesn't stop me from missing Vern or the life I wish I were leading now, but it feels like I'm honoring him with this service. The wonderful years we had together, caring for him during those hard cancer years, losing him all made me who I am today. I would give it all up if it would bring Vern back, but I have believed from the very beginning that I need to live my life in a way that honors him. Serving the widowed community through my volunteer work with Soaring Spirits and my widow mentoring in Brave Girl University definitely honors him.

CHAPTER EIGHTEEN

OUR HOPE

Be like the birds, sing after every storm.

-BETH MENDE CONNY

Hope is the fuel that propels us forward, urges us to get out of bed each morning. It is the promise that tomorrow will be better than today. Is hope possible in the aftermath of loss? If so, where do we find it?

*

TANYA CAMERON
Tanya's 43-year-old husband Ivor
died of a heart attack in 2013

Hope for me is just trying to be the best mum I can, and seeing that my boys grow up to be happy and fine responsible young men.

*

JONATHAN DEAN
Jonathan's 36-year-old wife Cara
died of double pneumonia in 2010

I hope I will continue to help those less fortunate for a long time.

*

BONNIE FORSHEY
Bonnie's 43-year-old husband Carl
died in a car accident in 2005

I know that things can always get worse. We have to make the best out of every situation and keep on moving forward. We are so much stronger than we give ourselves credit for.

*

STEPHEN HOCHHAUS
Stephen's 51-year-old wife Kathy
died of soft tissue sarcoma in 2011

Hope is to me basically the fantasy of "what if?" Hope is the desire for something that has yet to come. One could say that they hope the pain will end when they are so grieving. They may say hope is to be reunited once again with their loved one. What I see is that hope is a desire that keeps me going. It makes me work toward that desire if I could effect it coming true. When I was younger, I used to think that I was in control and hope was meaningless because I could do anything I wanted. Death has a way of making you realize that you are not and never were in control. Hope is the very essence of optimism.

*

MARLISE MAGNA
Marlise's 36-year-old partner Blaine
died by suicide in 2010

The Bible states there is ALWAYS hope, faith and love. Hope to me means things can only get better and that this, too, shall pass.

*

DIANE MCKENZIE-SAPP
Diane's 65-year-old husband Ron
died from renal failure in 2006

I hope my rings change the way we grieve. They answered the question, "What do I do about my rings?" I hope to heal broken hearts, ease the transition, and give widows an identity.

We are invisible because we are unconnected individuals. I hoped the widow ring united individual widows as a group co-sharing grief and crushing loss. I hoped the rings could heal broken hearts, transforming widows to be a visible and significant group that deserves respect. I hoped for meaning because "widows matter." We erect tombstones and memorials, small crosses dot the roadsides and tattoos are forever inked into skin. Individually we remember but still remain invisible.

The world does not "see" widows. They don't want to KNOW a widow. Widows remain invisible and insignificant to the world and that needs to change. We need to be the change we wish to see. Social media gives you a voice - use this voice. Call out government, business and society, our numbers are significant and until now we have accepted the second class status, but no more. My experience in being invisible: The widow's ring concept was rebuffed by the jewelry industry as "very little profit to be made." QVC and HSN said their audience does not need this product. Oprah and Ellen did not answer emails. Shark Tank does not see widows as marketing opportunities. Amazon has no category. Jewelry shops dismissed the market as insignificant. Funeral directors, flower shops, and department stores didn't want a widow's inventory.

What is my hope? Hope is the vision of an achievement, supposedly making a better tomorrow. My deepest hope is that someday there will be a place just to support grieving new widows. Wouldn't it be marvelous to walk into the Ministry of Widowed? As you enter you are greeted by sympathetic eyes and refreshments. Young children can play in the toy room with a children's grief counselor nearby while you register a "change of status." All you need to do and know is in the Ministry's Data Base. Registering you the first time and last time as you check off the box that says [ ] widow.

All is accessible in the one-stop Ministry office.

- Each death certificate is transmitted to the corporations who require them
- Banking requirements and funds are allotted immediately to a new personal account
- Insurance company is data searched and claims are initiated
- IRAs, bonds, certificates and company stock plans are consolidated and transferred
- Bills that are required to be paid by the estate are listed by importance
- Bills that are requested and not mandatory are sent a "Quit Pestering Me" notice
- Apply and Fast Track for Financial Support i.e. rent subsidy, food stamps, medical insurance
- The Department of Motor Vehicles title and registration are automatically sent out
- May join the League of Widowed Voters to ensure your rights and reasonable taxes
- Federal 1040 adds [ ] Widow a separate taxpayer status and removes [ ] Single

- Your interests are noted and with permission email invitations from similar interest groups
- You are added to the official Federal DO NOT CALL LIST
- A legal team will help with bills, wills, estates and name changes if you desire
- Link with the Home and Automotive Co-Operative For Widows:
    o Automotive team safety checks and maintains your vehicle for a small fee
    o GPS and Emergency Road Service are scheduled for your automobile
    o Volunteer list to winterize your home, shovel snow and make repairs or plumbing
    o The gas and electric company and water company offer a monthly subsidy
    o The phone company and the cable company offer special subscription rates
    o The mortgage is amortized with new lower payments at lower rate
- Social and Personal:
    o Grief counseling provided that does not rush you to get over "your illness"
    o Your discount code for a widow's ring is validated
    o You schedule Facebook time with other widows who have met challenges
    o Volunteer sitters donate several hours a week for grocery shopping, classes or Christmas gifts
    o Massage, reiki, herbal tonics and acupuncture is offered free or minimal rates
    o Wednesdays are "Widows Day" and the restaurants, movies, nail salons and carry outs offer discounts
    o Enrollment of children in the after school programs allowing you to continue to work full time

- o Free training for skilled employment is offered by the community college
- o Application to Workplace Bereavement Program funds up to three months of leave to settle your affairs and adjust
- o Follow up appointments with previously widowed counselors to continue transition support

You walk out of the Ministry of Widows (MOW) feeling hopeful and not hopeless, alone, or invisible. You take a deep breath and feel empowered to face tomorrow. All the confusing post funeral details are sorted and prepared for in one meeting. As a society we fund groups with less need. I will continue to hope for the improbable.

*

JULIE MJELVE
Julie's 42-year-old husband Cameron
died by suicide in 2011

My definition of hope lies in the future. My life, and who I am is not defined by any one singe act in the past or the present. Hope, for me, is that there's always a chance for change, for something amazing to happen. I look at the smiles on my children's faces, and know that there is a future, a future filled with hope.

*

LISA OWENS
Lisa's 50 year-old husband Greg
died of pancreatic cancer in 2014

Hope is knowing that one day I will see my beautiful husband again, hold him in my arms and know we will never part.

*

MARY POTTER KENYON
Mary's 60-year-old husband David
died of heart failure in 2012

Knowing there is far more to life than what we see here on earth, that there is meaning in everything, and knowing that we will see our loved ones again. To me, that is hope.

*

NANCY REDMOND
Nancy's 40-year-old husband Kevin
died of a heart attack in 2012

Hope for me is living my life in such a way that I would make Kevin proud of me, and in such a way that I'd want Kevin to carry on with his life if the situation were reversed. Hope is getting up each morning and wanting to make the best of each day so that I can fulfill God's plan for my life. Hope is knowing when I leave this earthly existence, I will be reunited with my husband, my love, and will be with him for all eternity. Hope is knowing the sun will come out after the storm. Hope is knowing that after even the darkest, coldest winter, spring and sunshine will return.

*

MARY LEE ROBINSON
Mary Lee's 63-year-old husband Pat
died from a sudden stroke in 2013

Hope for me is to leave the world a better place for the widowed. I would like to educate the non-grieving world to better understand and support us. I would also like to establish a nationwide network of social clubs for widows and widowers. I want them to be a safe vehicle for "stepping back into the sunshine" and re-establishing a social life, and form new friendships, a place to meet companion travelers on the healing road. My personal experience opened my eyes about how grievers are treated in our culture. I'd like to do something about that, and have several projects underway to further that healing and education.

*

CAROL SCIBELLI
Carol's 56-year-old husband Jimmy
died from lymphoma in 2006

Google lists these following words as synonyms for hope: chance, expectation, likelihood, confidence, expectation, optimism, and anticipation. I would have agreed with that slanted list before my husband died and before I lived through other devastating losses. These days, hope to me means wishing. Wishing holds no magic power. It's the outcome I desire. I'm not negative. I'm just no longer positive. It's a happy surprise when life goes the right way.

*

KRISTI SMITH
Kristi's 48-year-old husband Michael
died from cardiac arrest in 2011

What is my definition of hope? If you would have asked me a couple of years ago how to define hope I would have told you that hope was a whimsical word that well-meaning people threw around. To me, hope was like a cheap-suited Santa tossing candy from atop his sleigh on Thanksgiving Day. Hope was in the sugar candies that were wrapped in brightly colored foil that we scooped up off of the pavement and popped into our mouths. Oh, there was the initial short term rush of pure sweetness, but it was quickly followed by the inevitable and more powerful sugar crash.

To me, hope was a yoyo ride of ups and downs. It was true that hope could make people feel good for a little while, but it had no sustaining power. Just like those tasty sweets from the local street parade, hope could not provide any lasting value to my life. Hope was a cheap carnival trick that amused adults and persuaded children to believe in fairy tales. I know I sound cynical, but hope was an illusion; a mirage. Only fools and desperate people would fall for hope… and then only because it was all they had to fall back on. Hope was a folk legend like some elusive prize-winning fish that never really existed, but still got men up at the crack of dawn in search of it. To me hope was a waste of time and money; like spending hard earned cash to buy a "one chance in a million" lottery ticket. Personally, I have never known anyone who won the grand lotto, but I have known plenty of people who have won the small prizes just often enough to keep them coming back to buy more tickets. Scratching for hope. Pathetic.

When my husband died was a time when I could have lost all hope. But to tell you the truth, it was precisely the moment when I found hope. It was strange standing there while everything I ever believed in was washed away in the blink of an eye and all I had ever known as secure, solid, and predictable vanished. Hope was all that I had left. No longer a mirage or trick of the eye, hope stood directly in front of me. Hope was not like a fly-by-night salesman like I had expected. Hope was here and it was not going anywhere else. Hope was as forever as the tattoo on my back. Hope could be as light as the breeze on my neck or as heavy as the heartache I carried. There are still days when hope surrounds me like a well-worn quilt with soft, frayed edges to comfort me in my darkest moments. I have no proof of this hope. No evidence. No x-ray or test result or lab report. I can't show hope to you. All I know is that hope is what gets me out of bed in the morning, and hope is what allows to sleep at night. Hope is tangible, palatable, and unending. Hope provides energy to help me face the day-to-day challenges. I would not last a minute without hope. I will say it plain: without hope I am a goner. Done. Cooked. Fried. Flambéed.

So if you ask me how to define hope now, I would tell you differently. Hope isn't a flimsy card trick. Hope is the real-est thing I know. Hope has legs and weight, and stands in the center of everything there is. Hope is solid and predictable and sure. Hope is lasting. Hope is eternal. Hope gives me peace in the middle of the storm, and is the anchor that keeps me from getting lost at sea.

Hope stabilizes me when I have no strength. Hope is the guiding light that leads me onward and keeps me on the path. Hope never deceives me, but always points to what is true and good and lovely. Hope teaches me to wait patiently and ask kindly and forgive quickly. Many people have asked me, "After what you have gone through, what is the most important message you want to share with people?" And I reply, "Hope."

What is my definition of hope? Hope is the source of every living thing, and we cannot live without it. Hope feeds our souls and lifts our spirits. Hope contains everything that we need to endure, triumph, and prevail. Hope is powerful. Hope is as important as the breath we breathe. Without hope, we would surely die. I pray you will find hope. Enough hope for every breath. Hope on every step. Hope around every corner. What is hope? Hope is not the compass to guide us home, hope is home.

*

DIANNE WEST
Dianne's 69-year-old husband Vern
died from multiple myeloma in 2010

Hope is what allows me to get up each morning and face a new day with gratitude and peace, trusting that I am where I am supposed to be. I didn't feel this way early in my loss, but my faith sustained me even then. Hope and faith are intertwined for me – along with love. I believe I will see Vern again one day, and how I live my life now makes a difference. Hope is the belief that I am here for a purpose, that God has a plan for me now that I am alone, and I just need to be still and listen, knowing that my sweet Vern's spirit is with me always.

*

CHAPTER NINETEEN

OUR JOURNEY

Be soft. Do not let the world make you hard. Do not let
the pain make you hate. Do not let bitterness steal your
sweetness.   -KURT VONNEGUT

Every journey through loss is as unique as our fingerprint, for we
experience life through different filters. Although we may not see
anyone else on the path, we are never truly alone for more walk
behind, beside, and in front of us. In this chapter, writers answer
the final question: What would you like the world to know about
your grief journey?

*

TANYA CAMERON
Tanya's 43-year-old husband Ivor
died of a heart attack in 2013

No matter what, you can get through this. It is not an easy
journey, and nothing can prepare you for it. Everyone grieves
differently and you do it how you feel you need to. The people who
tell you to get over it, well you don't need those people in your life.
Please seek professional help if you need to, and join a group to talk
to others who have been where you now are. Whether it's a social
media site or face-to-face in a group, please remember that you are
not alone. Take comfort in the people around you.

*

JONATHAN DEAN
Jonathan's 36-year-old wife Cara
died of double pneumonia in 2010

That I want to be accepted with the life I lead now and not with the life I had before.

*

BONNIE FORSHEY
Bonnie's 43-year-old husband Carl
died in a car accident in 2005

I have had so much grief in my life and have survived. At times I wanted to give up, even attempted suicide, but it just wasn't my time to go. I now have been blessed with two grandsons that I adore. Life has new meaning for me.

*

STEPHEN HOCHHAUS
Stephen's 51-year-old wife Kathy
died of soft tissue sarcoma in 2011

I would like the world to know every emotion and every achievement I have experienced in the last four and a half years of my grief's journey. I would like it to read as a book describing the rise of a man who lost his reason for living, yet crawled up from despair to live again. For the world needs to see how the loss of such a deep love does not have to be an end, but a beginning.

The pain of loss is caused by love itself. We risk pain by allowing our love to be so deep. Once I accepted that truth, I could begin finding ways to honor my wife by living on. What I wish is for others to see that I am still standing and still very much in love. Life is for now and death is eternal. I will see her once again. All in good time.

*

MARLISE MAGNA
Marlise's 36-year-old partner Blaine
died by suicide in 2010

I've learned to take things slowly - ten minutes at a time if I must. Even though at times it feels like there is no hope and your life is over, time does heal. Also, love is everything and a small smile or act of kindness helps you feel better. Most of all, have no expectations. Hope for the best, expect the worst, and you will end up somewhere in between. Life goes on.

*

DIANE MCKENZIE-SAPP
Diane's 65-year-old husband Ron
died from renal failure in 2006

Once I became a widow, my journey with grief and my path has been crystal clear, it was to design a ring just for widows. As an artist, I was to create a widow symbol that showed wordlessly who she was and her innermost emotions. I nailed it. I built the best widow's ring ever. They say build a better mousetrap and the world will beat a path to your door. I am guessing the first mousetrap builder had no world, no path and no door. It is impossible to search for something that you do not know exists. My designs are for widows and widowers until mothers and daughters claim the broken hearts as their own. A broken heart is the universal and singular pain felt by everyone death has touched. More designs were created that appeal not only to widows and widowers but to anyone struggling with grief. Below is the "Widows Rings and Expressions Of Grief" elevator speech as presented to Shark Tank on television.

"Hello. I am Diane, owner of Expressions of Grief by Diane. My website is ExpressionsOfGrief.com. I am a widow, but you can't tell from looking at me, UNLESS you notice my widow's ring, I design widows rings because they need to BE. In today's world these rings answer the widow's question: "What do I do about my rings?" I would like to change how we grieve. Widows should be seen and heard. The engagement and wedding rings on your ring finger tell the story of your life. And the fact that you didn't die; just half of you died. Instead of hiding your feelings under a mask of "I'm fine" simply show your heart is broken. People treat you as if you are invisible and if you take off your wedding rings, you become invisible. My rings are a part of a new ritual that gives a face to the grieving. Remove your ring? No, you add a third ring: a widow's ring, to tell the entire story. Your broken heart should be a visible and touchable symbol of your unending love. I design wearable art that tells a story. Within the designs of my mourning rings, each has a story to tell. Listen with your broken heart.

- The Broken Heart. Teardrops form the broken heart of this patented setting.
- The Broken Heart Legacy set.
- The Widows Legacy set.
- The Widow's Third Ring. Adding a third ring finishes the story told on your finger.
- The Serenity Prayer- Accept /Change Courage and Wisdom inside a black mourning band.
- Spinning ALWAYS IN MY HEART & SOUL supports movement while still connected.
- Spinning Serenity Prayer. This ring supports acceptance and change.
- The Heart Of Steel. This ring supports the young widow with children.
- Forget-Me-Knot. This ring remembers grandparents and others with a steel string on your finger.
- Twin Hearts. This design remembers soul mates and kindred spirts.
- Dark Journey. This ring represents the unending dark journey path of grief.

- Rainbow Footprints. Shows hope and remembers those who supported us.
- Fallen Heroes. This ring is a patriotic half-mast ring for fallen heroes from the military, police, fire.

The designs appeal not only to widows and widowers but mothers, daughters, sons and grandchildren. My market is everyone who death has marked with a broken heart. Over the past four years, I have sent over one thousand rings all over the world. I was told by the bereaved that their precious ring slowed their tears, saved their sanity and gave them peace. My passion is Expression of Grief and is only a hobby, with no profits. I reinvest everything into the design and production of new rings. I take no salary and have no employees. I work from my computer, and the inventory is on my back porch. Product awareness and marketing are not this artist's strengths. I need business people to make a business from a widow's dream, so all the world will know there is a special place just for grieving souls. Which shark can nurture my legacy into the next century?"

Needless to say, you won't be seeing me on Shark Tank. I didn't get a callback or an invitation. I am not wrong; they missed an opportunity. My only solace is the parable paraphrased, "It is harder for a camel to fit through the eye of a needle, than it is for a rich man to enter the Gates of Heaven.

*

JULIE MJELVE
Julie's 42-year-old husband Cameron
died by suicide in 2011

I would like the world to know first and foremost that grief is indeed a journey. It is not a one-time event, it is something I will carry with me for the rest of my life. While it will move from the foreground to the background, it will still be there. It's not something I will get over, and most certainly not in two to three weeks. I would like the world to know that the initial intense grief lasts more like two to three years. I would like the world to know that this is okay, normal, expected. I would like the world to know that my grief journey is about remembering my loved one, not trying to come to the point where I've pushed him out of my mind to the point where I've pushed them out of existence. My loved one lived, and their existence doesn't end because their physical life ended. I loved my loved one, so please, please, allow me to continue to express my love for them by allowing me to grieve, and expecting me to grieve.

*

LISA OWENS

Lisa's 50 year-old husband Greg
died of pancreatic cancer in 2014

I want people to know to take it one moment at a time until it becomes hours and then days; you're a lot tougher than you think, and life is a blessing! Hold on tight to family and friends! You will never get over it! You will always have a piece of your puzzle missing, but you look at the whole puzzle and see the beauty of your life!

*

MARY POTTER KENYON

Mary's 60-year-old husband David
died of heart failure in 2012

I think back to those awful first months full of terrible pain and anguish, and I want those who are beginning their grief journey to know that they will not always feel that way. We would die, too, if we did. Yes, grief can still hit with a vengeance. It sideswipes us with its fury, but we don't have to live with that agonizing pain forever. We must not waste that pain, either. Use it. Reach out to others. Take someone's hand. Give a hug. Write a card or note to someone else who is in pain. I am a different person than I was. I like who I have become. It took a lot of darkness to bring me into the light. I think about what someone said to me recently, after several weeks of extra stress when I was holding down two jobs and spending my weekends promoting a new book. I burst into tears when they asked how I was doing. Later, they e-mailed me, professing concern. "You need to get professional help," they wrote. "Your grief is not healthy. It is ruining your life." I had to laugh; I am a productive woman with a job, four books out, speaking all over my state, and I'm not allowed to cry once in a while? Particularly after four hellish weeks of job stress? How dare anyone judge us on our grief! This is MY journey, and if I want to cry about being a single parent nearly four years after my husband dies, then by golly, I'm going to cry.

*

NANCY REDMOND
Nancy's 40-year-old husband Kevin
died of a heart attack in 2012

I would like the world to know how important it is to not sweat the small stuff, and most of what we allow to get to us in this life is just that -- small stuff. I would like everyone to know the implications and ramifications of words spoken in anger. These words can be the last your loved one ever hears and, likewise, loving words can also be the last words ever shared between you. I would like the world to know how proud I am of the progress I've made toward being whole again; it's a long, lonely journey and I stand proud when I look back at how far I've come. I would like the world to know that I have chosen LOVE, rather than resentment or anger over Kevin's death, and I have chosen to carry on and be the best mom, grandma, and ME I can be.

*

MARY LEE ROBINSON
Mary Lee's 63-year-old husband Pat
died from a sudden stroke in 2013

While death was no stranger in my own family life, this most personal and intimate of losses brought with it a devastation and pain I could never have come close to fathoming before. A friend and fellow widow said something a while back that resonated with me. "Widowhood has led me to discover the coolness of friends and the kindness of strangers." It's true. The people I counted on, the people I was just certain would be there for me, were not. One woman in my community even went out of her way to be cruel, spreading nasty rumors about the decisions I had to make about Pat's life support. Other people, the people who are worth knowing, have been a godsend. There are a bunch of them. One in particular is a special friend and a sister-in-arms. She is my collaborator-in-chief on my widow projects. Without the latter group, I may well have followed Pat into an early demise. Onlookers need to know that even the smallest of kind gestures matter. They can make an enormous impact and foster healing in ways the givers may not ever hear, but they do matter. Do those small gestures, even when you don't know what to do. Do them even when you don't feel like doing them. They are important. Someday, someone may return the favor.

*

CAROL SCIBELLI
Carol's 56-year-old husband Jimmy
died from lymphoma in 2006

I wanted my old life back for the longest time. I didn't expect Jimmy to pop in and say, "Hi, hon. What's for dinner?" Still, I ached for familiarity. This yearning for normalcy was constantly countered with, "Your normal doesn't exist anymore. Now, you must accept your new normal." I detested that expression.

I tried two bereavement groups at four months. I left each one after three sessions. It was beyond upsetting for me to see so much pain and hear horrible stories, all with an awful ending. Eventually, after three years and private bereavement therapy beginning at eight months, I grasped that "new normal" did define my life. I relaxed. I accepted that I was a widow. I began to look more to my future than to our past. Three years was a breakthrough time for me.

Mean Jean was my nickname for my bereavement shrink because she was tough. I joked with friends that she must have gone to the "snap out of it school for shrinks." She was not the type to allow me to lie on the couch and suck my thumb. Her no-nonsense approach worked for me because every so often she tossed me a gem. Once she told me, "When women remarry, often they go to the cemetery to ask permission." I said, "I can understand that." She laughed, "It makes sense to you to ask permission from a dead man? Just for the record, Sweetie, none of the husbands ever say no."

I got it. My life was my own. I didn't have to lie to myself; Jimmy would want me to buy that leather jacket. And I know he'd be thrilled when I start dating. Reluctantly, coupled with a tinge of exhilaration, I signed up for several dating sites. Shopping for a man online was safe. I could look and not have to worry about what to say, what to wear. At first I was only attracted to men who looked like Jimmy. There was Asian Jimmy, Black Jimmy, Spanish Jimmy and Jewish Jimmy. Writing my profile forced me to articulate who I am and what kind of man and relationship I was looking for. Again, Mean Jean's brutal honesty both annoyed and helped me. "When you begin to date, you will emotionally pick up at the age that you left off when you were last dating. In your case, eighteen." I'd be eighteen again? No. I refused to accept that I had the emotions of an eighteen year-old in the body of a sixty year-old. It certainly wouldn't be necessary to swat away suitors with that combo. I argued with Mean Jean. "I've been out in the world for a lot more than eighteen years. I know how to talk to people. And,

I'm funny. Men like funny." "Apples and oranges, Sweetie Pie, when it comes to seducing and being seduced. Flirting is an art. And did you ever stop to think that when a man says he's looking for a woman with a sense of humor, he might mean someone to laugh at his jokes?" She had me there. I was brought up in an era where girls let the guy win at checkers. Will this boloney be my new dance with someone?

Happily, MJ was wrong. I met a man who I am with to this day; he loves laughing at my silliness, and loves when I laugh at his. Mickey is wonderful and couldn't be more different than Jimmy in looks and in personality. Of course, I am different now, too. I often wonder how Jimmy and I would mesh if he came back. I am happy these days, not only because of the people in my life; I am content inside. Of course, I'm fortunate to share my life with a good man, have kind children and three sweet, fun-loving granddaughters. My close friends and one special nephew stayed with me through the rough times and helped me to be resilient.

I learned that there is nothing more important than being gracious, kind and loving. Always appreciate and celebrate the good occasions. If we hold on to our sense of humor, there is life after death. Living is not for wimps.

*

DIANNE WEST
Dianne's 69-year-old husband Vern
died from multiple myeloma in 2010

I have not shared my deep grief openly with friends and family. They have believed from the start that I am incredibly strong, and have sailed through my grief with hardly a scar. Oh, if that were only true. I wrote somewhat truthfully in my blog over these past five years, but always tempered my words with an expression of hope, regardless of how I was actually feeling. I write for others, for those in my cancer caregiver world who will follow me one day, and I want to make sure they see hope threaded throughout my grief. I don't regret that. I can't change that; it's who I am. But for those who may read my words in the future, I hope they will recognize what they see in their friends may not be the whole story. That they will reach out to those who are grieving, not turn away. That they will sit with them, embrace their grief, hear their unspoken words, love them.

I would love for those not widowed to truly understand that they are not promised tomorrow … that this life I'm living could be theirs … will be theirs … one day. We don't deal well with death here in North America. It's feared. It's uncomfortable. It's not spoken about. We tend to want to "fix" the person who is grieving so they can return to who they were before. And that is just not possible. We are forever changed by our loss.

So my hope is that we learn to accept that death is a part of life for all living things. And with that knowledge, that we find moments each day to cherish our loved ones, spend time doing the important things together, not the daily grind things our current culture portrays as being important – but those little precious moments of just being with the ones you love. May you live each day as if it is your last, sharing your love with friends and family openly, saying kind words, doing kind deeds, seeing the beauty that is present everywhere, showing compassion to your fellow humans. It's the only way to truly live until we die.

My great hope is to laugh as much as I cry;
to get my work done and try to love somebody and
have the courage to accept the love in return.
MAYA ANGELOU

*

CHAPTER TWENTY

FINDING THE SUNRISE

One night in my own journey, I had one of *those* dreams: a vivid nightmare that stays with you. I was running westward in a frantic attempt to catch the setting sun as it descended below the horizon. Rapidly advancing from behind was nightfall; foreboding and frightening, it was a pitch black abyss. And it was coming directly for me. I ran desperately, as fast as my legs could go, toward the sunset, but my attempt was futile; it descended below the horizon, out of my reach. Oh, the looming nightfall was terrifying! But it was clear that if I wanted to ever see the sun again, I had to stop running west and, instead, turn around and walk east to begin my journey through the great murky abyss, the nightfall of grief. For just as there would be no rainbow without the rain, the sun only rises on the other side of night. The message was clear: it was futile to avoid my grief; I had to allow it to swallow me whole. Then, and only then, would I find my way through it and out the other side.

I remember reading in a bereavement book that if we don't allow ourselves to experience the full scope of the journey, it will come back to bite us. I couldn't fathom how it could get any worse, but I knew I didn't want to test that theory. So I gave in and allowed my grief to swallow me whole. I allowed myself to wail on the my daughter's bedroom floor. I penned my deep emotions, regardless of who might read it. I created a national radio show to openly and candidly discuss our journeys with anyone who wanted to call in. And I allowed myself to sink to the bottom of the fiery pits of hell. This, in turn, lit a fire under me, so to speak, to find a way out.

Today, I'm often asked how I manage my grief so well. Some assume that because I have found peace and joy, I'm simply avoiding my grief. Others believe that because I work in the bereavement field, I'm wallowing in self-pity. Well, which is it?

Neither. I will miss my child with every breath I take. Just like you, I will always have my moments: the painful holidays, birthdays, death anniversaries, a song or smell that evokes an unexpected memory. But I have also found purpose, beauty and joy again. It takes hard work and determination to overcome profound grief, and it also takes the ability to let go and succumb to the journey. Do not be afraid of the tears, sorrow, and heartbreak; they are a natural reaction, and are imperative to your healing.

As you walk your own path, avail yourself to whatever bereavement tools that ease your discomfort, for each one was created by someone who walked in your shoes and understands the heartache. While there are many wonderful bereavement resources available, what brings comfort to one person might irritate the next. Bereavement tools are not one-size-fits-all, so if one tool doesn't work, find another.

Lastly, grief is not something we get "over," like a mountain. Rather, it is something we get "through," like the rapids of Niagara Falls. Without the kayak and paddle. And plenty of falls. But it's also survivable. And if others had survived this wretched journey, why not me? And why not you?

On the following pages are the baby steps I took to put hell in my rearview mirror. They took great effort at first, and lots of patience. But like any dedicated routine, it got easier over time, and the reward of finding balance in my life was worth every step.

1. VALIDATING OUR EMOTIONS

The first step is to validate your emotions. When we talk about our deep heartbreak, we aren't ruminating in our sorrow or feeling sorry for ourselves. By discussing it, we are actually processing it. If we aren't allowed to process it, then it becomes silent grief. Silent grief is deadly grief.

Find a friend who will patiently listen while you discuss your loss for fifteen minutes every day. Set the timer, and ask them not to say anything during those fifteen minutes. Explain that it is important for you to just ramble without interruption, guidance, or judgment. You need not have the same listener each time, but practice this step every day.

2. COMPASSIONATE THOUGHTS

Find yourself a quiet spot. It can be your favorite chair, in your car, in your office, or even in your garden. Then clear your head and for five minutes think nothing but compassionate thoughts about yourself. Not your spouse, not your children, not your coworkers, but yourself.

Having trouble? Fill in the blanks below, and then give yourself permission to really validate those positive qualities. Do this every day.

I have a _____

Example: good heart, gentle soul, witty personality

I make a _____

Example: good lasagna, potato salad, scrapbook, quilt

I'm a good_____

Example: friend, gardener, knitter, painter, poem writer

People would say I'm _____

Example: funny, kind, smart, gentle, generous, humble, creative

3. TENDER LOVING CARE

While grieving, it is important to consider yourself in the intensive care unit of Grief United Hospital, and treat accordingly. How would nurses treat you if you were their patient in the ICU? They would be compassionate, gentle, and allow for plenty of rest. That is exactly how you should treat yourself. Also, consider soothing your physical self with TLC as an attentive way to honor your emotional pain. This doesn't mean you have to book an expensive massage. If wearing fuzzy blue socks offers a smidgen of comfort, then wear them unabashedly. If whipped cream on your cocoa offers a morsel of pleasure, then indulge unapologetically.

Treating our five senses to anything that offers a perception of delight might not erase the emotional heartache, but it will offer a reminder that not all pleasure is lost. List five ways you can offer yourself tender loving care, and then incorporate at least three into your day, every day. With practice, the awareness of delight eventually becomes effortless, and is an important step toward regaining joy.

TLC suggestions:

- Shower or bathe with a lovely scented soap
- Soak in a warm tub with Epsom salts or a splash of bath oil
- Wear a pair of extra soft socks
- Light a fragrant candle
- Listen to relaxing music
- Apply a rich lotion to your skin before bed
- Indulge in a few bites of your favorite treat
- Enjoy a mug of your favorite soothing herbal tea
- Add whipped cream to a steaming mug of cocoa
- _____
- _____
- _____
- _____

4. SEE THE BEAUTY

Listening to the birds outside my bedroom window every morning was something I had loved since childhood. But when Aly died, I found myself deaf and blind to the beauty around me. My world had become colorless and silent. On one particular morning as I struggled to get out of bed, I halfheartedly noticed the birds chirping outside my bedroom window. My heart sank as I realized that they had been chirping all along, but I was now deaf to their morning melody. Panic set in as I concluded that I would never enjoy life's beauty ever again. Briefly entertaining suicide to escape the profound pain, I quickly ruled it out. My family had been through so much already, I couldn't dump further pain on them. But in order to survive the heartbreak, I had to find a way to allow beauty back into my life.

So on that particular morning as I lay in bed, I forced myself to listen and really *hear* the birds. Every morning from that point forward, I repeated that same exercise. With persistent practice, it became easier and then eventually effortless to appreciate the birds' chirping and singsongs. Glorious beauty and sounds have once again returned to my world.

Profound grief can appear to rob our world of all beauty. Yet the truth is, and despite our suffering, beauty continues to surround us. The birds continue to sing, flowers continue to bloom, the surf continues to ebb and flow. Reconnecting to our surroundings helps us to reintegrate back into our environment.

Begin by acknowledging one small pleasantry each day. Perhaps your ears register the sound of singing birds. Or you catch the faint scent of warm cookies as you walk past a bakery. Or notice the sun's illumination of a nearby red rosebush. Give yourself permission to notice one pleasantry, and allow it to *really* register.

Here are some suggestions:

- Listen to the birds sing (hearing)
- Observe pretty cloud formations (sight)
- Visit a nearby park and listen to the children (hearing)
- Notice the pretty colors of blooming flowers (sight)
- Light a fragrant candle (scent)
- See the beauty in the sunset (sight)
- Attend a local recital, concert, play, or comedy act (hearing)
- Wear luxury socks (touch)
- Wrap yourself in a soft scarf or sweater (touch)
- Indulge in whipped cream on your cocoa (taste)
- Enjoy a Hershey's chocolate kiss (taste)

5. PROTECT YOUR HEALTH

After our daughter's accident I soon found myself fighting an assortment of viruses including head colds, stomach flus, sore throats and more, compounding my already frazzled emotions. Studies show that profound grief throws our body into "flight or fight" syndrome for months and months, which is very hard on our physical body. Thus, it becomes critical to guard our physical health. Incorporating a few changes into our daily routine feels hard at first, but soon gets easy. Plus, a stronger physical health helps to strengthen our coping skills. Below are a few suggestions to consider adding to your daily routine to help your physical self withstand the emotional upheaval.

- Practice good sleep hygiene

- Drink plenty of water

- Take a short walk outside every day

- Resist simple carbohydrates (I'm a food addict, so I know that avoiding simple carbs is worth its weight in gold)

- Keep a light calendar and guard your time carefully, don't allow others to dictate and overflow your schedule

6. FIND AN OUTLET

For a long time in the grief journey, everything is painful. In the early days, just getting out of bed and taking a shower can be exhausting. Housecleaning, grocery shopping, and routine errands often take a backseat or disappear altogether. As painful as it is, it's very important to find an outlet that gets you out of bed each day. Finding something to distract you from the pain, occupy your mind, and soothe your senses can be tricky, but possible. Performing a repetitive action can calm your mood, and even result in a new craft or gifts to give. Beginning a new outlet may feel exhausting at first, just remember that the first step is always the hardest. And you don't have to do it forever, just focus on it for the time being.

Possible activities include:

- Learn to mold chocolate or make soap
- Learn how to bead, knit, crochet, or quilt
- Volunteer at a local shelter
- Learn a new sport such as golf or kayaking
- Create a memorial garden in a forgotten part of the yard
- Join Pinterest
- Doodle or draw
- Mold clay
- Learn to scrapbook
- Join a book club

Grief is hell on earth. It truly is. But when walking through hell, your only option is to keep going. Eventually the hell ends, the dark night fades to dawn, and the sun begins its ascent once again. Just keep going and you, too, will find the sunrise.

Lynda Cheldelin Fell

One smile can change a day.
One hug can change a life
One hope can change a destiny.
LYNDA CHELDELIN FELL

*

SURVIVING LOSS OF A SPOUSE

MEET THE WRITERS

*
TANYA CAMERON
Tanya's 43-year-old husband Ivor died of a heart attack in 2013
ivortan05@hotmail.com

Tanya Cameron grew up in the southern beachside suburbs of Adelaide, South Australia. At age twenty-one, she bought a business and after five long years working seven days a week, she knew there was more to life than the business and she wanted to spread her wings. She felt that she needed to find herself and her independence. After selling her business, she headed to the United Kingdom to travel and work. This is where she met the love of her life.

Tanya considers herself an amazing, strong, loving, caring, a wonderful mother and such a funny person. She works very hard but she can take things to heart and stresses out a little bit too much, even when things are out of her control. She would do anything to help people out, always putting the needs of others before her own. She is not a religious person but believes that things happen for a reason.

*
JONATHAN DEAN
Jonathan's 36-year-old wife Cara
died of double pneumonia in 2010
deanjonathan49@gmail.com

Jonathan Dean was born in 1970, in Montreal, Quebec. As a teenager, Jonathan was diagnosed with a learning disability and has a grade nine (Secondary Three) education with grade ten education in history. At age eighteen, he was forced to find work and was in and out of jobs until age twenty-three. At age twenty-five, Jonathan moved out of his parents' place to start his own life. At age twenty-nine, he met his wife Cara and in 2000, she moved in with him.

An avid animal lover, Jonathan considers himself a huge caring teddy bear and he loves to help people. He loves life and loves to make people laugh, which warms his heart.

*

BONNIE FORSHEY
Bonnie's 43-year-old husband Carl
died in a car accident in 2005

Bonnie Forshey was born in Lewistown, Pennsylvania, and raised in New Castle, Delaware. She later moved to Swainsboro, Georgia, and attended Emanuel County Junior College where she earned the Science Merit Award and graduated with her A.S. degree. Bonnie then attended Gordon State College in Barnesville, Georgia, earning a B.S. in Nursing. She spent most of her life working in medical-surgical, geriatrics, rehabilitation and long-term care facilities.

Bonnie raised two children and worked as a nursing assistant, unit secretary, and in medical records while putting herself through school. Bonnie currently resides in both Port Royal, Pennsylvania, and Brandon, Florida, and has two grandsons.

*

STEPHEN HOCHHAUS
Stephen's 51-year-old wife Kathy died of soft tissue sarcoma in 2011
lilacsandladybugs@msn.com

Stephen Hochhaus was born in Douglas, Arizona, in 1948, spending most of his life in the Phoenix area. He graduated with a B.F.A. in art from Arizona State University in 1972 where he started his own business which he still operates today. He became a commercial pilot in 1968.

Stephen married his first wife in 1970, raising two sons and now have six grandchildren. The couple divorced in 1990. He met his wife Kathy and they married September 22, 1998, and lived in Scottsdale, Arizona, where Stephen resides today.

*

MARLISE MAGNA

Marlise's 36-year-old partner Blaine died by suicide in 2010

Marlise was born <u>December 2,</u> 1978, in Johannesburg, South Africa and is the first of two children. Her life has been nothing but out of the ordinary as most people would describe it. She studied drama at South Africa's National School of the Arts before becoming a Jill of all trades. She's worked as a canine behaviorist, wedding planner, TV presenter,  matchmaker and dance instructor, to name a few. At age thirty-five, after two divorces and many suicide attempts, she finally found what she wanted to do and is currently studying to become a pastor. She has been instrumental in planting two churches involved in relationship counseling, praise and worship singing. She is also lead singer in her own Christian band.

Marlise is also director of an alternative clothing and interior design company, magazine editor, and proof reader. Marlise is an avid reader and loves nothing better than doing research and trivia games. Standup comedy and watching reality TV series is another favorite pastime. She lives with her mom and her beloved dog, Juke.

*
DIANE MCKENZIE-SAPP
Diane's 65-year-old husband Ron died from renal failure in 2006
widowsring@gmail.com * www.ExpressionOfGrief.com

Diane McKenzie-Sapp, a Maryland native, has been an airline stewardess, dental assistant, department store manager and buyer, and has been a hospice nurse, an Assistant Director of Nursing and an inspector for Medicare. She can handcraft Christmas ornaments, crochet, quilt, paint ceramic nativity sets, canvas, wood, glass and mailboxes, and she trained for ten years to teach and make porcelain dolls. She reads medical and herbal texts for fun. Ron and Diane's village included three children, a family of parents, siblings, friends and pets. Asked why she could not settle on one career, she cited Matthew parable 25:14-30 "Talents" and the consequences of neglecting a God-given talent. She broke tradition by crafting new unconventional solutions. Seeing an unattractive photo of an open-mouthed tearful girl, she stopped crying at age four. At age six she decided being ticklish was a weakness. She was relentless until her "why nots" were answered. All suffer a broken heart with grief. Finding a way to heal that heart, the child became stronger than the widow. That unwavering determination for solutions to problems by challenging with "Why Not?" led to unconventional ways to view grief and offer widow's rings to the world.

*

JULIE MJELVE
Julie's 42-year-old husband Cameron died by suicide in 2011
Grieving Together
www.grievingtogether.ca * julie@grievingtogether.ca

Julie (McCargar) Mjelve was born in Edmonton, Alberta, Canada. She completed her BSC in Physical Therapy in 1992. After working as a physical therapist for ten years, Julie spent almost eight months traveling Europe before returning to Edmonton to complete her Master's in Education, specializing in teaching English as a Second Language. In 2007 Julie married James Cameron Mjelve. Julie and Cameron went on to have three beautiful children, one boy and two girls. As the demands of child raising increased, Julie's work shifted from teaching English as a Second Language to Internationally Educated Nurses to working as an academic strategist with a local college. Following the birth of their second child, Julie became a stay-at-home mom, focusing on the care and attention her children required. Currently, Julie has started her own business, along with two other partners, called Grieving Together which provides mourning symbols to those who are grieving.

*

LILIAN MORTON
Lilian's 58-year-old husband Michael died in a plane crash in 2012

Lilian was born in a small town where she lived most of her life. She has three beautiful children who are all grown and on their own. When she was in her late thirties, she began her journey across the country. She moved to Florida with her husband and three children where they lived for five years. They relocated to the suburbs of Chicago for two years, and then moved to San Antonio in 2010, where Lilian and her husband had purchased a business. Lilian worked with her husband running the business. They met while both were working at another company and they enjoyed working together. A year after her husband's tragic death, Lilian moved back to her home state to be closer to her family and support system where she still lives today.

*

LISA OWENS

Lisa's 50 year-old husband Greg died of pancreatic cancer in 2014

lisagreg2004@gmail.com

Lisa Owens was born in Savannah, Georgia, and moved to Rome, Georgia, at age seven. She graduated high school in 1983. After a few retail jobs, she found her niche working with adults with developmental disabilities. Lisa has worked for a state hospital, group homes, and day programs, and has been at Network Day Service Center for the past sixteen years. Lisa and her husband Greg moved into an apartment in her parents' home when Greg quit working twenty-three months prior to his death. Lisa provides support for her elderly parents, and is the proud parent of two fur babies (cats), Sam and Little Girl.

Lisa is trying hard to make her husband proud by continuing on, forcing herself to live the life he fought so hard for. She is trying hard to "Finish Strong" a saying engraved on Greg's headstone because he finished his journey fighting.

*

MARY POTTER KENYON
Mary's 60-year-old husband David died of heart failure in 2012
marypotterkenyon@gmail.com * www.marypotterkenyon.com

Mary Potter Kenyon graduated from the University of Northern Iowa and is a reporter for the Manchester Press newspaper in Iowa.

She is a widely published author, workshop presenter and sought after public speaker. Familius has published four of her books: *Coupon Crazy: The Science, the Savings and the Stories Behind America's Extreme Obsession*, *Chemo-Therapist: How Cancer Cured a Marriage*, *Refined By Fire: A Journey of Grief and Grace*, and is co-author of *Mary & Me: A Lasting Link Through Ink*. Several of Mary's devotions were published in Zondervan's *Hope in the Mourning* Bible and an essay about the connection between grief and creativity was published in the January / February issue of *Poets & Writers* magazine. Mary lives in Iowa with two of her eight children.

*

NANCY REDMOND
Nancy's 40-year-old husband Kevin died of a heart attack in 2012
PlumeriaMoon@msn.com

Nancy Hammink Redmond is a mom to three wonderful children, one grandson, and is a resident of Oakdale, Minnesota. She is a medical secretary and medical coder, specializing in ophthalmology, orthopedics and pathology.

When not working, her hobbies include agate hunting on Lake Superior and photography. Her favorite photography subjects include her grandson and macro shots of flowers and the magic of raindrops.

*

MARY LEE ROBINSON
Mary Lee's 63-year-old husband Pat died from a sudden stroke in 2013
www.MaryLeeRobinson.com * mary-lee-robinson.myshopify.com

Mary Lee Robinson is a native of Towson, Maryland, graduating from high school there and going on to attend Virginia Tech.

Mary Lee has lived in Maryland, Pennsylvania and West Virginia. She now resides in South Carolina, where she retired (she thought) with her husband shortly before his death.

Mary Lee is a Certified Grief Coach, a member of the American Association of Christian Counselors, the author of *The Widow or Widower Next Door*, co-author of *Grief Diaries: Surviving Loss of a Spouse*, co-author of *Grief Diaries: How to Help the Newly Bereaved*, and the owner of Rings of Remembrance. She also organizes social clubs for widows and widowers, and hopes to see chapters all over the country one day.

*
CAROL SCIBELLI
Carol's 56-year-old husband Jimmy died from lymphoma in 2006
www.CarolScibelli.com

Carol Scibelli is a humor writer and popular comedic speaker for all occasions. Known as the funniest widow on earth, Carol is a sought after performer at grief conferences because she is irreverent and funny! She has had numerous essays published in *The New York Times*, *Newsday*, *The Hartford Courant* and dozens of weekly publications.

Carol's one-act plays have been performed throughout New York City. Carol's memoir, *Poor Widow Me: Moments of feeling & dealing and finding the funny along the way*, is a collection of eighty-four small moments that had a big impact on her. Each one captured her experience of widowhood. Carol writes a monthly humor column for *Pathfinder*, an online widows magazine.

She has been a proud member of the Friars Club since 1998, a committee chairperson and a contributor to their distinguished magazine. Carol has a grown daughter and son and three fun-loving granddaughters. She lives in Manhattan with her Morkie, Tony Baloney. They rescued each other.

*

KRISTI SMITH

Kristi's 48-year-old husband Michael died from cardiac arrest in 2011

www.dreamsmithbooks.com * kristi@dreamsmithbooks.com

Kristi is a dreamer with a vision of Speaking Life, Cultivating Courage, Sparking Laughter, and Awakening Dreams. She does this through both writing and speaking. For more information or to book Kristi for a speaking engagement, please go to www.DreamsmithBooks.com.

Kristi is the author of the #1 bestselling book, *DREAM...a guide to grieving gracefully,* with five keys to unlock the grip of grief. DREAM pairs each of the five stages of grief with an exact key to unlock that stage. DREAM is about more than mere survival – it is a new way of living. DREAM empowers grievers to propel their lives forward with dignity, strength, and grace. DREAM is not about the trauma and tragedy of her story. It is about hope and how to infuse energy and victory into your story.

A degree in Psychology combined with thirty-plus years of ministry experience provides Kristi with a solid knowledge of how the mind, body, and spirit work together. It is this spiritual perspective that transcends the traditional view of grief.

Kristi relocated from Ohio to Charlotte, North Carolina, and loves uptown living. Kristi's greatest joy is being the mother to two beautiful adult daughters, Abbi and Faith.

*
DIANNE WEST
Dianne's 69-year-old husband Vern died from multiple myeloma in 2010
www.soaringspirits.org * bravegirlsclub.com
amyelomawidowsjourney.blogspot.com dianneinnv@gmail.com

Originally from a small town in southeast Michigan, Dianne married at eighteen and was blessed to share forty-one years with her husband, Vern. She was his caregiver for over four years as he fought multiple myeloma, a blood cancer that attacks the bone marrow. Widowed in 2010, Dianne has dedicated her post-loss life to giving back to the widowed community. In 2013, she was asked to become the National Volunteer Coordinator for Soaring Spirits International, a nonprofit organization committed to providing resources and peer support to people who have lost a spouse or life partner. She currently serves as the administrator of Widowed Village, an online community, and coordinates volunteers for Camp Widow weekends held in Tampa, San Diego and Toronto each year. Additionally, she oversees the Soaring Spirits Regional Group program, local communities of widowed friends throughout North America, and co-leads a group in the Las Vegas area. Dianne retired from the Las Vegas Valley Water District in 2015 after twenty-nine years of service, and has joined the Brave Girl University teaching team as a mentor and resource for widows.

THANK YOU

I am deeply indebted to the writers who contributed to *Grief Diaries: Surviving Loss of a Spouse*. It required a tremendous amount of courage to revisit such painful memories for the purpose of helping others, and the collective dedication to seeing this project to the end is a legacy to be proud of.

I very much appreciate author Annah Elizabeth's assistance in framing the start of each chapter. I'm also grateful to our Grief Diaries village and the very lovely souls I consider dear friends, collaborative partners, mentors, and muses. I treasure each and every one of you!

There simply are no words to express how much I love my husband Jamie, our children, and our wonderfully supportive family and friends for being there through laughter and tears, and encouraging me at every turn. None of this would have been possible without their unquestioning love that continues to surround me.

Finally, I am indebted to our daughter Aly for being my biggest cheerleader in Heaven. Her bright star continues to inspire me, and I feel her love through the thin veil that separates us as I work to offer help, healing and hope around the world. My dearest Lovey, I love you to the fartherest star and beyond. XO

Lynda Cheldelin Fell

Shared joy is doubled joy;
shared sorrow is half a sorrow.
SWEDISH PROVERB

*

ABOUT

LYNDA CHELDELIN FELL

Lynda Cheldelin Fell is an international bestselling author, radio and film producer, and inspirational visionary who is passionately dedicated to serving those struggling with life's challenges.

Lynda is CEO of AlyBlue Media, is board president of the National Grief & Hope Coalition, and the creator of the Grief Diaries brand of books, radio, film and webinars. Considered a pioneer in the field of inspirational hope in the aftermath of loss, Lynda creates ground-breaking projects dedicated to raising awareness and compassion, teaching others that they hold the power to change someone's life with just one smile, and inspire hope that life can be full and rich in the aftermath of loss.

Lynda believes that inside every human is a story worth telling, and is passionate about helping people share their journeys through life's most challenging losses.

lynda@lyndafell.com   *   www.LyndaFell.com

Humanity's legacy of stories and storytelling is the most precious we have.
All wisdom is in our stories and songs.
DORIS LESSING

*

ABOUT THE SERIES

It's important that we share our experiences with other people. Your story will heal you, and your story will heal somebody else.   -IYANLA VANZANT

Grief Diaries is a series of anthology books exploring true stories about the intimate side of life. Created by international bestselling author and bereaved mother Lynda Cheldelin Fell, the series began with eight titles exploring unique losses shared by people around the world. Over a hundred people in six countries registered for those first eight titles, and the books were launched in December 2015. Following their release, organizations and individuals began asking Lynda to create additional titles to help raise awareness about their plights. More than thirty anthology titles are now in the works.

"By sharing stories, we go beyond raising awareness. When we give others an opportunity to see beyond the edge of their own life into the tapestry of our hidden challenges, we offer crucial insight that opens the dialogue," states Lynda. "Allowing society a firsthand glimpse is a critical step towards improving existing support, benefitting everyone for generations to come."

Now a 5-star series, a portion of profits from every AlyBlue Media book is donated to a national organization serving those in need.

ALYBLUE MEDIA TITLES

PUBLISHED 2015:

GRAMMY VISITS FROM HEAVEN	ISBN: 978-1-944328-05-4
MY GRIEF DIARY: A WORKBOOK	ISBN: 978-1-944328-10-8
GRIEF DIARIES: SURVIVING LOSS OF A CHILD	ISBN: 978-1-944328-00-9
GRIEF DIARIES: SURVIVING LOSS OF A SPOUSE	ISBN: 978-1-944328-01-6
GRIEF DIARIES: SURVIVING LOSS BY SUICIDE	ISBN: 978-1-944328-03-0
GRIEF DIARIES: SURVIVING LOSS OF A PARENT	ISBN: 978-1-944328-07-8
GRIEF DIARIES: SURVIVING LOSS OF A SIBLING	ISBN: 978-1-944328-02-3
GRIEF DIARIES: SURVIVING LOSS OF AN INFANT	ISBN: 978-1-944328-04-7
GRIEF DIARIES: SURVIVING LOSS OF A LOVED ONE	ISBN: 978-1-944328-13-9
GRIEF DIARIES: LOSS OF HEALTH	ISBN: 978-1-944328-08-5

FORTHCOMING 2016 TITLES (PARTIAL LIST):

COLOR MY SOUL WHOLE

FAITH, GRIEF & PASS THE CHOCOLATE PUDDING

GRIEF DIARIES: MESSAGES FROM HEAVEN

GRIEF DIARIES: LIVING WITH A BRAIN INJURY

GRIEF DIARIES: RAISING A DISABLED CHILD

GRIEF DIARIES: LIVING WITH D.I.D.

GRIEF DIARIES: THROUGH THE EYES OF FALLEN HERO WIVES

GRIEF DIARIES: THROUGH THE EYES OF AN EATING DISORDER

GRIEF DIARIES: SURVIVING LOSS BY HOMICIDE

GRIEF DIARIES: LIVING WITH RHEUMATIC DISEASE

GRIEF DIARIES: THROUGH THE EYES OF CANCER

GRIEF DIARIES: SURVIVING LOSS OF A CLIENT

GRIEF DIARIES: LIVING WITH LEARNING DISORDERS

GRIEF DIARIES: LIFE AFTER RAPE

GRIEF DIARIES: LIFE AFTER CHILD SEXUAL ABUSE

GRIEF DIARIES: GRIEVING THE MISSING

GRIEF DIARIES: SURVIVING INFIDELITY

GRIEF DIARIES: LIVING WITH A MENTAL ILLNESS

GRIEF DIARIES: LIVING WITH ALCOHOLISM

GRIEF DIARIES: LIVING WITH ADDICTION

GRIEF DIARIES: LIVING WITH DEMENTIA

GRIEF DIARIES: SURVIVING LOSS OF MY FAMILY

GRIEF DIARIES: SURVIVING CLERGY MOLESTATION

GRIEF DIARIES: SHUNNING THE WIDOW

GRIEF DIARIES: SHUNNING THE BEREAVED

GRIEF DIARIES: MY CHILD WAS BULLIED

ALYBLUE MEDIA

HEALING TOGETHER PROGRAM

Dedicated to raising awareness and offer comfort and hope in the aftermath of painful experiences, AlyBlue Media's Healing Together Program donates a portion of profits from each title to a national organization serving those in need. The nonprofit recipients were determined by votes by the writers who contributed to the series. To date, recipients of AlyBlue Media's Healing Together Program include:

Grief Diaries: Surviving Loss by Suicide
Recipient: American Foundation for Suicide Prevention

Grief Diaries: Surviving Loss by Homicide
Recipient: National Center for Missing & Exploited Children

Grief Diaries: Surviving Loss of a Child
Recipient: Cry For Me, No More

Grief Diaries: Loss of Health
Recipient: Global Healthy Living Foundation

Grief Diaries: Surviving Loss of a Sibling
Recipient: The Compassionate Friends

Grief Diaries: Surviving Loss of a Parent
Recipient: Save the Children

Grief Diaries: Surviving Loss of a Spouse
Recipient: Soaring Spirits International

Grief Diaries: Surviving Loss of an Infant
Recipient: St. Jude Children's Research Hospital

Grief Diaries: Grieving the Living
Recipient: National Grief & Hope Coalition

Grief Diaries: Surviving Loss of a Loved One
Recipient: The Grief Recovery Institute

Grief Diaries: Surviving Loss of a Pregnancy
Recipient: Sufficient Grace Ministries

Grief Diaries: Memos from Heaven
Recipient: Friends for Survival

Grief Diaries: Through the Eyes of D.I.D.
Recipient: National Alliance on Mental Illness

Grief Diaries: Living with Mental Illness
Recipient: National Alliance on Mental Illness

Grief Diaries: Living with a Brain Injury
Recipient: Brain Injury Association of America

Grief Diaries: Loss at the Hands of an Impaired Driver
Recipient: AVIDD - Advocates for Victims of Impaired/Distracted
Driving

Grief Diaries: Through the Eyes of an Eating Disorder
Recipient: National Eating Disorders Association

Grief Diaries: How to Help the Newly Bereaved
Recipient: National Grief & Hope Coalition

To share your story in a Grief Diaries book, visit
www.griefdiaries.com

Published by AlyBlue Media
Inside every human is a story worth sharing.
www.AlyBlueMedia.com